Praise for *Conquering the Wireless World*

Doug Lamont deserves credit for writing the best book that I have seen about the trillion dollar m-commerce wager that enough individuals and groups will take to using wireless Internet while on the "go."

Philip Kotler
S.C. Johnson & Son Distinguished Professor of International Marketing, Kellogg Graduate School of Management, Northwestern University Illinois, USA

In my work (marketing studies) I need hard data. Professor Lamont's work reveals why mobile Internet will play such a crucial role in the future of marketing studies: data-points can be gathered at the individual level, and related to proximity, timeliness and commerce activities. This is an eye-opener: in the future, you cannot do marketing without taking the mobile Internet into consideration.

Ing. S. Meacci
President, Italian Marketing Association-AISMCEO Databank, Italy

No one understands and explains the market dynamics and forces of m-commerce better than Professor Lamont. While I've been well aware of the implications of m-commerce in the small, only this book gave me the big, whole picture. This book is the definitive reference for mobile marketing.

Steve Tendon
General Partner, Tendon Consulting Group, Sweden

Everyone agrees that the mobile Internet will create a paradigm shift in the ways that we work and live. There is less agreement, however, in where the business opportunities and pitfalls can be found in the wireless place. Douglas Lamont's *Conquering the Wireless World: The Age of M-Commerce*, offers a clear and analytical plan to help wireless leaders develop winning marketing plans and strategies.

David Jacobson
Partner, Sonnenschein Nath & Rosenthal & Organizer of First Tuesday and Mobile Wednesdays in Chicago

Other books published by Professor Douglas Lamont:

- *Managing Foreign Investments in Southern Italy*
- *Foreign State Enterprises: A Threat to American Business*
- *Forcing Our Hand: America's Trade Wars in the 1980s*
- *Winning Worldwide: Strategies for Dominating Global Markets*
- *Global Marketing*
- *Salmon Day: The End of the Beginning for Global Business*

CONQUERING THE WIRELESS WORLD

DOUGLAS LAMONT

CONQUERING THE WIRELESS WORLD

THE AGE OF M-COMMERCE

CAPSTONE

First published 2001 by
Capstone Publishing Limited (A Wiley Company)
8 Newtec Place
Magdalen Road
Oxford OX4 1RE
United Kingdom
http://www.capstoneideas.com

CIP catalogue records for this book are available from the British Library and the US Library of Congress

ISBN 1-84112-138-X

Typeset in 11/16 pt Bodoni Book by
Sparks Computer Solutions Ltd, Oxford, UK
http://www.sparks.co.uk
Printed and bound by
TJ International Ltd, Padstow, Cornwall

This book is printed on acid-free paper

Substantial discounts on bulk quantities of Capstone books are available to corporations, professional associations and other organizations. For details telephone Capstone Publishing on (+44-1865-798623), fax (+44-1865-240941) or email info@wiley-capstone.com

Dedication

The book is dedicated to my mother, Filomena Katherine, my first teacher, who died during the preparation of the manuscript.

Let all professors be as successful in transmitting knowledge to the next generation.

Contents

Preface

Today, Americans are less enthusiastic about mobile phones, m-commerce, and the wireless Internet than are the Japanese, Europeans, and the Chinese. In fact only 33 percent of Americans have cell phones versus up to 90 percent in some European countries. The book proposes a tried-and-true marketing approach for conquering the wireless world that will take Americans and others into the age of m-commerce.

About two years ago, business associates in Japan and Europe showed me the possibilities of wireless technology from NTT DoCoMo and GSM. Then several trips to China, Hong Kong and Singapore convinced me of the wide use of and the possibilities for mobile phones throughout East Asia. Moreover, my colleagues at DePaul University, Albert Muñiz and Zafar Iqbal, and my good friend at Northwestern University, Philip Kotler, corroborated my gut feeling that marketing's most important victory in the 21st century will be to turn Americans and others into consumers of m-commerce. Lastly, several meetings among venture capitalists at First Tuesday confirmed that money could be made through wireless when marketers target market segments, position products, and carry out a carefully crafted 4 Ps marketing strategy.

Recently, Steve Tendon flew from Sweden to Chicago because he had heard about my wireless manuscript. He read it, made important suggestions, and pronounced the book helpful for his own work in Europe.

All of these wireless marketing applications were discussed in my MBA classes at DePaul University both in Chicago and in Hong Kong at the International Bank of Asia. Several key ideas were tested among my children, Katherine and Kristine, as they became proponents of Gen-Y commitments to cell phones over landlines. My profound thanks to students, colleagues, friends and family who put up with my habits of detailed research, daily writing and fast-paced editing during the time the manuscript moved from being a good idea to an important book.

Douglas Lamont
Chicago, Illinois USA

How to be an M-Marketer

ANYBODY WHO IS A GOOD MARKETER also can become a good m-marketer. Mobile phones, m-commerce, and the wireless Internet change the skills required from the marketing manager, but not so fundamentally that good wireless marketers are not also good marketing managers. Here are some marketing qualities that are even more important today for mobile Internet marketers.

1   *Product marketing.* Marketers introduce miniature information appliances with unique interactive content to m-commerce customers.

2   *Promotion marketing.* Marketing managers provide customers with value-added intangible product attributes that are included as part of their smart handheld devices.

3   *Price marketing.* Marketers offer both commodity and higher value-added prices as marketing managers divide m-commerce customers into those who do virtually everything on-line and those who prefer personal services from telecom, content, and financial service providers.

   Although marketing professionals speak of rolling out a 4 Ps (product, price, promotion, and place) marketing strategy, price marketing is by far the most important of the four in terms of creating value for m-commerce. During the next few years, marketers must teach those customers who prefer personal services to adjust to substantially higher fees, including paying for content, or to join the rest of the world in preparing for virtual transactions on-line through mobile phones, m-commerce, and the wireless Internet. This is the essence of the *new* marketing concept applied to rolling out a *new* marketing strategy for m-commerce.

4   *Segmentation.* Marketers divide like groups of people across national frontiers into those who have the income, are the correct age, live in the right neighborhoods, and belong to modernizing ethnic groups as candidates for the purchase of miniature information appliances, 3G telecom services, and interactive Internet content.

5   *Targeting.* Marketing managers assemble smaller like groups of people who are bound together by their professions, such as entertainers, or by their skills, such as athletes, and by their personal tastes, habits, and values, such as info-tech geeks.

6   *Positioning.* Marketers match possible on-line Internet products with probable customers; the former offer the latter enhanced customer relationships to try out m-commerce and the mobile Internet.

Although marketing professionals speak of segmentation, targeting, and positioning as one continuous effort, targeting specific like-minded groups is by far the most important of the three in delivering value to present and potential customers of m-commerce. During the transition years between 2001 and 2005, marketers must teach m-commerce providers about how on-line stock trading firms effectively use customer relationship management (CRM) to jump ahead of on-line Internet bankers in the quest for more revenue from customers who are committed to m-commerce. This is the application of real options analysis to marketing m-commerce in Japan, Europe, the US, China, and elsewhere in the world.

These six fundamental marketing ideas are discussed throughout the book in chapters one through six. The book is written for marketers who want to sell mobile phones, m-commerce, and the wireless Internet to a new generation of telecom customers. Let's start with the executive summary of the chapter and then work through several critical issues facing wireless marketers.

EXECUTIVE SUMMARY

Marketers train m-commerce customers to use mobile phones and to interact with unique content from the wireless Internet. If traditional financial rules are followed, marketers make money from m-commerce. Here's what they must do:

- Design new and different interactive content for the wireless Internet.
- Form fixed-wireless alliances among telecom and content providers.
- Turn iMode and WAP phones into miniature information appliances.
- Sell cell phones to the following age segments: Gen-Y (twenty-somethings); Gen-X (thirty-somethings); and 'boomers' (forty-somethings).
- Market anytime, anywhere voice and data communications, and transaction capabilities to the following values and lifestyles target groups: "Supli" teenage Japanese young women, unmarried American info-geeks, married European business executives, Chinese bureaucrats, and others.
- Build brand communities as product-based experiences for users by carrying out segmentation, targeting, and positioning strategies in Japan, Europe, the US, China, and elsewhere in the world.

Best deals money can buy

The following financial rules from the venture capital market judge the quality of an investment in the wireless Internet. The "burn rate" of cash is no more than eight months. Positive cash flow starts within two years. Sales produce earnings in the third and following years after the initial investment. Marketers and financial investors label these rules an analysis of real (or strategic) options. Here are the best deals discussed throughout the book.

Initial round of investments
- Web-based phones, whose screen or "home deck" shows books, CDs, airplane tickets, and other items to purchase, from Finland's Nokia and Sweden's Ericsson;
- W-CDMA or CDMA 2000 from America's Qualcomm;
- distribution alliances for connections and content from Japan's NTT DoCoMo's-AOL Japan;
- electronic wallets from Finland and Sweden's Merita-Nordbanken; and

- on-line stock trading from Charles Schwab and other non-bank financial institutions.

Today, these m-commerce deals create value for marketers, beat out competitors, grow sales rapidly, build market share, make money for business firms, and help investors conquer the wireless world.

Future rounds of investments

- Dual-protocol GSM and iMode phones in Europe from Japan's NTT DoCoMo and its Dutch partner, KPN Mobile;
- investments in the US wireless market by DoCoMo with the goal of introducing 3G wireless technology sooner than 2005;
- on-line hotel and travel services from the Hyatt and other hotels;
- Portals in Europe, such as Vizzavi, itself a joint venture of the UK's Vodafone and France's Vivendi, morph into wireless service; and
- Internet banks from global and local banks in East Asia, Europe and the US.

Tomorrow, these mobile Internet deals may create value for marketers, might make money for business firms, and may help investors conquer the wireless world.

Investment in an innovative and highly disruptive technology

- Wireless Ethernet network from America's Aerzone and Wayport for the Red Carpet Clubs of United Airlines, the lobbies of five-star hotels, and intranets for business offices, university campuses, and Starbucks coffee shops.

If Aerzone, Wayport, and others who sell wireless Ethernet networks produce burn rates of eight months or less, positive cash flow within two years, and earnings from sales in the third and following years, then existing fixed-wireless and satellite technologies, and wired systems for PCs and cable-ready TV's will become second-best options and possibly obsolete. The wireless Ethernet network is the most important, new, disruptive technology to come along that it may be the deal breaker for all other m-commerce investments by telecom and content providers in the world of the mobile Internet.

Recommendations

Marketers must spend a great deal of time creating and delivering value about mobile phones, m-commerce, and the wireless Internet. The devil is in the details on how and when interactive content, distribution, and platforms morph into interactive m-sports, m-entertainment, m-banking, and all other possible money-making mobile Internet deals. Events do come along to disrupt the best laid plans of marketers, technologists, and venture capitalists. Therefore, marketers must develop segmentation, targeting, and positioning strategies for such new, innovative technologies as wireless Ethernet networks as well as for tried-and-true fixed-wireless and satellite technologies.

INTRODUCTION

Here is our *new* 4 Ps marketing strategy for m-commerce:

- Sell mobile Internet technology in competition with fixed Internet technology. The wireless Internet is in the expansion phase of the product life cycle, and mobile Internet will grow even faster when telecom providers introduce packet switching, 3G technology, and more interesting content. For a few telecom providers sales growth is doubling every year, but for most the burn rate of cash has been extended into the second year and positive cash flow is not in sight. Therefore, the better managed wireless firms will be acquiring the more poorly managed firms, and both will be looking for alliances with content providers.
- Create new market space. Sell "always on" connections, content specifically designed for the mobile medium, and even a daily *manga* cartoon to both wired and wireless telecom firms. These providers must reconfigure the value chain of price-quality-service, provide location awareness, offer microbilling on the phone bill, and collect a rich monthly fee from customers. The content providers must transform latent into real demand. Email

and short messaging services may be killer applications for mobile phones. Of course, no finish line exists for telecom firms, because new market space must be created and re-created all the time.

- Control the value proposition delivered to customers. Marketers have some control over mobile products and the roll-out of 3G wireless service. However, they have almost no control over pricing strategy because the mobile Internet is transparent for all to check prices and make bids on their own. Therefore, marketers are in a competitive environment in which margins are shrinking for bankers, insurance brokers, stock brokers, advertisers, entertainment firms, and many other companies.

- Establish brand communities for the wireless Internet. *Mobile* is a universal word. It is used by most people in the world as an exclamation. *Mobile* has no subject or object. *Mobile* means answer the phone, chat through the phone, do business on the phone, buy goods and services with the phone. The vocabulary of *mobile* keeps expanding no matter which language, dialect or accent is used. Hence, GSM users are one brand community, iMode users are another brand community, and CDMA may become a third. Predict consumer choices for each of these brands for one, three and five years into the future. Forecast the impact of discontinuous change, especially when GSM shifts to 2.5G (and later 3G) in Europe, iMode becomes an appropriate substitute for GSM within Europe, or W-CDMA or CDMA 2000 becomes the UMTS wireless standard throughout the mobile world.

- Target twenty-somethings (Gen-Y), do deeper data mining, and collect demographic data, and values and lifestyles information. Teach thirty-something (Gen-X) customers to pay for content. Encourage forty-somethings (boomers) to try the mobile Internet with the hope the latter might follow their children into using m-commerce, mobile phones, and the wireless Internet. Teach older customers that their technology phobia about the mobile Internet can be overcome by use of the new phones, and these more senior boomers also will prosper by using m-commerce.

- Position mobile products and their 4 Ps marketing strategies based on the success stories, e.g., on-line stock trading, and fixed wireless alliances. These money-making deals offer rich content for making things happen properly, growing sales, and making some money. Learn from the failures of on-line Internet banking, many dot-coms, and other Web-based firms. Through all of this, marketers will be teaching new customers how to benefit from the *new* economy of the mobile Internet.

Prediction

Right before your eyes the rules of the telecommunications game are changing. When all is said and done – that is, in about ten years – the mobile wireless Internet will have replaced today's fixed-wired Internet.

MARKETING'S ROLE IN M-COMMERCE

In October 2000, *The Economist*, a well-respected magazine for most people in the know around the world called m-commerce the biggest gamble in business history. Its leader article said this:

> *"Over the next three or four years, [telecom companies in Europe] will invest more than $300 billion bringing together the two hottest technologies of the moment: the mobile telephone and the Internet … What makes this a leap in the dark … is that nobody knows if consumers will want the new services [and pay for them] – or even exactly what they will be."*[1]

In the latest poll of 1700 Americans by Jupiter Communications,

> *"a majority reported that they wouldn't use or wouldn't pay for m-commerce … Of those who don't own cell phones, 56 percent expressed such unwillingness. Even among cell phone owners … 48 percent indicated similar resistance … Only 10 percent said they would make retail purchases on the wireless Web, and fewer still would make stock trades."*[2]

Why this negative response? Right now the mobile Internet is slow; it gives really poor-quality service; and it has too many incompatible standards.

Hence, the US has few m-commerce sites. Whereas Europe has a good number of sites using GSM, the single continent-wide standard. Of course, Japan has many m-commerce sites using iMode, the all-important, single national standard. Whether more European customers will use m-commerce sites in greater numbers, and whether American customers in any significant number will use m-commerce sites for retail shopping and stock trading, of course, is another question. Marketers are still searching for the answer to the question: "Who wants m-commerce?"

Glossary

What is known about cellular mobile phones is as follows:

- 1G analogue telephones in the US are useless unless you are willing to pay a lot of money for lost voice connections and roaming connections outside your local calling area.
- 2G voice GSM phones in Europe are on the verge of becoming obsolete technology. However, European mobile customers love GSM's short messaging service (SMS), and American users enjoy their ability to roam to 70 countries worldwide with their home telephone number. Next year GSM in Europe must be converted to UMTS (universal mobile telecommunications system), or die. Of course, most American cell phone customers use CDMA (code division multiple access) or other 2G technologies that are incompatible with one another, and this legacy fiasco puts the US behind in the race to dominate mobile communications.
- 2.5G gives Japanese W-CDMA (wideband code division multiple access) and European GSM users breathing room to do a little better with voice and limited data communications until more bandwidth comes along in Japan in 2001 and in Europe in 2003.
- 3G, which starts in Japan in May 2001, puts Japan ahead, especially NTT DoCoMo, in the race to convert cell phone users to "always on" wireless Internet connections. DoCoMo's iMode cell phone offers these "killer applications": packet switches; faster and speedier voice, data, and transaction capabilities anytime, anywhere (or 24/7 time); and one monthly bill

for line usage, content choice, and Web purchases. Thirteen million Japanese customers love iMode phones and DoCoMo's mobile services, and the recent addition of instant messaging and the "buddy list" from AOL, and worldwide content from AOL/Time Warner. More users will go mobile through the DoCoMo-AOL partnership in Europe by 2003 and in the US by 2005.

▨ 4G is pie in the sky, but Nokia and Ericsson, and other European firms are thinking about it for the five years between 2006 and 2011.

Dialing for dollars

Today, DoCoMo earns half of its revenues from transactions and from data traffic, at least two years before European telecom companies, and more than four years before American telecom firms can try their hand at 3G mobile phone service. DoCoMo knows what it's doing. A river of money will flow through DoCoMo and AOL, and their telecom and content providers. All the big venture capitalists want a piece of the action of cellular positioning, stock-trading on the run, wireless gambling, a browser in everyone's pocket, hassle-free shopping, and fun-and-games commuting. The DoCoMo-AOL Japan alliance is dialing for dollars as they look for other content providers. None of this should be lost on European telecom companies that have paid a lot of money for their 3G licenses and must get a return from transactions and data communications sooner rather than later. Japan will be ahead of Europe for at least two years.

Possible unanticipated futures

Let's be clear. Investments in mobile phones, m-commerce and the wireless Internet are a big gamble. Even the most expected futures arrive late and in unexpected ways.

For example, Hutchison Whampoa, a Hong Kong firm, pulled out of its wireless license in Germany because it could not see how it could make money from wireless telecommunications in the heart of Europe. Is this a financial signal about lower than expected returns on 3G investments? AT&T Wireless that gave the market TDMA (time division multiple access) may be sold to others for its customer list and not for its legacy technology. Is this a signal about wrong guesses in technology and the failures that lie ahead? Pacific Century Cyberworks renegotiated its wired, wireless and content deal with Telstra after the former's "burn rate" of cash sped up too fast even for the most risk-taking venture capitalists. Is this a signal that the salad days of easy money chasing any dot-com deals are over?

Thus not all telecom firms that have made wireless investments will survive; some might have to be broken up to pay their 3G bills. The latest word is that NTT DoCoMo is already on the prowl for partners and deals in Europe together with AOL or KPN Mobile, DoCoMo's Dutch partner, or both. The outcome in Europe is uncertain. No one has done the hard work of finding out what European consumers want from 3G wireless Internet. The marketing questions remain unanswered.

Plan of book

This is the plan of the book. Section I is about how marketers create value within and for the wireless Internet. First, we will examine m-commerce products such as connections and content (Chapter 1). Then we will discuss how to create new market space for the m-commerce world (Chapter 2). Finally, we will explore pricing issues, especially as they relate to specific m-commerce industries (Chapter 3). We will ask these questions: What do customers want, what connection speed and content will they pay for, and do telecom and content providers have these products ready to go once 3G is in place?

Section II is about how marketers deliver value. First, we will carry out segmentation analysis in international telecom markets to determine whether there are similar market segments across national frontiers, such as Japan, Europe, the US, China and elsewhere in the world. Here we need to look at demographic data, and values and lifestyle information to see whether similar patterns of m-commerce consumption exist as part of the global reach of wired and wireless telecommunications. If similar market segments exist across national boundaries, then the start up costs for 3G can be spread over a wider global market in which partnerships play a key competitive role in the success of m-commerce (Chapter 4).

Then we will do targeting analysis of narrowly focused age groups where gender, occupation, and personal choices play a significant role in national markets (Chapter 5). Here we need to look at the following target groups:

- Japanese teenagers who are fond of short messaging services (SMS);
- upwardly mobile young Swedish professionals (Gen-Y) who want data communications around the clock; and American professional athletes, their agents, and hangers-on who want to be connected at all times;
- middle-level Finnish executives (Gen-X) who want electronic wallets to complete their purchases of cola drinks from vending machines, or pay for their parking spaces; and American professional coaches who want to send play schemes to their athletes and receive scouting reports from their spotters; and
- senior British, German and American executives (or the younger boomers) who want voice, data and transaction capabilities from their cell phones; and American professional team owners who want the same, but cannot get them with 2G telephones.

Lastly, we will show how positioning analysis works in local business markets. The concept of always being on is very powerful. It means all the barriers are coming down as the cell phone merges with wireless laptops and personal digital assistants (PDAs), and they together create a new network of social structure. Positioning means business executives must make choices about technology, investments, and markets; and then they must decide whom they are to serve, how to serve them, and what needs to be done to get them to pay for 3G broadband connections, good, bad or indifferent content, and all the unexpected goods and services in the future (Chapter 6).

Marketers have some good answers for today, but they must learn new answers for tomorrow. What do we do with fast connections? How do wireless devices fit into our lives? How much divergence in information appliances can we incorporate into our lifestyles? Should we depend on the wireless Ethernet network for all our future connections and content? 3G technology, burn rates of Web investments, marketing miniature information devices, and content creativity for virtual worlds are the new rules of the game for both investors and marketers alike. Learning for them is similar to bandwidth – only too much seems to be enough. No doubt the wireless Internet will surprise us all as we fit it into our lifestyles and then command it to change our lifestyles for the better.

Customer information

In all of this, let's remember the customer is the data. We need to know a great deal more about users of m-commerce before we can predict whether they will buy mobile connections, wireless content, and data transactions in the numbers necessary to pay back the cost of spectrum licenses and 3G infrastructure investments. Right now everybody in the wireless Internet business is making it up as they go along. Telecom firms and content providers need to understand that customers want more than just part of the answer – they want solutions.

New marketing concept

To be successful in implanting new market space within the wireless Internet industry, marketers must introduce the *new* marketing concept. That is, they must teach themselves and their customers how to use new 3G connections and how to gain the most from the content provided through their mobile phones. Then marketers must implement a *new* 4 Ps marketing strategy for fixed-wireless services in Japan, Europe and the US. That is, they must make each of the marketing functions (product, price, place and promotion) fully transparent among competitors and between them and customers. Finally, marketers must create a *new* marketing organization, one that is responsive to m-commerce on the Web from entertainment, stock trading and banking firms.

INFORMATION APPLIANCES

The cell phone offers voice communications on the run. Whether you are in an elevator, walking downtown, driving down the highway, or getting off a plane, you can pull out your mobile and talk. This has captured the imagination of all teenagers because they can talk to their hearts' content, and in Europe and Japan get short messages, too. Continuous, instantaneous voice communications is the killer application for cell phones.

Voice communications also are in demand from mothers of younger children and professional business women who want safety and security as they travel for business. Most don't care whether the voice service is analogue (1G), primitive digital voice (2G), or advanced digital voice and data (2.5G) communications so long as they can talk with friends, children and loved ones all the time.

Then comes the demand for advanced voice and data communications from younger (Gen-Y) managers and upwardly mobile (Gen-X) professionals. Most care about their service and expect it to get better quickly. Whether Qualcomm's W-CDMA (or CDMA 2000) or Europe's GSM wins the telecom technology race is immaterial to customers so long as they can talk with business associates and get their reports done. These services have built up demand for even faster connections with more content as global positioning by wireless satellite connections enters into the conscious habits of users in Japan, Europe and the US.

For mobile phones to work well as information appliances cell phones must do several things:

- connect users to the World Wide Web;
- offer an easy-to-use voice browser, such as Hey Anita and TellMe;
- provide short-range wireless communication, such as the wireless Ethernet network that allows computers to talk with printers, cell phones with headsets, Palm Pilots with vending machines, and each of these devices with the Internet;
- give users peer-to-peer computing in which directories and files are stored on individual PCs, such as how Napster and Gnutella parcels music among PCs, workstations, servers, and cell phones; and
- work with XML, or extensible markup language, that permits users to display information (HTML) and to manipulate information by encoding it in a standardized way so Web sites can talk with each other.

Thus users are living through a paradigm shift in their lifestyles. Only recently, they were in the Information Age in which stand-alone PCs were simply word processors or number crunchers. Then they were plugged into the Internet and customers learned how to use wired PCs in new and different ways. Advances in speed and mobility took the functions of PCs and information appliances to iMode, GSM, and other mobile phones. Today, the wireless Internet is unfolding as users learn new ways to gain, use and market information to improve their lifestyles through m-commerce. This paradigm shift puts all demographic segments, target groups, and local customers into the Network Age.

CONTENT INVESTMENTS

Yet wireless Internet users ask that nagging question: "What do I get?" So far their answer is "Not much." According to Justin Post, Internet media analyst at Deutsche Banc Alex Brown in San Francisco, "It costs more to [encode, store, and deliver multimedia content] on the Internet than you can monetize," and this does not include the production and marketing costs.[3]

Neither marketers nor investors know how much disposable personal income will be set aside by customers for their monthly microbills from telecom firms. What customers see today is Internet content that is neither exciting or unique, but all too similar to what is seen on network and cable TV. Simply put, marketers have no idea what customers will like and be willing to pay for on a long-term basis.

Intangibles make or break deals

The task ahead is to marry Silicon Valley capital and info-tech brainpower with LA storytelling and distribution, and bring them both together with wireless telecom firms so content makes it through the final mile to offices and homes. The trick is to burn cash for no more than 12 months and show positive cash flow within 18–24 months. The odds are still against success because 3G is unavailable in most parts of the industrialized world, and customers have yet to weigh in on their preferences, tastes and habits for content via the wireless Internet.

These m-commerce investments are made in good faith to gain first-mover advantage. However, many fail to get enough wireless business so they can move quickly up the expansion curve of the product life cycle. Most dot-coms raised substantial cash before the market collapsed in March 2000. They put all the cash into marketing their Web sites. Their burn rates were much longer than six–eight months, and their estimates of positive cash flow were far beyond two years in the future. So they went back to the market for more cash, got none, and, similar to the failed new-media company DEN, went out of business.

Intangibles destroyed these deals. No buzz among users. No content of interest for customers. No brand community among users. No new technology from Silicon Valley info-geeks. No more rounds of investments from venture capitalists. No mega-IPO. No market capitalization.

Wireless is the answer

Outside the US, m-commerce, mobile phones and the wireless Internet are fast becoming the only lifestyle for those target groups who want fast voice and data communications. The testing ground is Japan's NTT DoCoMo with its non-GSM mobile Internet service in which jokes, photos, and many other things are swapped, bought and sold. "Wireless is going to become the preferred business-to-business communications medium, not just for voice but also for data," says Nigel Deighton, a wireless industry expert for the Gartner Group in Europe.[4] Successful wireless companies have one thing in common. Their executives believe that the wireless Internet of the future is and will be different from the fixed-wired Internet of the past. This conceptual leap gives wireless its power to destroy wired cable and DSL services, and build a completely new mobile world, rich in content and speedy access for all who can pay to join the network.

BRAND COMMUNITY

What do two Hollywood stars, Ben Affleck and Matt Damon, tell marketers about building brand community among wireless broadband users?[5] They won their Oscars for best screenplay of *Good Will Hunting*, and they have gone on to do other money-making films. Affleck is 28 and Damon is 30, older Gen-Y and younger Gen-X respectively. Both are what everyone expects from these age groups – that is, info-tech geeks. Affleck knows wired computers, routers, and servers, and Damon knows wireless computers and the Internet. As with many of their age group in LA, especially those with friends in the Silicon Valley, they are deeply involved in information technology for personal and business use. Where they differ from most of their age groups is that they both have very high levels of personal disposable income (from their films) to spend on anything they want.

Here's how they spent their money. The two stars set up their own production company, and then put its assets into a breakout new-media company with Chris Moore, a former promising agent to movie stars at ICM turned Hollywood producer, and Sean Bailey, another young 30-year-old producer. Together they organized LivePlanet, a wired and wireless broadband entertainment company.

Content investment

Let's look at the deal. Affleck and Damon, and their Hollywood movie studio backers provide access to top-tier talent and content, and the muscle to get the results distributed around the country. They can do traditional movies, TV and cable projects; translate them for viewing on Web sites; and put the results out through a fixed-wireless infrastructure. Their goal is to do it all in the world of real-time sports, music and other live entertainment events, and on the Internet. The team took their business plan to the Silicon Valley buyout firm, Silver Lake, got US $2 million in seed capital, and a lot of technical advice on info-geek stuff, rounds of investments, OK (but not great) burn rates of 12–18 months, positive cash flow within two years (or by 2002), and the potential for an IPO, sometime in the future when the stock market is again ready for a new media broadband company.

Affleck's info-tech IQ is truly impressive, and Damon's is above average. Together, they represent a new technophile set of customers who are waiting to be dazzled by wireless broadband events in real time. This is a target group well worth pursuing because of its high net worth and ability to get deals done. It includes Hollywood stars, producers, and directors, their agents, and venture capital investors – that is, a marriage of LA and Silicon Valley, California cultures. In Chapter 5, we talk about actionable targeting and the emergence of another high disposable personal income target group among professional athletes, their agents, coaches, team owners, and all the hangers-on in this piece of show business. This target group lacks the info-geeks that one finds in the other target group. However, both target groups are bi-coastal people with business deals percolating on both sides of the North Atlantic and around the Pacific Rim basin. They are the new rich who support winning teams, such as Michael Jordan's Chicago Bulls, Wayne Gretzky's LA Kings, and soccer's Manchester United, have mega-frequent flyer points with one or more airlines, stay in high-tech hotels around the world, and insist on wireless email, on-line stock trading, and m-Internet banking. Affleck and Jordan, Damon and Gretzky, and many others are the early adapters of fixed-wireless broadband technology.

Will others follow? Let's take a preview look at probable customers for m-commerce and the wireless Internet.

Mass affluents

These upper-income middle-class folks also have money; of course, they don't have as much as the new rich movie stars and professional athletes. But the former are comfortable. They live in easily identifiable areas known by their ZIP or postal codes, such as 60614 (Lincoln Park, Chicago) and SW2 (Knightsbridge, London), or by their neighborhoods (Shibuya, Tokyo, or Mid-Levels escalator or "Soho," Hong Kong). If the mass affluents follow the early adapters into wireless broadband technology, then we have a sustainable product with decent positive cash flow and some free cash. The mass affluents also demand wireless email, on-line stock trading, high-tech hotels, and m-Internet banking; these five-star requests must be met for them to spend their money. The self-reference criteria (SRC) of the mass affluents include being as early in on the venture capital deals as possible so they might get pre-IPO or friends and family stock. For example, LivePlanet has set aside 20 percent of its stock for employees who will be part of the team to turn an idea of four people into a strong wireless broadband competitor. Even the mothers of Affleck and Damon, their dates for Oscar night, will get stock in their sons' business.

Mass-market folks

However, even with backing from early adapters and proactive choices from mass affluents, fixed wireless broadband technology is not guaranteed a success. The wireless Internet and m-commerce could stall during the expansion phase of the product life-cycle. Will mass-market folks pay monthly fees to their content providers, such as DoCoMo in Japan, for new media over wireless broadband networks? Will they forego the known technology of cable modems and DSL telephone lines for the relatively unknown satellite wireless technology? Will they view the new broadband media as substantially different than what is available today in the movies and on the TV? Will the mass market folks from the American Midwest (Chicago's 100 million hinterland) join West and East Coast people in forming a brand community for LivePlanet?

Right now the brand name LivePlanet is for the purpose of differentiating the company and its products from other broadband technology firms. The brand name LivePlanet has not become aspirational – that is, mass-market, middle class folks want to share in the reflected glory of the two Oscar winning stars as they do by wearing Michael Jordan's Nike athletic shoes. And, of course, the brand name LivePlanet does not reflect the values and lifestyles of the middle class. All these changes in what the brand means to the mass market must happen before fixed-wireless broadband technology moves up the expansion phase of the product life cycle as a fast-paced, newly successful media-based product.

Target groups

Throughout Section II of the book we talk about segments and target groups. Some are based on age – e.g., teenagers, Gen-Y, Gen-X, and boomers. Others are based on values and lifestyles – e.g., teenage Japanese girls, younger professional women managers, newly married men, and senior business executives. They too want what the others are getting from fixed-wireless broadband technology because they know what others are doing with these new information appliances for entertainment, news, and stock prices. They too want the transactions advantages of m-commerce and on-line stock trading. However, they don't have an interest in on-line Internet m-banking because they prefer the social value of their traditional banking relationships.[6] In this one industry, m-banking, customers are not learning what bankers are trying to teach. More on this in Chapter 6.

Decisions

Good value-based marketing decisions come about by answering three questions. The first is about the *context* of a decision. Mobile phones are merging with the Internet to give users fixed-wireless Internet capability with 2G (primitive digital), 2.5G (advanced digital) and 3G (broadband) infrastructure. 3G broadband wireless technology together with iMode phones and AOL content will either remake or destroy the old-line games businesses.

The second is about the *object* of a decision. Do wireless telecom firms and content providers encourage European users to switch from 2G to 2.5G when 3G is just around the corner for Europe? They probably will. However, if European customers act rationally, this is a poor investment for users because 2.5G phones will have to be thrown away as new 3G information appliances come to market. If these customers act irrationally, extra revenue will go into the pockets of mobile phone manufacturers, wireless telecom firms, and content providers so they can pay down the US $300 billion in debt they accumulated in setting up 3G for Europe. In either case, northern Europe will be first within the European Union to remake or destroy old-line, traditional industries, such as chemicals, paper, and automobiles.

The third is about the *impact* of a decision. Will Japanese and European firms that are 3G proficient bring their technology and content to the US? They definitely will. These companies will change the competitive landscape in the US and probably will drive prices down for 3G connections and content. However, this use of first-mover advantage by Japanese and European first will not dethrone American-owned entertainment, on-line stock traders and m-banks.

My bet is that US firms will adapt quickly to broadband wireless technology once it becomes clear how much muscle the federal government will use to recapture spectrum given away in a previous simpler world.

Forecast

The question remains: What do probable users want from broadband wireless technology?

Without fixed-wireless broadband availability most of the money being spent on m-entertainment will be wasted. 3G broadband wireless technology comes to Japan in 2001, in Europe 2003, and the US in 2005. Once broadband wireless is up and running, then the question will be whether 3G suits the content that is being distributed. And if it does, can older boomers and seniors, who hate doing anything technologically complicated, master how to download music, books, games, news, sports, and their stock quotes on their new miniature information appliances. Probably not with any ease. Thus marketers may face a difficult diffusion problem, as a large group of potential customers, who are high net worth individuals with huge amounts of disposable personal income, hesitates in, postpones or decides against the purchase of new 3G compatible mobile phones.

Here's the data we have so far.

- *Japan.* Retirees use so few iMode cell phones that they are invisible in sales reports. The same is true for senior business executives. The following show up in sales reports for iMode mobile phones: teenagers who want to chat; younger women business executives who have a need for greater security; and business commuters who surf the Web on their long train journeys between home and office.
- *Europe.* Here too retirees consider GSM mobile phones a luxury item that Germans and British who live in Spain and Italy respectively rarely use. On the other hand, senior executives view cell phones as a nice-to-have item for their business, and something they quietly give up when they too go into retirement. Teenagers and junior business executives insist mobile phones

are a necessity, and they are the customers who are pushing for the fast introduction of 3G broadband wireless technology.

- *US.* Although about 33 percent of the population has cell phones, older people in the third age of adulthood (65–80) or the very elderly (81–95) tend not to have tried them and cannot conceive of any time when they might use them to call great-grandchildren, grandchildren, or their children. Folks in the second age of adulthood (40–64) might have used cell phones in their business work, and when an emergency exists in their cars they try out their mobile phones. Given their lack of familiarity with cell phones and the general absence of helpful call centers, these middle aged people tend to abandon the new technology with a sense of frustration and an "attitude of never again." Teenagers, junior business executives and newly married couples in the first stage of adulthood (20–39) know how to use analogue and primitive digital cell phone technology, and they probably will shift to 2.5G advanced digital mobile phones and 3G broadband wireless technology when the latter becomes available in 2005. However, this is too far in the future for any good marketing predictions.

- *Other places in the world.* None of these diffusion issues as they pertain to age groups, especially the 50-year interval between retirees and teenagers, are crucial in China, India and elsewhere in the world. In most places, no landline legacy systems exist and the first phone anyone will use is a wireless mobile phone. For example, "mama traders" in the cash-only markets of West Africa, gold traders in Bombay (Mumbai), India, and export-import factors in southern and coastal China all use cell phones for business without regard to income, age, and technological confusion.

Thus our forecast must help us get answers to the following questions:

- How long will it take teenagers as younger business managers to translate their techno-geek skills with fixed-wireless telecom services into broadband wireless technology?
  Very fast.

- How long will it take Gen-Y as mid-career business executives to translate their info-geek skills with broadband wireless technology into m-entertainment, m-stock trading, and m-banking?

  Fast.

- How long will it take Gen-X as more mature business executives to translate their information technology skills with computers into wired e-commerce?

  Not very fast.

- How long will it take boomers as senior business executives to translate their word processing and spread sheet skills into good Internet search skills?

  Not very fast.

Detailed answers are found in Section I of the book.

- Which younger age groups will lay the groundwork for actionable segmentation and are ready right now to create value within a world of fixed-wireless broadband technology?
- Which professional groups will put up the superstructure for actionable targeting and are ready right now to deliver value in business news, sports events, some games, and pornography with this new technology?
- Which products and services establish actionable positioning as the vehicle for putting mobile phones, m-commerce, and the wireless Internet into play among venture capitalists in the pre-IPO market?

Answers are found in Section II of the book.

The problem is that nobody in marketing knows a great deal about the demographic data, and values and lifestyle information that underpin consumer decisions about m-commerce. Boomers hold on to their visions from the 1980s in which they became adults with PCs on their desktops. The trouble with this vision is that it provides little guidance on the boring business of using wired laptops by Gen-X, linking up to the wired Internet by Gen-Y, and going over to wireless computers, email, and the wireless Internet by teenagers; then deciding how much to produce for each target group; and finally setting a range of price, for connections and content. Investments in on-line ventures have piled up, but nobody has made money except the porn kings.

Today, older professionals tell you that phones are only for phoning among all age groups, and teenagers shout out that phones are for talking, sending messages, and getting data. This wide gap about the use of wired and cell phones between age groups complicates the creation and delivery of value for broadband wireless Internet. This diffusion of technology problem is as old as marketing itself.

Will Affleck and Damon succeed with LivePlanet and its new media broadband wired and wireless technology? Will it gain market share? Will it make money? Nobody knows.

USER-FRIENDLY PRODUCTS

Mobile phones, m-commerce, and the wireless Internet together are creating a unique new medium. First, the mobile Internet is designed for people on the move; these include teenagers, business commuters, and other Japanese target groups. Second, the content that shows up on the handset is designed for small phones that fit in the pockets of users; these are *manga* cartoons, seaweed-covered rice balls with mayonnaise, and other quick purchases, late night snacks from the hub of m-commerce in Japan, the 7-Eleven *combini*. Third, wireless providers must deliver innovative revenue-generating applications through innovative content partnerships; several good examples include the alliance of NTT DoCoMo-AOL Japan, and 7-Eleven's deals with Softbank and Yahoo! Japan.

The coming revolution

The widespread mobile telecommunications revolution is about to humble governments, the religious establishment, and businesses. It is coming to us with all its wonders and woes. The mobile Internet is creating new goods and new ways of living in the world. It is not erasing the past or changing human nature, but it is replacing previous forms of communications. Most things wired telephone firms do are irrelevant to a mobile future.

Preparing yellow (or golden) pages, hiding unlisted numbers, ordering plug in service and home wiring, presenting unintelligible bills, managing phone inventories, staging elaborate campaigns to connect even more dissatisfied landline users: these traditional wired-telephone functions and their complex infrastructures, which absorb perhaps half or more of wired telecom revenues and thus represent an expense to telephone subscribers, will not abruptly vanish. But they will become increasingly marginal to the extent that phone calls are delivered without wires; some folks already use analogue 1G, others use primitive digital 2G, and a few now use digital 3G. Should digital mobile Internet become dominant, as I suspect it will within the decade, these traditional functions will be contracted out to specialized firms, while wireless firms concentrate on essential mobile connections and the enhancement of their Internet Web strategies.

The new mobile technology will alter the way we communicate. The number of wireless users will increase greatly as new 3G technology delivers "content" – video, music, writing of all kinds, or mastery of everything – instantaneously and at negligible transportation cost to remote corners of the world, awaking the desire and imparting the skills to talk to friends, do business, and visit with the family anytime, anywhere. For better or worse, emerging mobile technologies will extend Hollywood's vast capacity to entertain, Silicon Valley's strong commitment to bringing new technologies to the market, and Wall Street's in-depth ability to finance it all wherever they are found: in the US, Europe, in East Asia and Australia, and in South Asia. Whoever prevails in tomorrow's digital mobile Internet marketspace, today's baffled and lumbering wired telecom conglomerates in their current configuration face certain extinction.

The digital mobile Internet future is not a matter of choice for telecom firms. To the extent that they forego this future, independent wireless content providers will claim it for themselves.

GSM versus iMode

Can 13 million iMode users in Japan be right about which cell phone technology will predominate at home and abroad? Since there are only 2.6 million worldwide WAP users, is it possible that this ubiquitous European mobile technology has reached the mature phase of the product life cycle prematurely, may start declining in numbers of users, and eventually give way to iMode or something else?

Yesterday, through the Nokia 7110 mobile phone, GSM supported voice communications, SMS text, data transfer, and Web gateways to the Internet. Today, through the Nokia GPRS Communicator, GSM gains speed and with Web 2.0 the GSM mobile phone becomes a usable device for Web content. At least, this is what the boosters say about GSM. Of course, the sales of handsets for GSM-only phones from Ericsson, Nokia and others are in decline. Those who do the forecasts for Hollywood, Silicon Valley, and Wall Street are putting some money behind NTT DoCoMo's iMode technology. They cannot afford to be left out in the cold should GSM falter, and iMode pull even or get ahead in the race to dominate mobile Internet.

Here are some of the things DoCoMo is doing today. It has taken a minority stake in KPN Mobile, the Dutch mobile operator, and it has other deals pending in Europe. If DoCoMo goes with KPN Mobile and GSM in Europe, the former will have to translate iMode content, which is based on compact HTML (cHTML) computer language, into WAP's wireless mark-up language (WML). iMode would be run over KPN's existing system, and this approach enables KPN to introduce the same content and style of services that have proven popular in Japan. Or DoCoMo might use two separate protocols in Europe, that is, GSM and iMode, over KPN's existing system. Users would have access to both technologies through a single handset that contains browsers for both.

Let's be clear. There is not a great deal of difference between WML and cHTML. WAP, as a subset of XML, may move us closer to the mainstream evolution towards XML, the single Internet standard that enables PCs, mobile phones, digital TVs, and other miniature information appliances to communicate with one another. However, iMode's cHTML is close to HTML fixed-Internet language, and software developers easily can add tags to existing HTML language to link up with XML. This is an important advantage for iMode over GSM.

Unfortunately for GSM telecom providers in Europe, their advertising and promotion campaigns have suggested that the GSM-based mobile Internet is the same as the PC-based fixed-wired Internet. It is not. Fixed-wired Internet and wireless mobile Internet are two different media, and attempts to put the former's content on the latter's handsets are a mistake. Yesterday's, GSM wireless Internet content was just text whereas the wired PC Internet content is text, video pictures, music, and many other interesting things. Moreover, GSM technology is still based on circuit-switching technology whereas iMode technology is based on packet-switching technology. Only packet switching offers "always on" mobile phones, the hallmark of iMode handsets in Japan.

Today, in Europe, GSM mobile links mean business executives need not carry a laptop computer and phone their offices so often. The same is true for iMode in Japan. This is a big plus for mobile Internet.

GSM applications in Finland

"We're pure *users*," says Kenneth Raman, head of trading at the Finnish forestry and paper production company UPM-Kymmene. "We're really not interested in the technology ... but in the value it can give us ... It's useful, but it's not revolutionising our lives."[7]

UPM's business is capital-intensive. Hence, Raman needs to put funding in place and take care of the associated foreign exchange and interest rate risks. Raman and his team manage trading from Finland, but many of their transactions are completed out of hours in New York, London, or other markets. Good risk management requires that deals should be put into the back-office treasury system as soon as possible after completion; confirmations come in as the deals occur; and any errors or mis-matches are taken care of quickly.

"Of course, we don't know where the markets are heading any more than before ... But life is more certain,"[8] says Raman. This funding support system is a GSM product that is priced right for international firms that do business both within Europe and elsewhere in the world. If iMode is priced right for international firms in Europe would their executives switch from WAP to iMode? The question is still open. A positive answer scares GSM telecom providers.

Promotion marketing

GSM mobile advertising depends on good access to demographic data, and values and lifestyle information about segments, target groups, and individuals. The typical GSM user is one with a lot of disposable personal income who needs high quality information. Thus the ads must be tied to what they want in terms of services and what can GSM do right away: short messaging services, text not video, and new personalized services. GSM users elect to receive messages about their favorite brands (so-called, "permission marketing") that is highly targeted and adds value.

According to Sonera, Finland's largest mobile telecommunications operator, 70 percent of Finnish users are open to wireless advertising if it is timely and personalized or if it keeps costs down. Sonera has pioneered the use of GSM advertising through Zed, its mobile portal. With the availability of electronic wallets in Finland, electronic cash is readily available to pay for premium ad placement, promotion exclusivity, and even discounts to stimulate immediate sales. As soon as 3G is widely available in the Scandinavian, Baltic, and northern European countries, GSM-based permission marketing will become a "push" system for getting product information to users.[9] Right now GSM promotion marketing is dependent on the willingness of users to "pull" products onto their GSM handsets.

User-friendly GSM products already are in place in northern Europe and similar iMode products already are in place in Japan. If iMode decides to compete in Europe, especially with the coming of 3G, then iMode could run a strong competitive race against GSM in its home market, Europe. Given the *nihonjin* or "We Japanese" value in Japan, GSM has no chance of mounting a serious challenge to iMode in Japan. Therefore, iMode will strike at GSM in Europe, and take market share and future revenue from GSM. In the end, iMode will be a stronger competitor at home and in all overseas markets because it has money to invest from its conquest of markets in Europe.

M-COMMERCE TRANSACTIONS

Here is the impact of m-commerce on the 4 Ps of marketing.

- *Products.* Real time wireless Internet transactions force products to become commodities, core assets to become peripheral, and valuable assets
  to become loss leaders. Recognize that goods and services from wireless
  content providers tend to be the same in the minds of the buyers. Marketers
  must create competitive transparency to succeed. This is the *new* approach
  of marketers towards product marketing.

- *Price.* Real time m-commerce transactions base prices on demand at the
  time of sale, and these prices change continuously. Deliver the lowest possible prices and minimum transactions costs for goods and services from
  content providers. Users demand this competitive pricing structure in return for maximum purchases. Marketers must establish financial nakedness to succeed. This is the *new* approach of marketers towards price marketing.

- *Place.* Real-time wireless Internet transactions give all sellers power in
  the channel of distribution. Provide the maximum number of suppliers and
  minimum inventory levels. Customers insist on success in fulfillment or
  the delivery of accurate orders. Marketers must put in place distribution
  exposure. This is the *new* approach of marketers towards place marketing.

- *Promotion.* Real time m-commerce transactions push well-established
  brands out of the market and into the dead brands society. Increase marketing openness as the norm for customers who want promotion and advertising to provide information rather than new entry barriers. Marketers must
  convert traditional pull advertising to push promotions that are targeted
  to specific individuals through permission marketing. This is the *new* approach of marketers to promotion marketing.

Together, these make up the *new* marketing strategy for using GSM, iMode and
other mobile phones on the wireless Internet. Done well they train customers
on how to get ready for the migration from 2G and 2.5G to 3G. If customers
learn enough to make 3G a part of their lifestyles, then marketers have done
a good job in putting the *new* marketing concept into use for speeding up the
transition to 3G.

Real options

Let's regroup these marketing opportunities into three categories of options based on the data, information, and knowledge we have concerning international segmentation, national target groups, and local positioning efforts for products and services.

Option 1: pursue

Put first-round investments into technology-rich hotels, horse racing and other forms of gambling, and voice portals. Add to investments in the NTT DoCoMo-AOL Japan alliance. Rebalance mobile Internet assets with more money going into iMode and less going into GSM.

Which of these investments will have double-digit growth in sales revenues and profits? Apply these questions to interactive TV and LivePlanet. Are they in the expansion phase of the product life cycle? Does the expansion phase show fast-paced growth (a concave curve) or slower growth (an S-curve)? After first-round investments are made by venture capitalists, is LivePlanet's "burn rate" of cash within the norm of six–eight months, and will it have positive cash flow within two years?

Follow the advice of Hutchison Whampoa: "Every investment must pay its own way in the shortest period of time ... We are not in the business of subsidizing loss-leaders."

Option 2: postpone

During future rounds of investments, convert what remains of Dell's wired real time ordering and inventory system to the wireless Internet, and gradually put all on-line stock trading and some Internet m-banking up as alternative channels of distribution.

Observe how some sports entertainment, especially the Olympics, are unable to guarantee their audience size for advertisers. Then ask the questions: "Are TV personalities unable to produce interesting content that competes favorably with big-event programs, such as *Survivor*? Is this a good time for push promotions and permissions marketing in the new media of mobile Internet? Or has the product life cycle for big-event sports programs entered its mature or no growth phase even as commercials shown during these big events convince more people to join the brand communities favored by the athletes?"

Follow the advice of venture capitalists: "Get it done fast." Don't worry about TV production values or when the mass market might be awake to watch the big-event sports program. Put the results out now before both wired and wireless Internet spread the news and scores to the world.

Option 3: terminate

Don't invest any more money in the current awkward ways of trying to make plane reservations via primitive digital phones. Keep away from the firms without content, such as Pacific Century Cyberworks.

The application of real options to marketing helps turn marketing opportunities into successful strategies for creating and delivering value for customers, marketers and investors alike. The crucial question in this analysis is: "What do I get?"

MONEY-MAKING DEALS

Let's summarize the deals we will discuss in detail in the following chapters.

1   Marketers are selling mobile Internet technology in competition with fixed Internet technology. The wireless Internet is in the expansion phase of the product life cycle, and mobile Internet will grow even faster when telecom providers introduce packet switching, 3G technology, and more interesting content. For a few telecom providers sales growth is doubling every year, but for most the burn rate of cash has been extended into the second year and positive cash flow is nowhere in sight. Therefore, the better-managed wireless firms will be acquiring the more poorly managed firms, and both will be looking for alliances with content providers.

2   Marketers are creating new market space. They are selling "always on" connections, content specifically designed for the mobile medium, and even a daily *manga* cartoon to both wired and wireless telecom firms.

These providers must reconfigure the value chain of price–quality–service, provide location awareness, offer microbilling on the phone bill, and collect a rich monthly fee from customers. The content providers must transform latent into real demand. Email and short messaging services may be killer applications for mobile phones. Of course, there is no finish line for telecom firms because new market space must be created and re-created all the time.

3   Marketers have the most control over the value proposition they deliver to customers. They have some control over mobile products and the roll-out of 3G wireless service. However, marketers have almost no control over pricing strategy because the mobile Internet is transparent for all to check prices and make bids on their own. Therefore, marketers are in a competitive environment in which margins are shrinking for bankers, insurance brokers, stock brokers, advertisers, entertainment firms, and many other companies.

4   Marketers must create brand communities for the wireless Internet. *Mobile* is a universal word. It is used by most people in the world as an exclamation. *Mobile* has no subject or object. *Mobile* means answer the phone, chat through the phone, do business on the phone, buy goods and services with the phone. The vocabulary of *mobile* keeps expanding irrespective of language, dialect or accent. Hence, GSM users are one brand community, iMode users are another brand community, and CDMA may become a third brand community. Marketers must predict consumer choices for each of these brands for one, three and five years into the future. Marketers also must forecast the impact of discontinuous change, especially if and when iMode becomes an appropriate substitute for GSM within Europe, or W-CDMA or CDMA 2000 becomes the UMTS wireless standard throughout the mobile world.

5   Marketers must target twenty-somethings (Gen-Y), do deeper data mining, and collect demographic data, and values and lifestyle information. Marketers must teach thirty-something (Gen-X) customers to pay for content. And marketers must encourage forty-somethings (boomers) to try the mobile Internet with the hope the latter might follow their children into using m-commerce, mobile phones, and the wireless Internet. Mar-

keters must teach older customers that their technology phobia about mobile Internet can be overcome by use of the new phones, and these boomers also will prosper by using m-commerce.

6   Marketers must position their mobile products and their 4 Ps marketing strategies based on the success stories, e.g., on-line stock trading, and fixed-wireless alliances. These offer marketers rich content for making things happen properly, growing sales, and making some money. Marketers also must learn from the failures of on-line Internet banking, many dot-coms, and other Web-based firms. Through all of this marketers will be teaching new customers how to benefit from the *new* economy of the mobile Internet.

These six chapters provide investors with a well-marked road map. Risks must be taken at the beginning of the trip, especially if we take some wrong detours and must double back. Rewards will come along as we journey towards robust sales and good profits. When all is said and done – that is, in about ten years – the mobile wireless Internet will have replaced the fixed-wired Internet.

MARKETING IN THE *NEW* ECONOMY

The application of financial theory to marketing information now provides standards of proof across the full range of practical problems. We can compare rewards and risks of each of the 4 Ps or all of them together; measure the successes and failures of traditional telecom providers; and speculate on the potential ups or downs of non-traditional wireless telecom and content providers. We can study how segments across national frontiers react to the migration from 2G to 2.5G or 3G, the willingness of national target groups (by income, age, lifestyle preferences, etc.) to use WAP or iMode, and whether local products are positioned properly to take advantage of the more rapid acceptance of technological diffusion among Gen-Y twenty-somethings, less rapid among Gen-X thirty-somethings, and much slower acceptance of discontinuous technological change among boomers or forty-somethings and fifty-somethings.

Of course, in each of these positioning statements, we may have omitted a crucial variable that provides valuable information. Were boomers engineers, computer scientists or technically-trained personnel, and thus more willing than their peers to accept the introduction of new technology? Were the boomers senior executive officers of business firms who within the last two decades brought a computer and keyboard into their offices so they could keep up with their middle managers in terms of word processing, financial spreadsheets, email, and, most recently, Internet-based applications? Did the boomers as parents train their twenty-something children at an early age to work with new technology even if the kids preferred to play ball, go on stage in a rock band, or be an artist? Therefore, the age of twenty-somethings may mislead us into concluding they are all from Silicon Valley and expert in every nuance of info-geek rather than from Stamford, Lake Forest or Palo Alto.

Marketing in the *new* economy means choices among two or more options, such as pursuing an investment for target group that will pay out within one year or postponing an investment for another target group that will pay out within three years, or terminating an investment for a third target group that will pay out within five years. Choices have to be made among investments in Japan's May 2001 use of 3G, versus Europe's coming of age with 3G in 2003, versus America's drift towards 3G in 2005. In the decision about Europe, another choice has to be made between GSM and iMode, or something entirely new, CDMA 2000. It is entirely possible that the macro factors influencing 3G decisions for Europe may not be the same as the micro factors that lead Europeans to stay with GSM or abandon it for iMode. Financial legitimacy is a necessary (though not sufficient) condition for the credibility that marketing still lacks outside its own domain.

Marketers who mine data until they find "proof" to support virtually any conclusion about m-commerce, mobile phones, and the wireless Internet give marketing a bad name. Real options force marketers to take advantage of a state-of-the-art method for financial analysis in which we can rank options and decide whether to pursue, postpone, or terminate them. If marketers make the best choice, then their investments will throw off double-digit growth in sales, positive cash flow and better than average returns on investments, and improvements in US productivity.

Myth making

The Internet, wireless communications and computer networking have become so quickly a part of our lives. Although these have the earmarks of a revolution in values and lifestyles, similar to the introduction of the telephone, radio, TV and the car, all revolutionary products must face market forces at some time in the near or distant future. The mobile Internet myths are as follows:

■ Wireless m-commerce is different.
■ Prospects about potential sales are better than current earnings.
■ Exponential growth is going to accelerate almost for ever.
■ Wireless telecom and content providers aren't subject to ordinary economic forces, such as a slower economy and higher interest rates.
■ IT companies, computer hardware manufacturers, software developers, wired and wireless telecom providers, and content developers all can generate breathtaking gains in earnings, sales, and productivity for years to come.

In reality, growth slows, the business cycle matters, and first-movers lose control over markets.[10] In the second half of 2000, many wireless IT competitors got hurt and were carried off the field with career-ending injuries, similar to NFL football players. They won't be getting first-round investments from venture capitalists, and they won't be issuing friends-and-family stock in anticipation of now dead-in-the-water IPOs. That is, they won't be doing this in early 2001 or anytime in the future until the next set of myths becomes the gospel truth for mobile Internet.[11]

Grow and invest

Let's give up our myths about IT, computers, e-commerce, fixed-wireless Internet, and m-commerce for the reality of sales growth, real options investments, 4 Ps marketing strategy, an earnings stream, value creation and value delivery. Although capital efficiency is important in investments, a more important number in mobile Internet is how many more users with a higher value have been added to a firm's stable of customers. Both DoCoMo and AOL do a great job getting users to spend more money per month on content and other services; together, they will be a formidable competitor in Japan, perhaps in Europe, and maybe even in the US too. The task of marketers is to get customers to yield a positive cash flow return on investment, and to convince their finance colleagues that more investments yield more growth and more growth yields higher positive cash flow returns on investments.[12]

CONCLUSIONS

How to conquer the wireless world? Apply a *new* 4 Ps marketing strategy to m-commerce, especially to the existing wireless platforms of GSM, iMode and CDMA, and to those mobile Internet platforms that are coming soon with 3G technology in 2001, 2003 and 2005. Here is a checklist of things to do:

- Put information appliances in the hands of m-commerce users, and upgrade these enhanced mobile phones as 2G and 2.5G systems move to 3G technology.
- Build market share with a *new* 4 Ps marketing strategy that is transparent, and carefully adapted to the expansion phase of the product life cycle.
- Offer customers training on crucial salient product attributes, such as location awareness, voice and data transmissions, and transaction capabilities, and implement the learning requirements of the *new* marketing concept for mobile Internet.
- Create and deliver interactive value by mixing and matching the old and new economies, and adapting them both to the needs of m-commerce, mobile phones, and the wireless Internet.

Let's look at how marketers create value in the new wireless world unfolding before our very eyes.

Value Creation

CHAPTER 1

Marketing Wireless Products

EXECUTIVE SUMMARY

MARKETERS OFFER MINIATURE INFORMATION APPLIANCES with unique interactive content to m-commerce customers. Here's what is involved:

- They offer iMode and GSM phones as smart handheld devices for location awareness (or 24/7 anytime, anywhere availability).
- They build brand community for Japanese users of iMode phones with *manga* cartoons, Pokémon images, and the purchase of goods at 7-Eleven stores.
- Marketers design tangible product attributes (e.g. voice and data communications, and transaction capabilities) for European users of GSM phones.
- They sell cell phones to early adapters in the US who put up with some negative product attributes, such as the loss of signal, until better, more reliable products come along.
- They market short messaging services (SMS) to teenagers, data communications to frequent flyers, and m-retailing to women business executives in Japan, Europe and the US.
- They answer the fundamental customer question "What do I get from miniature information appliances?" and explain their unique interactive content, and the messages they bring to customers at the point of need.
- Marketers carry out a *new* 4 Ps marketing strategy that offers marketers data-based customer relationship management, and provide investors with the option to build, expand or delay investments in the mobile Internet.

Invest in product marketing deals

Do the deals answer fundamental marketing questions? What do I get as customers or users? How rapid is the increase in sales especially during the expansion phase of the product life cycle? Are revenues substantial enough so market share can be measured? Are revenues sustainable after initial start-up? Do these sales revenues grow market share? Also do the deals deliver appropriate financial results in terms of the burn rate of cash, positive cash flows, and earnings from sales? Do the following product marketing deals create and deliver value?

- Add tangible benefits to the distribution alliance for Japanese customers between Japan's wireless telecom provider, NTT DoCoMo, and America's content provider, AOL Japan. This deal answers important marketing questions and delivers crucial financial results. After a careful review of existing product marketing deals, the alliance is the best business model for the emerging m-commerce wireless Internet world.

- Offer Finnish customers Nokia Web-enabled cell phones with wireless Ethernet networks and with screens or "home decks" that provide electronic wallets, show books, sell CDs, and distribute e-airplane tickets. This deal also answers important marketing questions and delivers crucial financial results. However, an open question exists among customers from outside Finland and Sweden whether others will accept small screens, difficult-to-read text, and 3–12 key strokes to gain access to e-airline tickets and other on-line products.

- Establish the logo of iMode mobile phones outside of Japan, particularly in Europe and the US. This deal depends on the acceptance by local customers of iMode technology, and the willingness of DoCoMo marketers to promote and advertise its benefits to European and American users. At the moment, this deal has not generated a large number of sales, but the firm is burning cash without positive cash flow from Europe. However, if DoCoMo's success in Japan is any indication of its future success elsewhere, then we can expect DoCoMo to begin growing sales revenue in Europe, perhaps by the end of 2001, and about two to four years later in the US.

- Increase the brand awareness of GSM phones in the US by deepening the foreign direct investments of European telecom firms in American wireless companies, such as UK Vodafone's acquisition of California-based AirTouch. However, do recognize that the use of the WAP standard in the US faces strong competition from CDMA. Currently, the AirTouch subsidiary contributes positive cash flow and strong earnings to its parent, Vodafone. This may not continue. The pending takeover of loss-ridden VoiceStream Wireless by Germany's Deutsche Telekom may not be completed because the latter's stock price is nearing its bottom collar price, at which time the deal could be terminated by VoiceStream.

Recommendation

Wireless telecom marketers are getting ready for the fast expansion in demand for m-commerce products in the years between 2001 and 2005. If they attempt to depend on corporate structures, strategies and people from the traditional wired telecom industry, that is, Deutsche Telekom, AT&T and British Telecommunications, these marketers ill serve their wireless firms. Theirs is a failure to respond in a timely fashion to changes in alliances, technology, brand names, and customer demands.

Here is the marketing assignment for wireless marketers.

- Segment digital customers across national frontiers in Japan, Europe, the US and China, and elsewhere in the world.
- Target upwardly mobile, relatively affluent customers who have similar personal values and lifestyles, e.g., teenagers, senior business executives, and others.
- Position iMode and GSM phones with new unique wireless content, fully Web-enabled 3G phones, exciting new logos, deeper brand awareness, location awareness, voice and data communications, transaction capabilities, and short messaging services.

The overall task of marketers is to accelerate the change from wired to wireless telecommunications. The survival of wireless firms beyond their start-up years demands tough decisions about which investments to make in technology and content, how to increase sales, how to grow market share, how to capture the right kind of customers, how to slow down the burn rate of cash, how to speed up positive cash flow, how to generate earnings, and finally how to manage the new wireless business effectively.

No lifetime of happiness exists for today's group of wireless telecom firms as it did in the past for the giant, wired telecom monopolies. Only hell on earth is the future for wireless firms, but that is better than being dead in the water as are the wired firms, whose executives could not or would not transform their wired firms into entrepreneurial, start-up wireless firms.

INTRODUCTION

Here's our product marketing strategy:

- Provide Web-based data communications anytime, anywhere to senior business executives in Finland, Sweden, the UK, and Germany. Offer SMS and fun content to pre-teen kids, teenagers, and Gen-Y (twenty-somethings) in Japan and Europe. Give business commuters m-commerce transactions at Tokyo's, London's and Chicago's train stations, and Narita, Heathrow, and O'Hare airports. Turn an interest in the wireless Internet into an addiction for miniature wireless appliances.

- Create value with iMode in Japan and GSM in Europe. Note that both are in the expansion phase of the product life cycle; however, sales of iMode phones are growing faster than sales of GSM phones. Transmit data rapidly with packet switching and the introduction of 3G. Deliver content-rich iMode phones to affluent and middle-income users. Package GSM phones with short text messages as commodities for teenagers; offer added value with MP3 and keyboards for Gen-Y; and sell water-resistant and drop-resistant mobiles for Gen-X boaters and construction workers respectively. Decide which wireless standard will do a better job in building brand community in the US and China.

- Invest in telecom platforms, wireless distribution alliances, and content providers that grow sales, build market share, increase turnover, and, perhaps, make money, too. Offer customers what they want from m-commerce, such as location awareness, voice and data transmissions, and transaction capabilities. Support a single iMode standard for Japan, and a dual-protocol GSM and iMode standard for Europe, and decide on one standard for the US.

- Manage m-commerce that mixes and matches assets from the old and new economies. Follow the example of Manchester United and its fans in London and Shanghai who use Web-enabled GSM phones to check scores and order merchandise. Increase the return on invested capital for the wireless telecom and content providers, and for sports entertainment firms that sell merchandise through m-retailing.

DUMB INVESTORS

Let's test my favorite theory. When will American-owned wireless firms compete effectively against Japanese- and European-owned mobile phone carriers in the former's home market, the US? Ask telecom executives to select from the following range of choices: third quarter 2001; first quarter 2002; third quarter 2002; first quarter 2003; third quarter 2003; even farther out in the future. About 95 percent of the guesses from the telecom executives of US-owned analogue and primitive digital wireless firms were for years beyond 2003 when most of them will be retired, bought out by foreign firms, or out of the telecom business altogether.

This is a victory for dumb investors. These business executives spend corporate earnings on investments that eventually destroy shareholder value. The US wireless industry is being overwhelmed with an influx of poorly informed wired telecom investors – dumb investors in academic jargon. During the rush to convert the US to wireless m-commerce, investors from the wired telecom world are promoting new market space for the wireless telecom world. However, they are rushing ahead into wireless without the innovations in mobile commerce, the range of content for wireless Internet, and the richness in pricing of e-services now available in Japan and Europe.

AT&T Wireless, Sprint PCS, Verizon and others want to connect more customers and build up their networks of users. They believe connections grow sales of basic wireless service; hence they give away mobile phones and precious minutes per month. Bundled pricing precludes these American-owned wireless firms from charging customers for continuous on-line connections, short messaging services, packet switching, daily downloads of favorite *manga* cartoons, and wireless links to favorite Web sites, electronic wallets. Also bundled pricing precludes these US firms from charging on-line firms for access to the two crucial targeted market groups in the initial roll out of fast 3G wireless service. The early adapters are the young, technologically sophisticated, affluent, urban-based teenagers and young adults, and their boomer parents, executives who need wireless connections in their business, for home, and at play.

By focusing marketing strategy on increasing sales and growing earnings, AT&T, Sprint and others are not paying attention to what is absolutely important when firms create new market space for a technologically superior industry, the return on invested capital from target market groups. Either the wired firms benchmark the best strategies from highly successful firms in other industries, or the former will face new entrants from Japan and Europe in the US wireless industry. Currently, NTT DoCoMo from Japan, Vodafone AirTouch from the UK, and other foreign-owned telecom firms are coming to the US using marketing and financial strategies employed successfully by Enron, Pfizer, and Hutchison Whampoa.

Return on invested capital

The benchmark tool is return on invested capital. Business firms create value not from physical assets alone, but from intangible assets, such as anytime, anywhere 24/7 connections, packet switching, buying and *selling* licenses, putting a collar on the underlying options, and a self-reinforcing network of users, that offer the potential of far higher returns on investment. Such real options analysis works well with the big strategic marketing risks facing a new, technologically superior industry, such as m-commerce or the wireless world.

The collective opinion of the dominant wireless firms in Japan and Europe is superior to that of the individual wired and wireless firms in the US. The former get the market right when they act individually to establish one multinational standard, such as GSM in Europe or W-CDMA (wide-code division multiple access) in Japan. Unfortunately, the latter got it wrong when they started copying each other and invested too much in AT&T's TDMA (time division multiple access), Qualcomm's CDMA, or something else. Not only did they get the technology wrong, but they created non-compatible wireless technologies across the US. Today, only 33 percent of potential American users of wireless have shifted their primary telephone usage from wired to wireless. The individual wisdom of the wired telecom firms in the US was to confuse potential customers. Confusion is always a dumb marketing strategy, and each year the strategy of confusion continues it becomes an even dumber m-commerce strategy.

The obscene success of GSM in Europe and W-CDMA in Japan says nothing more than the underlying shift to m-commerce in both regions is real. Without new foreign-owned entrants into the American wireless market, the US will remain an abject failure in the wireless world of m-commerce for the next two years or longer. To speed up the transition to wireless in the US, the American-owned wired firms must start benchmarking themselves against the best companies worldwide, or go out of business.

Competitive advantage

The GSM-based firms in Europe have a deep respect for competitive advantage, cash flow and return on capital. Their chief executive officers are successful because they pay attention to the cash their firm generates for each dollar the capital lenders and shareholders have sunk into it. On the other hand, AT&T expended earnings only through costly investments that destroyed shareholder value. Successes include:

▪ Dell Computer, which gave shareholders a return on invested capital of 223 percent, new market space in channel strategy, inventory velocity and stock turns of three days, and pricing down the cost curve; and

■ Vodafone, which purchased AirTouch from Pacific Bell of California and turned AirTouch into an American-based GSM source of high returns on invested capital.

Real options

In m-commerce, real options are used to value wireless firms such as telecom carriers as probable providers of 2G, 2.5G and 3G (generation) wireless networks. They can extend the capacity of their existing 2G networks by expanding into 2.5G or 3G, or both, or decide to hold back for a short or longer period of time. Also these wireless firms can acquire built-out networks or lease capacity or do both. Moreover, they can transmit a little or a great deal of content, such as daily *manga* cartoons and e-retailing sites, electronic wallets for the purchase of soda and parking slots, and e-banking services for insurance, home mortgages, and money market funds. The value of real options to m-commerce is to give wireless firms the ability to price out one or more delays in the introduction of the infrastructure, content and worldwide connections until market share sustains additional wireless investments.

In academic jargon, real options are known as contingent value rights, or a series of put or sell options. They buttress the price of an acquisition when a possibility exists of a delay in turning 2G into 3G, or shifting from TDMA to GSM. These rights are not publicly traded, but are held by the seller and, if need be, they can be hedged through one or more offsetting options. The optimum set of options permits wireless firms to make just enough investments in the US to raise their returns on invested capital to the level of Dell without suffering the slow earnings growth of AT&T.

Prospect theory in m-commerce

The American-owned wired firms are loss averse. They have an asymmetric attitude to gains and losses. They do not measure risk consistently. Currently, AT&T and others are taking fewer risks; they won't end their fixation with older wireless technology and call this investment a sunk cost; and these wired firms with wireless operations are regularly miscalculating the probabilities of the success of new entrants from Europe and Japan. The worst of it is these American-owned telecom firms are assuming a GSM outcome for the US has no chance at all of happening. Behavioral finance explains this irrational behavior by showing how the American-owned telecom firms think they are winning by increasing connections and sales, and by growing earnings, which gives them less incentive to keep working on increasing the returns on invested capital.

Their business executives have a mental account of what happened in the past. Their wired firms were on top; the cash flow was great. Now the wired firms are at the bottom. Their return on equity is slipping. These managers are using short-term solutions to increase sales and raise earnings without paying attention to what credit lenders and shareholders expect from them over the longer run – substantial increases in returns on invested capital. When these senior executives are presented with a report on the link between invested capital and market valuation, they usually scrawl "I don't get it," across the document and send it back to their internal finance and marketing strategy committee.

Notwithstanding the corporate cultural problems facing executives with new ideas, the future success of the wireless race is not yet apparent; no one knows for sure which technology will win out. Thus these "I don't get it" managers stick with what they know because they don't want to go into retirement as losers. Unless these executives have stock options which vest at some time in the future if and when the price of the stock reaches a certain higher level, the cost to them of sticking with primitive wireless technology and not going into 3G wireless technology is virtually non-existent. Some call this rational choice within an irrational world, or say business executives are trying to be rational even when they make the same mistakes over and over.

On the other hand, some executives are from the "I don't get it, but I'm willing to try something new" school of experimental decision making. Enron and Pfizer all put a high premium on trying something new with the expectation that the capital employed would yield higher returns on invested capital. Therefore, the behavior of key executives, their committees of internal experts, and the investment choices made by established firms and new entrants in the wireless telecom industry must be incorporated into models of the real world of m-commerce. This is the competitive thrust of NTT DoCoMo, Vodafone AirTouch and other foreign-owned wireless carriers as they do battle for market share in the US with the tired, wired giants of America's past.

The three chapters in Section I (marketing mobile products, promoting new market space, and pricing m-commerce services) are about the irrational investment behavior of the American-owned wired telecom firms and the rational investment behavior of the foreign-owned wireless telecom firms. The latter's acquisitions of the wireless divisions of the former is driven by business goals (e.g., gain revenues from the US) and influenced by the emotion of the possibility of dominating US firms in one important new technology. The refusal of the American-owned wired firms to see the threat from abroad and to do something constructive about it is influenced more by emotions and irrational decision making than by financial and marketing goals.

The use of values and lifestyles and the choices made by customers are well established in marketing as marketers collect data and process information on purchasing decisions among targeted market groups. The use of psychology, sociology and human behavior, and the choices made by users are less well established in finance, as executives make crucial investment decisions. Both attitudes are incorporated into these three chapters. The behavior of wired and wireless executives and customers in the real world of telecom competition must be understood before we can get a good sense of what is to come in 2001, 2003 and beyond.

PRODUCT ATTRIBUTES

All m-commerce products have more attributes than meet the eye.[1] For example, if the wireless Internet is indeed the world-changing technology as telecom players suggest, then you can do the following with your smart devices:

- find a parking spot for your car;
- search out the best bargains for your family;
- transfer medical records to your physician;
- permit mothers to breast-feed their babies on time and at work;
- scan inventory and make the close on sales;

- download music recommended by your friends;
- chat with your friends;
- read your email;
- pay bills while you commute to the city; and
- transfer funds from you checking account to your savings account.

Add to the list and find out what is important to you.

Probable customers

Also those persons who already have mobile phones are probable m-commerce customers. They know how to use smart telecom devices. Their behavior is to upgrade technology products as soon as they can with little regard to price. About half a billion people now use cell phones;[2] they are early adopters of anytime, anywhere technology. These customers see little or no risk in purchasing m-commerce products. Here are the most important product attributes for the probable consumers.[3]

Salient attribute

Of course, wireless communication is intrinsic to the m-commerce phones. Customers get information at anytime, so-called 24/7 time; and they get voice, data and Web-based ideas anywhere. The killer application is location awareness.[4]

- *Are your m-commerce customers on an airplane in business class?* Let them get the facts and do a deal.
- *Are they in a subway car?* Let them change the time and place for the next appointment.
- *Are your wireless Internet customers in a boring high-school class?* Let them do their email and chat with friends.

Look at these possible transactions, and calculate what you can charge for them.

Microbilling as a marketing innovation

For example, NTT DoCoMo, Japan's wireless telecom firm, charges customers for the minute-by-minute connection time used, a monthly "packet" access fee for both incoming and outgoing connections, and a monthly content fee for each subscription to a service of an Internet provider, including the monthly *manga* cartoons. All these appear on the customer's monthly bill from NTT DoCoMo, and such microbilling amounts to between $75 and $155 per month. This telecom firm also takes nine percent of the total content fee from the Internet provider as a service charge for acting as middleman, credit bureau, and fee collector. Microbilling is an important marketing innovation for m-commerce in Japan.[5]

Positive and negative attributes

The managerial task ahead for European and American telecom firms is to uncover and define how their customers will use their m-commerce products. Broadly speaking: if you are a business person with substantial corporate resources behind you, you are a member of the market segment called business executives. If you are a frequent flyer, then you are a member of the target market group called frequent flyer business executives. Therefore, telecom firms position their m-commerce products with the attributes preferred by their target customers, especially at 31,000 feet in the air.

Now for the tricky part. You can load your wireless Internet products with all the attributes possible. Some are non-negotiable for customers (e.g., continuous, on-line access similar to iMode phones). Others are tolerable (e.g., banner ads). Still others are negative (e.g., dead spaces in buildings and along highways). Most attributes should be positive so customers eventually will buy today's m-commerce products and later upgrade them to streaming or Packet Video, laptops with a wireless connections, or any and all of the coolest new things that are coming down the road.

WHAT DO I GET?

What do I get? A mobile phone? A consumer electronics device? Smart mobile makers must ask this question today. The next generation of mobile phones will be a new form of product with elements such as electronic games and video bundled in. Eiji Aono, an analyst at Goldman Sachs, asks "whether the consumer of the future comes to regard a handset as a mobile phone or a consumer electronics device ... If it is the former, Nokia, Ericsson, and other European manufacturers will have a considerable advantage. If it is the latter, [the Europeans] will have plenty"[6] of competition from Japan and South Korea.

"What do I get?" is always in the mind of customers. It is the question they ask themselves when manufacturers present them with new technologies, new products, and new services. "What do I get?" is a universal question because consumers want something better at a good price that offers them something they could not get before.

Handsets in Japan are two-thirds the size and weight of their European counterparts because Europeans prefer long battery life and the Japanese don't care about battery life. Also Japanese handsets have more functionality for both fun (e.g., *manga* cartoons) and business (i. e., data communications) than do European handsets. Motorola, the US mobile maker, prefers profitability at the expense of volume production.

iMode phones as CRM devices

Moreover, the iMode mobile phones receive content from AOL Japan including access to AOL's "Buddies List." This distribution alliance, especially the latter link, is crucial because it forms the basis of providing Japanese users with tailored messages and information. "Bring the message directly to the customer at the point of need,"[7] is the mantra of iMode. In Japan, DoCoMo offers subscribers access to 10,000 iMode sites, such as, restaurant locators, ski-condition reports, hotel reservation systems, on-line auctions, airline ticketing services, and many others.

For marketers the 4 Ps of marketing (product, promotion, price, and place) are constantly changing, always transparent, and mostly borrowed from alliance partners. The constant flux of the 4 Ps means all marketers become direct marketers – that is, the crucial person to make a success of customer relationship management or CRM. These *new* direct marketers must reposition messages, build new databases, upgrade IT legacy systems, create new middleware, and tailor messages to the ever-changing needs and lifestyles of customers. By providing the Japanese with a ubiquitous Internet (i.e., the Internet is accessible from almost anywhere in Japan), iMode-AOL becomes the mobile intermediary of choice to build ongoing digital relationships, reconfigure value chains, and to charge a premium price for contextual marketing in Japan.

This alliance answers important marketing questions and delivers crucial financial results based on the real business of the wireless Internet. It is the best non-US deal to promote contextual marketing; other overseas deals include electronic wallets from Sonera in Finland, and the mobile recipe book from Unilever. US-deals include Amazon.com, Mobile's Speedpass, Dell's link to ZDNet and CNET, and FedEx.

After a careful review of existing product marketing deals, the distribution alliance between NTT DoCoMo and AOL Japan is the best contextual marketing business model for the emerging m-commerce wireless Internet world.

Mobile phones as commodities

Japanese mobile makers already have priced their phones down the cost curve. Their price is so low they will capture a large market share. On the other hand, Deutsche Telekom, France Telecom, Vodafone and other operators are trying to shift some of the costs of building the networks, especially the costs of the new licenses, on to Nokia, Ericsson and Siemens. The operators want the infrastructure companies to provide vendor financing – that is, sell their mobile phones at low prices and defer full payments until sometime in the future. These equipment manufacturers are becoming lenders of last resort because the capital markets have quit funding telecom providers.[8] This poses substantial financing risks for Nokia and other mobile makers. European mobile phones are at the point of becoming commodities and the equipment manufacturers will have little or no control over price.

Slowdown in expansion phase of product life cycle

Nokia and Ericsson are firms from Finland and Sweden respectively. Over 65 percent of the population have mobile phones. In the year 2000 growth in mobile phone sales dropped to about 10–12 percent a year, a predictable slowdown in new subscribers. A sales slowdown will occur in other European countries as market penetration hits 60–70 percent for GSM phones, 95 percent in Finland. These European-made mobile phones will have to offer consumer electronics fun or watch Japanese-made GSM-compatible phones push the former out of the market with fun and games as consumer electronic devices.

New product life cycle

If both European- and Japanese-made dual-band iMode and GSM mobile phones become consumer electronic devices, then a new expansion phase in a new product life cycle will begin in Europe for mobile consumer electronic phones. The old mobile phones will be obsolete, and they will be replaced by the new consumer electronic devices. Right now Japan is poised to get the lion's share of the market in third-generation technology. European customers will get what they want at the expense of European mobile makers.[9]

VALUE-BASED MARKETING DECISIONS

Here are the value-based decision opportunities open to top management at the wired and wireless telecom firms throughout the world:

What is the context of a decision?

The telecom industry is shifting from narrowband to broadband technology, from 2G to 3G infrastructure, and from wired to wireless service. This is evident in Japan, Europe and elsewhere in the world. Although the telecom firms in the US talk a good game, their commitment to substantive change – namely, building the 3G infrastructure – is behind both Japan and Europe.

What is the object of a decision?

Japan will be the first country off the mark with 3G infrastructure. Some of the European counties, such as the UK, Germany and France, will be a close second as most EU and central and eastern European countries are holding auctions to give licenses to wireless telecom providers. The US has to decide whether to import the GSM digital standard of Europe, its upgrade called UMTS (or Universal Mobile Telecommunications Services), or the W-CDMA digital standard of Japan, or put in place nationally the current upgraded CDMA 2000 digital standard as the national standard in competition with GSM and UMTS.

What is the impact of a decision?

Each telecom firm must make individual decisions about acquisitions in its home and in overseas markets, and in the amount of money it will pay for new licenses in each country. European firms are seeking acquisitions in the US and in other EU countries. Japanese firms are seeking minority partnerships both in Europe and the US. American firms are doing deals at home and overseas. The competitive structure of the operators' portion of the telecom industry is up for grabs; because their commitment to setting up outside one's home country (via direct investments or through licenses) is proving to be more expensive than top management had thought just a few months ago.

Decision opportunities

Lastly, none of them know with certainty what customers want in wireless service, and what they will pay for on a long-term basis. If the mobile phones do indeed become commodities, their prices in the B2B and B2C markets will be at cost or below. If the same thing happens to the cost of wireless phone service, many telecom firms will never recoup the cost of the licenses or the acquisition of foreign telecom firms. Sometime within the next decade a shake out will occur among telecom operators, and their fate will be similar to the fate of AT&T in the US or British Telecommunications in the UK – that is, both were once two great local and long distance firms that made acquisitions and sold off divisions, but they never found the key to making money after deregulation. This is when smart competitors from outside the home country, such as from Japan, Germany, France, or Spain, come in and reconfigure a country's telecom value chain.

Reconfiguring the value chain

Such thinking helps in three ways:

- Firms can recognize and identify decision opportunities across the industrial world for wireless telecom service.
- Firms can create better alternatives for making good decisions either through alliances and partnerships, or through direct investments, or both.
- Firms can establish a set of competitive principles for the firm as they seek to conquer the wireless world in the age of m-commerce.

If these decisions are made properly, the firms together will put in place a new value proposition for the wireless telecom industry. This value proposition will put customers at the center of the decision making for new 3G technology, new consumer electronic devices, and new voice, data and transaction capabilities over mobile phones. If they do so, they will make money from m-commerce transactions and create new value through the wireless Internet.

ACTIONABLE SEGMENTATION

Marketers spend a great deal of time looking for meaningful differences among groups of customers and then identifying them. For example, hard data on demographic information say something about level of income, education, and ZIP (or postal codes). Soft data or values and lifestyle information say something about attitudes, beliefs, and habits.[10]

Hard data

In the US, income and education play a tiny role in a decision about whether to buy a mobile phone and the accompanying service package. For the working poor who live in dangerous neighborhoods they rent a wireless phone on a monthly basis because the wired telephone company will not provide service to their neighborhoods. Therefore, an analysis of ZIP or postal codes is the best use of hard data.

Soft data

On the other hand, for kids under 20 soft data are most important to marketers. These American teenagers want to be in contact with their friends through voice and email connections. An analysis of their attitudes towards how they want to live their lives – their lifestyle – is the best use of soft data. Furthermore, kids under 20 are keepers because they will continue to be wireless phone users throughout their lives.

Their parents – business executives who are over 40 – want both voice and data communications, and some ability to do transactions. An analysis of their habits towards work – their business life – is the best use of soft data. However, note this caveat: should they give up work and retire, these former business executives may not continue to be mobile phone users.

Bad news from needs analysis

"A lot of [Americans of a certain age] think the wireless Internet is a PC screen just squished down to a phone," says Callie Nelson, a senior analyst for wireless and mobile communications at the research firm, International Data Corporation. "There's a lot of education to be done."[11] Americans need a cozier relationship with their mobile phones similar to that of the Japanese with their iMode phones and what the Europeans are beginning to develop with their GSM and UMTS phones. At the moment, Americans think of the mobile phone as a business tool and not a necessity while the Japanese and Europeans think of the cell phone as a digital lifeline.

Of course, this is bad news for the mobile phone industry. In the US most people see no compelling reason to give up their wired phones and PCs for another, largely unproved electronic wireless device.

Better news from actionable segmentation

Therefore, for the US market, it is necessary to bring together a limited amount of demographic information together with a large amount of value-based information, and combine them into an actionable segmentation strategy. The collective traits of the working poor segment force telecom firms to offer relatively low prices for mobile phones. On the other hand, the collective habits of the teenage segment encourage telecom firms to request higher prices for their services. Lastly, the collective habits of business executives provide telecom firms with a bonanza of riches in their pricing strategy. Given the latter's group proclivity to drop mobile phone service once they leave the work force, promotion marketing strategies become all important in keeping them within the family of wireless Internet users. Thus price marketing is the most important of the 4 Ps in rolling out an effective marketing strategy for the next few years.

CUSTOMERS ARE THE CENTER OF THE M-COMMERCE UNIVERSE

These wireless Internet products are artifacts around which m-commerce customers have lifestyle experiences. Sophisticated users expect superior product offerings; they will collaborate with m-commerce firms to get what the former want from the latter. Daily in the age of m-commerce, whether the time is 2G, 2.5G and now 3G, wireless telecom products are created in real time as firms obtain continuous feedback about consumer purchasing behavior.

Target market group: kids under 20

For example, kids under 20 already have a mastery of machines that no age group before them can match. They have been using Game Boy and cell phones as they moved into their teenage years and later into being Gen-Y or the net generation. Theirs is a omni-connected world that includes music, chat rooms and email. They get what they want right now, no questions asked.

Target market group: business executives who are over 40

Of course, the kids have parents. These business executives are frequent fly-ers, but they need a bit of coaching, tutoring or training in how to use these m-commerce devices. They "learn" by doing. This is the *new* marketing concept in which firms educate their customers in how to use and get the most from Internet wireless phones.

Target market group: executives who want anytime, anywhere telecom service

Good marketing firms know what the preferences are of one or more custom-ers. From these data points the former develops a new targeted market group based on a synthesis of the preferences of similar users – namely, frequent-flyer business executives who want anytime, anywhere telecom service. This group wants location awareness 24 hours each and every day during a seven-day working week.

When the 24/7 targeted group clicks on a Web guide about hotels and restaurants in the arriving city, these Internet transactions provide information to those marketers who carry out data mining. Good market researchers make predictions from these data on the use of m-commerce smart telecom devices by the 24/7 group.

In summary, customers become data. Then data become customers. Fi-nally, both customers and data migrate to real time.

M-COMMERCE TRANSACTIONS

Look at the previous list of ten possible transactions (see the section on product attributes, pp. 48–9) and how NTT DoCoMo charges for use of its wireless network for what you wireless marketers could do with smart telecom devices in Europe and the US. Through data mining sales personnel know the product preferences of their best and most probable customers. Then the former check product inventory and try to match it with customer needs. At this point, sales personnel make the offer in terms of product, quality, price and service. Finally, sales personnel do what they do best: they close on the sale in real time. Such IT functionality reaches almost 80 percent perfection at Maytag and Ford, and almost 100 percent perfection at Reuters and Bloomberg.

Impact on the 4 Ps of marketing

- *Products.* Real-time wireless Internet transactions force products to become commodities, core assets to become peripheral, and valuable assets to become loss leaders.
- *Price.* Real-time m-commerce transactions base prices on demand at the time of sale, and these prices change continually.
- *Place.* Real-time wireless Internet transactions give all sellers power in the channel of distribution.
- *Promotion.* Real-time m-commerce transactions push well-established brands out of the market and into the dead brands society.

Sales personnel know that goods in inventory for any length of time lose their competitive value. Theirs is the new world of building to order in real time.

Today, Dell uses a hardwire Internet system for connecting with probable customers. The firm keeps no more than three days of inventory velocity (or stock turns) as it reorders parts on the basis of actual orders from customers. As prices fall on chips and peripherals, Dell comes up with better deals for customers; if it did not, other sellers would take customers away from the firm. The firm delivers the computer order within 48 hours; with the aid of handheld smart telecom devices, Dell sends support personnel to take care of after market service problems. Otherwise, Dell could find itself similar to Compaq struggling to survive with one foot in the old channel of distribution and another foot in the on-line Internet channel of distribution.

Tomorrow, Dell will use a wireless Internet system for connecting with probable customers – that is, the kids who are turning 20. Now they are buying smart telecom devices for themselves and their parents. Next year these kids will be buying wireless products for their firms. They will be Gen-Y adults whose multi-million dollar purchasing decisions can make or break manufacturers of handheld devices, wireless laptops, LAN infrastructure, voice-recognition equipment, and content providers.

A forecast

- *2001*. Half a billion (500 million) people worldwide use mobile phones for voice and email transactions, some data transactions, and a limited number of Internet search transactions. Most of these customers live outside the US, in Europe, Japan, China and elsewhere in the world. The forecast for 2001 is a *continuing forecast*.

- *2003*. One billion people worldwide will use cell phones for voice, data and search transactions. The number of GSM users in Europe will jump to over 50 percent of the population; Japan's kids will take their addiction to short messaging services (SMS) into adulthood as *manga* cartoon characters show up on their iMode company phones. China, India and other countries in which landline telephone connections are few in number will explode in their use of m-commerce smart devices. The US will remain behind as only one-third of probable customers will buy the new wireless services or upgrade their current mobile phones. A great deal must be done in the US to acquire bandwidth from UHF and digital television companies, come up with compatible wireless technology, and convince most Americans that m-commerce is their future. The forecast for 2003 is a *doubling forecast*.

- *2005*. If US wireless firms employ the *new* marketing concept to train and educate Americans on how to use the coolest smart telecom devices and Americans buy into the salient attributes of these products, then all bets are off on the number of wireless m-commerce users in the world. Europe and Japan will become saturated with smart mobile phones and come to expect annual upgrades in quality and service. China, India and elsewhere in the world will explode from 10 to 20 percent of the population, or more if economic growth and government deregulation continues. The rate at which the US converts to m-commerce by the year 2005 is the great un-known for marketers.

Marketing wireless Internet m-commerce products

Today, most Americans are vaguely aware of wireless smart devices. They don't know what to make of the various offerings in the market. Americans are con-fused about the various, non-compatible standards They are not sure how to make their comparisons. Is it on the name of the telephone firm? Is it on price? Is it on range of service? Is it on the length of the contract? Or what? Such con-fusion has led them to ask themselves: "Do I really need this new gadget?"

The answer from Europe, Japan, China and elsewhere in the world is a resounding *Yes!* Of course, Europeans chose one standard, the WAP system for GSM phones, and the Japanese chose W-CDMA for iMode. No confusion ex-ists among customers in their centers of kids, young urban professionals, and business executive power. Instead, Europeans and Japanese make decisions based on the product, its quality, support service and price.

At some point between 2003 and 2005, providers of smart wireless tele-com devices will have enough data about why Americans are hesitant to make purchases, and know what the latter's preferences are for wireless products and services. Marketers of wireless goods will synthesize their data and infor-mation. Then they will reach out to probable and possible customers and ask them their present-day preferences for wireless products and services in real time. Such collaborative filtering will enhance m-commerce products with the newest information available from customers.

If done correctly and the data become customers, Americans will begin to replace their personal computers (PCs) and older cell phones with smart handheld wireless devices. These information appliances are able to do digital tasks, especially to tap into the Internet without the hassles of the PCs. This means the culture of the PC itself and the techies who control it must change to recognize that smart wireless devices can do digital tasks better than PCs. If all these changes take place, then the year 2005 forecast will be a doubling forecast, too.

MONEY-MAKING DEALS

Let's answer the product marketing questions with our current information on world-changing products:

Technology for sale

▦ *Can you have Web-based information anytime, anywhere?*
  Yes for business executives in Finland, Sweden, the UK, Germany and Spain? Yes for kids, Gen-Y and Gen-X in Japan? Not today, but maybe sometime in 2001 for some business persons and more teenagers in the US.
▦ *What is the probability that the US will catch up to Europe and Japan in 2001?*
  Very low, less than 10 percent.
▦ *What is the probability for the year 2003?*
  Higher, perhaps as high as 30 percent.
▦ *What is the probability for the year 2005?*
  A great deal higher, perhaps over 50 percent.

All available data suggest Americans will overcome their current reluctance to use wireless m-commerce smart devices and they will do so at an increasing rate. Hence, marketers predict a probable doubling for 2003, and a possible doubling forecast for 2005.

Here are the details behind the forecast. First, Americans may have to buy existing European and Japanese technologies, products and content. Second, even if America catches up with Europe and Japan in 2003 with extant 2001 technology, the US will still be two years behind. Unless European and Japanese firms take over American telecom firms, the former will be unwilling to give away their newest and coolest technologies by licensing US firms. The task facing American telecom firms is to abandon their obsolete cell phone technologies – consider these sunk costs – get new funds from the stock and venture capital markets, get ahead by investing in new technologies, and pray they have understood what are the most salient attributes preferred by probable American customers.

Only with a new investment strategy will US telecom firms be able to regroup and catch up with their competitors from overseas. This is a tall order.

Expansion phase of product life cycle

■ *Do the GSM in Europe and iMode in Japan effectively manage m-commerce to create value?*

Yes. Even though each uses different price strategies to gain market share, both are in the expansion phase of the product life cycle.

■ *Will CDMA do a better job for the US?*

This depends on the ability to transmit data rapidly, the availability of packet switching, and the introduction of 3G.

■ *Are other technologies, such as TDMA, finished as competitive wireless products?*

Yes.

■ *What is the probability that tried and true marketing practices will be used to extend the product life of GSM and iMode phones?*

Both technologies have had enormous success in the expansion phase of the product life cycle, and this phase is continuing through mid-2001. However, some slowdown is showing up in the number of new units of smart telecom devices planned for production in early 2001; that is, the rate of increase is slowing down, but the overall market is still growing. This could be a pause in the expansion phase. No evidence is available to suggest the GSM and iMode phones are in the mature phase of the product life cycle.

Skimming the cream

European marketers will therefore continue to promote their WAP phones as the top of the line telephone service, where every minute of use must be paid for at the high per-minute rate. The European telephone firms do not currently offer bulk rates as do both landlines and wireless cell phone firms in the US. European firms are making extraordinarily good profits from their mobile phone services in Europe; currently, they use GPRS which is built on the GSM network; at the moment, VoiceStream and AirTouch (the former Pacific Bell

Wireless) are the leading GSM carriers in the US. None of this has gone un-
noticed. The European firms have left themselves open to competition from
Japan's iMode service.

Pricing down the cost curve

The Japanese firm NTT DoCoMo plays its cards differently. Their approach is
to price their wireless telecom service three years down the cost curve. What
will be the cost structure underlying the price of the iMode phone when it has
built up market share in three years? Instead of skimming the cream off the
top of the market, as is the European practice, Japanese firms calculate what
their market share must be to get their costs down, and then price the product
accordingly in the first quarter of selling the new iMode phones. This prod-
uct-price market-share marketing strategy has proved to be unbeatable for
Sony, Matsushita, and others with VCRs and an assortment of home electronic
goods.

Data transactions demand packet switching

And what of American technology? Qualcomm's CDMA is based on the existing popular digital phone network in the US. Sprint PCS and Verizon (the
combination of Bell Atlantic and GTE) are the leading carriers in the US.
Qualcomm claims its patents on CDMA, W-CDMA (iMode), and some GSM
services will guarantee its competitive success against GSM and iMode. Time
will tell because the American-owned telephone companies still do not have a
great track record in handling data. They need to move to packet-switching –
the same system which is already in use in Japan by NTT DoCoMo.

3G future

Nevertheless, if US firms move quickly to set up third-generation (3G) wireless
services by 2002 rather than 2004 as planned, then they may catch up with and
perhaps get ahead of both the European and Japanese firms. Right now no will
exists among US firms to make these investments.

Rewards

- *What do customers want from m-commerce?*
  They want location awareness, voice and data transmissions, and transaction capabilities.
- *Will the current set of telecom, hardware, software and server firms be able to provide Web-based information anytime, anywhere, and create value?*
  They must invest in 3G technology, and build up their Web-enabled GSM, iMode and CDMA capabilities. Successful firms will grow sales, build share, increase turnover, and, perhaps, make money, too.

The rewards fall into several clear categories:

- creative destruction of existing technologies, e.g., landlines, hardwire Internet connections, TDMA (and its slow upgrade CDPD), and the PC-centered world;
- long-term sustainable competition among WAP, iMode and CDMA (and its faster upgrade CDMA 2000); and
- dominance by 3G compatible hardware, software and servers.

Probable European customers want location awareness so they can do their m-banking anytime, anywhere. This is the killer application. It revolutionizes the way we live, do business, and how we use the Internet. Location awareness is the most salient attribute in demand by customers who are early adopters. With packet-switching available from the telecom firms, customers insist on voice, data and purchase transactions. These three product attributes together with location awareness show telecom firms what they must do to gain and keep customers.

If customers get what they want, they will pay a monthly fee for voice and data services, give telecom firms a percentage of the transaction fees to do purchases on-line, and allow these firms to collect slotting fees from advertisers who want access to kids, young urban professionals, business executives, and other early adopters of 3G telecom services. Rewards are great for those firms that get in the market first, build up share by becoming #1 or #2 in offering 3G services, and collect licensing fees from all other competitors.

Risks

- *Is there a set of best practices for managing m-commerce or the wireless Internet?*

  Given the wireless Internet is a new industry and in the expansion phase of the product life cycle, a high level of risk is inherent in these m-commerce startups. Some will fail.

- *How do you manage product assets to create value?*

  Mix and match the old economy with the new economy, and Web-enable both of them with a 3G infrastructure.

- *Can you conceive of any new business strategies to add value to your m-commerce products?*

  Yes for Manchester United and its fans who use Web-enabled GSM phones to check scores and order merchandise.

- *Will these marketing efforts increase the returns on invested capital for the wireless telecom firms?*

  Of course.

The risk of a classic business failure is inherent in the wireless m-commerce business. Some technologies won't work. Others won't work fast enough. Still others may be too late to market. Their price may be too high. They have too many negative product attributes. Customers got use to some other technology and they don't want to change. The list is almost endless.

Also the risk inherent in customers not changing their behavior could bedevil the roll-out of 3G wireless m-commerce smart devices. Some customers may like what they have and not want to change. They are set in their routine social patterns – for example, they leave the office behind in the evening and watch TV, play cards, read a book, or chat face-to-face with family and friends. These customers don't want to be accessible 24/7, or anytime, anywhere.

Lastly, cell phone radiation constitutes an unknown risk to damage genes in blood cells. Microwave radiation at cell-phone frequencies may weaken the blood-brain barrier, and may cause tumors in the brain, effects on the immune system, and unknown genetic changes.[12] At the moment, nothing is proven. However, if anything comes from future FDA studies, handheld devices will have to give way to voice recognition systems in which the incoming and outgoing transmissions do not occur with an ear piece.

All of these favor the use of real options in deciding when to build, whether to expand, or choose to delay the expansion of the wireless world of m-commerce.

ACQUISITIONS MANAGEMENT

Why do wired telecom firms acquire wireless telecom businesses? Do these acquisitions transform and renew the wired firm? Do these acquisitions bring new technology and marketing capabilities to the wired firm? Does the wireless firm bring about cultural change in the wired firm?

US market

Throughout this book, wired firms will be acquiring wireless firms. AT&T acquired its cellular service so many years ago that people tend to forget this wired long-distance telecom firm did not create wireless capability internally. On the other hand, some of the Baby Bells originally formed a non-equity partnership to create mobile phone service. Then each in turn pulled out and either set up its own or acquired existing wireless services. For example, SBC Communications took over CellularOne and made it a leading provider of mobile phones. Pacific Bell was so successful with AirTouch that it sold it to Vodafone of the UK. Bell Atlantic together with GTE formed Verizon to offer wireless telecom services. Finally, many new telecom upstarts, such as VoiceStream Wireless, went into the wireless telecom as venture capitalists and saw this business as the way to make a great deal of money quickly.

Except for the last upstart telecom firm, VoiceStream Wireless, with its decision to use Europe's GSM mobile voice communications system, all the rest stayed with AT&T's slower TDMA system or Qualcomm's faster CDMA system. The use of TDMA did not offer much beyond the first product launch. When CDMA or GSM technologies became available and the new parent firm refused to treat TDMA as sunk costs and give it up, talented high-tech personnel left AT&T Wireless and the Baby Bells for new opportunities with the start-ups.

Rules for wireless acquisitions

Here are a few rules to live by:[13]

- Acquire firms with the best technology.
- Put this new technology to use immediately.
- Keep the personnel who developed this technology.
- Orient all acquisitions around people, not products.
- Plan for shorter product life cycles.
- Boost market share and profits quickly.
- Reinvest in new technology, and new versions of existing technology.
- Plan to leap ahead from one non-compatible technology to another.
- Try to go outside the company for technological insights.
- Institute quick decision-making.
- Resolve conflicts about technology and marketing quickly.
- Make it explicit that acquisitions mean cultural change.

American-owned firms tried their hand at acquiring wired European telecom firms in the UK, Poland, New Zealand, Argentina and elsewhere in the world. Most of these assets have been sold to other wired telecom firms from Europe's bigger countries. The big American-owned telecom firms learned very little from these acquisitions except how to spend the money of shareholders without showing an appropriate return on investment.

European market

Now the big wired telecom firms in Europe are bidding on licenses and acquiring telecom firms outside their home countries. For example, Vodafone of the UK bought Mannesmann of Germany, and France Telecom bought Orange of the UK. Both Vodafone and Deutsche Telekom have made wireless acquisitions, Pacific Bell and VoiceStream Wireless respectively, in the US, and NTT DoCoMo of Japan has taken a minority share in KPN Mobile of the Netherlands. Lastly, Hutchison Whampoa of Hong Kong is making acquisitions throughout Europe with the plan to build up wireless capacity in the UK, the Netherlands and Italy in 2001.

Success and failure

The mobile phone business with or without m-commerce is up for grabs in both the US and Europe. It's too early to confirm successes. It's too early to say for sure that the failure to use GSM or CDMA will cause failure. None of these firms that will be discussed in the book have carried out the basic marketing tasks of finding out what the customers want before acquiring new technologies, products, content, personnel and firms. These things we know already: acquiring technology by itself or applying marketing to inferior, somewhat out-of-date technology will not guarantee success. Doing one or both of them will guarantee that the acquiring firm will be left behind, e.g., AT&T and British Telecommunications. Nothing will be gained from following past practices.

Instead, mobile phones for m-commerce and the wireless Internet need to be seen for what they are in the minds of customers. The Japanese view iMode mobile phones as fun items to give them instantaneous communications with friends; the phones come in all colors with at least four different ways to access the Internet. Moreover, the content of iMode phones includes the user's favorite *manga* cartoon. Finally, iMode phones are easy to use with only two clicks required to get train schedules, news, and city guides.

The Europeans view GSM phones as both fun items for teens and young adults, and a quick way to talk with "mama" (in Italy), and do business deals throughout Europe. Older GSM phones are clumsier than the iMode phones because the former need five or seven clicks to do the same things the latter do in two clicks. Since NTT DoCoMo will introduce its special wireless capability into Europe in 2001, the Europeans are in for a classic competitive fight for market share and category dominance between the Japanese and European approach to wireless Internet.

Once the fight is settled in Europe, the next battleground will be the US. Will American firms be on the sidelines? Or will they start making decisions so that they will become wireless competitors in 2001? The time is short for US firms to get in on the m-commerce game, play well, and dominate some parts of the wireless Internet business.

MANAGING VALUE CREATION

Manchester United, the highly successful English soccer football team, exists in two marketing worlds. In the old economy, the team earns 99 percent of its income within Britain by selling tickets to matches, housing at team-owned motels, and sports merchandise (such as, branded towels, boxer shorts, T-shirts, posters, and replicas of its red-and-white uniform). Also it receives TV revenue from viewers in Asia and the Middle East, magazine income from its Thai-language magazine, licensing and partnership revenue from team Palmeiras of Sao Paulo, and tour income from Australia and China.

In the new economy, Manchester United's Web site attracts enormous traffic from users in China. Chinese fans follow their favorite team on a daily basis, especially, the Shanghai Supporters Club who can place an order for the team's new shirt just as quickly as fans who live close to the team's Old Trafford stadium in England. Both English and Chinese fans soon will be able to watch recorded highlights of games on their GSM mobile phones.[14]

Sports and GSM are made for each other because fans want instant access. How's Tiger doing at St Andrews? Is Michael Schumacher finishing first, second or third in the Formula One races? Sports content and IT technology through WAP are converging, and it's this convergence of sports entertainment and the "Internet buddy" called the GSM phone that creates value in today's marketplace.

By the year 2003 50 percent of all mobile phones will be Web-enabled so that everyone can be entertained through sports, Hollywood and politicians. All of us are just at the beginning of how the mobile phone connected to the Web will create additional m-commerce value for sports marketing.

CONCLUSIONS

How to conquer the wireless world? Apply traditional product marketing strategies to m-commerce, especially to GSM, iMode and CDMA. Here is a checklist of things to do:

- Put Web-based information out in the market anytime, anywhere with 3G-enhanced mobile or cell phones.
- Build market share with a 4 Ps marketing strategy that is carefully adapted to the expansion phase of the product life cycle, but don't over build.
- Offer customers crucial salient product attributes, such as location awareness, voice and data transmissions, and transaction capabilities.
- Create value by mixing and matching the old and new economies, and adapting them both to the needs of m-commerce.

Next we'll look at how to promote the new wireless world in national and global markets.

CHAPTER 2

Promoting New Market Space

EXECUTIVE SUMMARY

MARKETERS PROVIDE CUSTOMERS with value-added intangible product attributes that are included as part of their smart handheld devices. Here's what is involved:

- Build 3G universal mobile telecommunications standard (UMTS) in and bring packet switching to Europe, the technology now in place in Japan.
- Design intangible product attributes for "always on" technology in Japan, electronic money in northern Europe, and for "high loiter" areas in the US.
- Expand iMode's services of microbilling, one rate price marketing plans, and approved content sites on dual-band handheld appliances within Europe.
- Create new market space for frequent flyers and five-star hotel patrons, and promote contextual marketing in Japan, Europe and the US.
- Sell 2G and 2.5G m-commerce technology in the US to early adapters who are willing to put up with some negative product attributes.
- Delay m-banking because many customers are not ready to trust either e- or m-banking and are unwilling to give up the social context of their routine banking practices.
- Carry out a *new* 4 Ps marketing strategy that offers marketers the options to pursue, postpone, or terminate the roll-out of a succession of value-added intangible benefits in handheld miniature information appliances.

Invest in promotion marketing deals

Do the deals create new market space? Do they answer fundamental promotion and advertising questions? What information do I get as a customer or user? Can the rapid increase in sales be sustained with new approaches towards integrated marketing communications during the expansion phase of the product life cycle? Can the first-mover become the market leader? Will it become the number-one competitor in its product category? How long can the market leader grow market share without bringing in countervailing competitors who have newer technology, improved handheld devices, and better value-added intangible product benefits? Also do the deals deliver appropriate financial results, especially in terms of positive cash flows and earnings from sales? Do the following promotion marketing deals create and deliver value?

■ Add tangible benefits to the CDMA 2000-GSM dual-protocol, product partnership for European customers between Japan's wireless telecom provider, NTT DoCoMo, and the Dutch telecom firm, KPN Mobile. Tie this to the distribution alliance between DoCoMo and America's content provider, AOL Japan. These two deals answer important marketing questions for Europe and Japan respectively, and they may point the way towards deals in the US, too. Of course, at the moment, only the Japanese deal is delivering crucial financial results. After a careful review of existing product and promotion marketing deals, these alliances and partnerships among Japanese, European and American telecom and content providers are the best business model for the emerging m-commerce wireless Internet world.

■ Offer customers in Japan and northern Europe Web-enabled iMode and dual-band Nokia phones respectively. Give users wireless Ethernet networks and phones with screens or "home decks" that provide *manga* cartoons, Pokémon characters, electronic wallets, show books, sell CDs, offer stock trading, and distribute e-airplane tickets. These deals also answer important marketing questions and deliver crucial financial results. Although an open question exists among some potential customers in East Asia and southern Europe whether they will accept small screens, difficult to read text, and three to twelve key strokes to gain access to e-airline tickets and other on-line products, most customers in Japan, Finland or Sweden are not bothered with these negative product attributes. Begin now to think through how iMode or WAP phones or both together as dual-band devices might be sold in the US to wirelessly-challenged American customers.

▪ Establish the logo of Vodafone's AirTouch in the US, Germany and China, and of iMode mobile phones in The Netherlands, Germany, and the US. These deals depend on the acceptance by local customers of GSM or iMode technology or both together, and the willingness of Vodafone and DoCoMo marketers to promote and advertise their benefits to Dutch, German, and American users. At the moment, these deals have not generated a large number of sales, but the firms are burning cash without positive cash flow from Europe, the US and China. However, if the successes of Vodafone AirTouch and DoCoMo in California and Japan respectively are any indication of their future success elsewhere, then we can expect both Vodafone and DoCoMo to begin growing sales revenue in Europe, perhaps by the end of 2001, and two–four years later in the US.

▪ Increase brand differentiation and brand awareness of iMode phones in the US by deepening DoCoMo's relationships with Bell South and SBC, or by finding new partners for either DoCoMo alone or DoCoMo together with Dutch-owned KPN Mobile. Strengthen the brand relevance of GSM phones in the US by matching them to the aspirations of users and by adding to the number of foreign direct investments of European telecom firms in American wireless companies, such as the UK's Vodafone acquisition of California-based AirTouch. Grow brand equity and equate it with the values and lifestyles of users for both iMode and GSM mobile phones. Currently, only the AirTouch subsidiary contributes positive cash flow and strong earnings to its parent, Vodafone.

Recommendation

However, good burn rates, positive cash flow and strong earnings from both existing and potential key wireless players in the US are just over the horizon. 2001 could be a banner year for mobile phones, m-commerce, and the wireless Internet. Although only about 33 percent of Americans now own wireless phones, this is just the tip of the iceberg. Consumers throughout the US are about to shift from wired to wireless technologies, push for a free fall in long distance rates in favor of one-rate plans, and insist wired, regulated telecom providers no longer be given favorable exchange rates over wireless, unregulated new telecom providers.[1] Japan opened this path in 1999. Europe marched down the gravel road in 2000. The US is about to start paving the wireless highway in 2001.

Here is the marketing assignment for wireless marketers:

- Segment digital customers in terms of age, income and geography within Scandinavia, among northern and southern European countries, and between Europe and the US.
- Target middle-class American customers who have similar personal values and lifestyles, e.g., working women who want to chat with spouses and friends, and who think of wireless phones as secure, safety appliances; and men who want to keep in touch with other employees and who want to check the scores of their favorite sports teams.
- Position the older CDMA mobile phones, and the newer iMode and GSM information appliances as multi-functional handheld devices that include both PDA and wireless telecom functions.

Therefore get ready for the following wireless events: First, NTT DoCoMo together with KPN Mobile make a strong push in Europe for the popular iMode system as a dual-band system that includes both W-CDMA and GSM. Second, DoCoMo and an unknown American partner does the same in the US, and adds PDA functions to mobile phones. Third, prepare for bruising product and price competition among one or more GSM telecom providers from Europe, against NTT DoCoMo and its partners, and possibly against other unregulated wireless and PDA entrants. Today, no one knows the outcome of the battle. This is game theory at work in the mobile Internet industry, especially in Europe and the US.

INTRODUCTION

Here's our promotion marketing strategy:

- Create new market space with unencumbered spectrum in Europe for Web-enabled anytime, anywhere data communications among the GSM brand community. Turn valuable GSM assets into dual-protocol (GSM, and W-CDMA or CDMA 2000), value-creating, income-producing UMTS property. Apply lessons learned in Europe to the auction of encumbered spectrum (channels 60–69) in the US that are controlled by digital broadcasters, local school boards and the US Department of Defense. Interest venture capitalists in California's Silicon Valley and in Europe's new markets, and among European, Japanese, and American telecom providers in the roll-out of the wireless Internet throughout the industrialized, developed world.

- Promote wireless services as iMode's Japanese customers deepen their use of W-CDMA and as European users expand their use of GSM. Shape advertising campaigns to shift views about short messaging services (SMS) moves from being a fad to a fashion statement for kids, teenagers and young adults. Communicate to senior business persons who commute long distances, especially in Japan, that digital wireless services are a necessity. Begin pushing out informational pieces to American managers that the mobile Internet is required for success in business.

- Invest in global telecom brands. Here is a short list: iMode or dual-protocol GSM-iMode wireless services. Nokia, Ericsson, Siemans and Motorola wireless phones. Palm, Microsoft and Handspring PDAs. Use single-source data to measure the effectiveness of advertising, promotion, and integrated marketing communications to measure category dominance in 2001, again in 2003, and also in 2005.

- Manage a set of best practices for introducing new mobile products and creating new market space for m-commerce. Insist marketers meet the central strategic marketing challenge facing m-commerce – that is, to keep re-creating new Web-enabled markets. Show how airlines, hotels, and other business are deploying the wireless Internet for their customers. Ask this question: will wireless investors continue to make rational investments in a world dominated by irrational, increasingly irrelevant wired telecom firms?

CRAZY LIKE A FOX

Some dumb investors are crazy like a fox. Their approach to forecasting is unconventional. All agree that wireless telecom technology is here to stay. Users want anytime, anywhere voice communications. Currently, location awareness (or the wireless phone's ability to pinpoint the position of users) is the killer application for the new telecom technology; the engineers did their work well by rolling out networks of equipment at the lowest cost possible. Their day is over. Tomorrow, wireless will be about product content and marketing innovation. M-commerce is a marketer's dream come true.

Those dumb investors who are crazy like a fox don't pick favorite wireless technologies. Why worry today about which digital standard will dominate markets in 2001 in Japan, 2003 in Europe, and 2005 in the US? Investors don't care which standard takes control of the market so long as users get voice and data communications, and transaction capability. However, investors do care about the cost of European licenses as it nears $100 billion and about the cost of 3G infrastructure to the wireless firms as the sum approaches another $100 billion on both sides of the North Atlantic. Even with the current pressure on wireless margins, the resulting negative impact on earnings growth, and the reliability of the price/earnings ratio in valuing the telecom firms, successful investors buy into at least two or more of the competing digital standards. They try not to forget that most wireless services have yet to be invented, offered, priced and made popular. These investors who are crazy like a fox don't know which telecom providers will win and which will lose. Their investment rule is "Let the best one win out in the long run, and we will make money on all of them in the short run."

Cognitive dissonance

Some of these investors hold beliefs plainly at odds with the evidence. These are those who 'know' the industry. They made money in the telecommunications industry as it was deregulated in the US in the mid-1980s, and later in Europe and Japan. Their beliefs about the preference for wired links over wireless telecom services have been held and cherished for a long time. For as long as most of us can remember, investors have been influenced by suggestions from AT&T, then the Baby Bells, and, most recently, the European telecom monopolies. These wired players were no better informed about the future of wireless than those who came into m-commerce from the computer, pager and PDA industries. Also the wired telecom providers took big gambles to maintain the status quo when the best evidence suggested that the past was indeed over and all previous investments were sunk costs.

Wired telecom firms and their team of investors tended to compartmentalize their individual decisions on superficial grounds. They made choices about maintaining the existing wired network without taking account of the implications for the emerging wireless network. These wired fanatics were persistently over-confident, and they overstated the probability that wired service would always remain the dominant telecom provider. They saw patterns in data even when there were none. Thus AT&T and the other long-distance carriers argued with the Baby Bells over how much one should pay the other for connections, and then forced the Federal Communications Commission to establish a rule over who would pay what to whom and bill it all back to users. These players believed their testimony influenced events as if their collective actions could magically redirect the market away from wireless and back to wired services.

AT&T wanted to get even with the Baby Bells. The latter wanted to put "Ma Bell" in its place. Both acted emotionally. These wired firms got the most satisfaction from taking revenge on one another rather than trying to maximize their own financial gain by jumping with both feet into wireless. It's as if they made the wrong decisions on both sides of the investment, on the puts and the calls, and these choices were simply the dumbest financial decisions ever made by firms in the telecommunications industry. These wired firms are to blame for America's fate which is to be the long-term loser in the race to dominate m-commerce and the wireless Internet.

Prospect theory

Investors who are crazy like a fox bet on the long shots (VoiceStream, Power-Tel, etc.) over the favorites (Cellular One).They attach a high probability to unlikely outcomes and a low probability to likely outcomes. In the early stages of analogue wireless, most of these investors lost money, but a few beat the odds and did fabulously well. However, those who lost some money refused to leave the field and made their next set of investments in primitive digital services. Again the winners made higher returns than average investors. A few wireless investors have a huge appetite for risk while many do not. Even so those investors who are crazy like a fox demanded higher premiums for their investments in 2G, 2.5G and now 3G wireless infrastructure. Similar to Hutchison Whampoa these smart investors want to make money building up wireless services. However, if this is not possible within the framework of beauty contests and bids for wireless licenses required by governments in Europe and North America, these investors prefer to make lots of money rather than throwing it away on wireless telecom services that may not pay back investors for five–ten years in the future. Their investment actions may seem irrational to those who are fans of the wired or wireless firms or both, but those who do put their money on a wireless future are acting rationally in forecasting a new day for telecommunications.

The three chapters in Section I about marketing wireless products, promoting new market space, and pricing m-commerce services are about acting rationally in an emerging wireless world and existing in the irrational, increasingly irrelevant world of wired providers. Investors who are crazy like a fox will incorporate values and lifestyles, psychology and sociology, and brand communities and consumer behavior – all crucial marketing metrics or tools – into their decisions about wireless investments.

INTANGIBLE ATTRIBUTES

All m-commerce products have both physical and intangible attributes. In Chapter 1 we discussed the most salient product attribute of the wireless

Internet – that is, location awareness. In a recent advertisement, VoiceStream Wireless shouts out at the reader with this lead header:[2]

> *"Go to Helsinki.*
> *"Finland is just one of 70 countries you can do business in with one wireless phone number."*

The print copy reads:

> *"As a VoiceStream Wireless customer, you can now be reached over-seas at your US number ... We use the Global System for Mobile Communications (GSM), the standard in the most countries world-wide ... Why in the world would you use any other wireless ser-vice?"*

Actual customers

VoiceStream has 2.2 million subscribers and is the ninth largest provider of wireless voice service in the US. Compare this with Sprint PCS (6.6 million), and Verizon (the Bell Atlantic and GTE combination, 22 million), but AT&T Wireless is still the giant (66 million).

Forecast

VoiceStream owns licenses in 23 of the top 25 US markets with a potential 220 million subscriber base; unfortunately, VoiceStream and other wireless firms do not own the spectrum to transmit 3G wireless services. Nevertheless, VoiceStream adds subscribers at a growth rate of 18.8 percent per year; and they stay with the firm even though their cell phones don't work everywhere in the US. With some outside money VoiceStream could jump ahead of Sprint PCS by the year 2005.

Notwithstanding these figures, at the end of the year 2000, only 33 percent of the US population (or 90 million) uses some form of analog or primitive digital wireless – that is, only voice communications without access to email, data or text.[3] Moreover, only ten percent (or nine million Americans) use the European standard, or GSM. Compare this with Europe (52 percent, all on GSM) and Japan (60 percent, all on W-CDMA). By the end of 2001, VoiceStream, Sprint, Verizon, SBC Communications and others expect to have wireless systems in place to transmit data as fast as voice communications, too.

Global System for Mobile Communications (GSM)

In hindsight, VoiceStream Wireless's choice of GSM was a good business decision. As the firm got customers and built up market share, it gave them a bonus. Their US wireless phone numbers follow them to 70 countries in Europe, Asia and elsewhere in the world – all because VoiceStream is tied to the European standard, GSM. Such is the importance of one intangible attribute.

Today, VoiceStream is being acquired by Deutsche Telekom, one of the key GSM players in Europe. Although the corporate cultures are different – VoiceStream is a fast-paced start-up with West Coast venture capital money behind it, and Deutsche Telekom is a former government monopoly with over 50 percent of its shares still owned by the German government – the one thing neither has to worry about is its technology standards. Both use GSM. Today, Deutsche Telekom is building market share in Europe and the US.

One-rate pricing

Deutsche Telekom offers its customers the same rate no matter where they roam from Berlin to London, and now Berlin to Seattle (VoiceStream's headquarters). This pricing strategy is at variance with longstanding practice in the telephone industry, geography and distance pricing. It is another important intangible attribute that may make Deutsche Telekom a crucial competitor in the US market.

CDMA digital standard

Siemens, the German electronics conglomerate, which holds the #3 position in mobile phones in Europe after Nokia and Motorola, has decided to take a different tack in the US.[4] Siemens will not push GSM into the US as is Deutsche Telekom, another German firm. Instead, Siemens is launching mobile phones in the US that work on the US CDMA digital standard. To accomplish this task Siemens took a 15 percent share in a San Diego software developer, Neopoint, and together they are rolling out mobile phones in which design follows fun. The thought is that the consumer is always right even when they clash with the firm's engineers. In short, mobile phones have more in common with sports cars or Gucci handbags than the power plants, trains and light bulbs that made Siemens big.

Qualcomm, the inventor of a mobile-phone technology called CDMA, believes its digital standard will be the new 3G high-speed UMTS mobile Internet standard for wireless services across the world, because this technology uses the radio spectrum more frugally than do rival systems, such as TDMA and GSM. The firm supplies chipsets, which it contracts others to make, to mobile-phone equipment makers, such as Siemens.

In the early 1990s, most American telephone firms followed AT&T and went for TDMA while those in Europe went for GSM. AirTouch in 1993 and Sprint in 1995 were the first US telecom firms to adopt CDMA; of course, AirTouch switched to GSM when it was taken over by Vodafone. Today, in the US, CDMA is still in third place behind TDMA and GSM; CDMA has 13 percent of the world market. CDMA's crucial advantage is that it uses packet-based technology that may become the international standard for 3G services.

WHAT DO I GET FROM MICROBILLING?

What do I get? Microbilling is the new business model on how to get paid for Internet content. Yesterday in the US, in its PC-dominated world, providers of Internet content always gave it away free; because computer geeks would not pay for something that always had been free, and corporate advertisers did not think their banner ads on the Internet sites were driving sales. However, today in Japan, in its mobile phone-dominated world, providers of Internet content always charge a fee, and the fees for Internet content show up on the monthly phone bills for 13 million NTT DoCoMo, 1.7 million Japan Telecom, and 3 million KDDI Corporation subscribers.

What I do get are dozens of services from restaurant guides to ocean surf forecasts, weather, games, traffic conditions, stock quotes and cartoons. For a little under $5 a month for each Internet service, the fees are added to the monthly cellular phone bill. NTT DoCoMo has about 20,000 Web sites designed for its iMode service, and more are being added each month.

What I also get is convenience of payment. Subscribers do not have to give out credit card information over the Internet. Instead, the phone company provides its customers with a menu of mobile phone Internet services, and with a simple click of a button on the phone – that is, no URL and no Web address required – subscribers sign up for specific sites. Moreover, the phone company vets the Internet providers to give customers confidence that they will get the products or services they have paid for through the phone company bill. The telephone company checks out both sellers of content, products, and services; and the buyers of these goods; and the phone company acts as the credit reference bureau for both sellers and buyers. Such ease of payment obviates the need for content providers to advertise their presence on the Web because users can pay for and discontinue their monthly payments with one click on the mobile phone.

For some Japanese users of NTT DoCoMo mobile phones, they do not have wired phones at home, do not use the pay phones at the 7-Eleven convenience stores, and do not connect to the URLs on the Internet. Instead, they use their iMode phones to make phone calls, check the weather, exchange email, and click on Internet content. Their monthly bill averages between $75.00 and $155.00.

Marketing innovation

What do I get? The iMode mobile phone is given away as a commodity. The iMode consumer electronics device – that same phone – is in the earliest stage of the expansion phase of its product life cycle. More and more Internet content is available through this phone device, and Japanese consumers are willing to pay for it through their monthly phone bills. What do I get? New phone technology. More information. Most importantly, a reconfigured value chain has been created for billing these Internet content services. This important marketing innovation has made all the difference in the world to the success of iMode from NTT DoCoMo in Japan.

New revenue stream for NTT DoCoMo

First, NTT DoCoMo and Japanese phone companies charge for the higher use of air time by their customers who are surfing the Internet. Second, they charge their users a "packet" fee for the amount of information they send and receive over iMode; the average packet fee is about $16 per month. Third, the firm takes nine percent of what the content provider charges users as the fee for being the middleman and bill collector; this fee will drop as other Japanese telecom companies offer similar Internet content services. Finally, many of the Japanese companies that provided digital content to mobile phones plan to do deals with US- and EU-based venture capitalists, sell shares to the public as IPOs, or go into equity partnerships with firms that have access to the US market, such as NTT DoCoMo, AOL Japan, Yahoo! Japan, and Intel Japan.

Soon NTT DoCoMo will let users "download" money into their mobile phones so they can buy goods from vending machines or convenience stores, and can pay their credit and debit card bills. In this one item, the Japanese mobile phone companies will be following (rather than leading) the Finnish and Swedish telecom firms.

VALUE-BASED MARKETING DECISIONS

Here are the value-based decisions made by northern European wireless telecom firms, and open to top management at wireless telecom firms in Japan and throughout the world.

What is the context of a decision?

Wireless telecom firms in Europe are turning their mobile phones into electronic wallets through which users can do their banking, pay their rent and car park fees, buy wine, etc. Virtual money is stored in the electronic wallets, and with clicks on two keys money is transferred from the bank account of the buyer to that of the seller. Bank transfers, checks, and now cash are becoming obsolete forms of money wherever mobile phones are in wide scale use among European consumers. Their preferred form of exchange is through electronic wallets.

What is the object of a decision?

At the moment, Europe is not Japan. Each European country has a different set of Internet providers, different types of content, a different number of keys to click, and different arrangements for bank transfers – in short, within the European Union and in central and eastern Europe, a hodgepodge of wireless arrangements exists so that an Estonian's electronic wallet cannot pay rent and parking fees from their Estonian bank account in Italy, France or Spain. Once the 3G network is built within Europe, then these electronic wireless devices should work effortlessly anytime, anywhere in the emerging 24/7 mobile phone environment.

Europeans want what the Japanese have today: microbilling from their mobile phone companies in which the funds are automatically deducted from their bank accounts. If this is not possible because Europe comprises many nation-states with different regulatory authorities, then will Europeans, want electronic wallets, at least, that shift funds from buyers to sellers with two clicks on the mobile phone.

What is the impact of a decision?

The number of wireless m-commerce subscribers is going to rise from 44,000 at the end of 1999 to over 900,000 in early 2001, and if the doubling forecasts are correct, to about 50 million in the year 2004. Here are several examples:

- 1000 Estonians pay their parking fees with their electronic wallets from the Estonian Mobile Telephone Co.

- Italians participate in wireless auctions to bid for holiday packages and high-tech products with their electronic wireless devices from Omnitel, a unit of Vodafone AirTouch of the UK.
- Spaniards buy inexpensive products – such as, newspapers, hot dogs, and soft drinks – by punching a few keys on their mobile phones from Telefonica, SA.
- The French use a special cell phone with a built-in credit-card slot from France Telecom SA to make wireless payments.

Decision opportunities

M-Internet banking is one of the most important product attributes that mobile phones offer customers. Leonia Bank Oy of Finland lets wireless users pay rent, phone or electricity bills via their cellphone keypads. The bank sends a short message to the customer's cell phone whenever a bill becomes due. The user authorizes the payment with two clicks on the keypad, and the money is deducted from the person's bank account.

Reconfiguring the value chain

How all 15 nation-states of the European Union and those countries that seek EU membership resolve their legal, regulatory and cultural differences and pursue a single set of strategies for m-commerce is unknown. The leaders of the 15 member states held a Year 2000 summit in Lisbon, and they presented an outline of how to accomplish the goal of a single European framework for the use of mobile phones. These details need to be worked out before private-sector banks and firms can decide on how their several wireless Internet services will be integrated with one another.

Although GSM permits universal voice connections and UMTS will permit universal transaction capabilities within a 3G infrastructure, and these two commitments will keep Europe ahead of the US for the next few years, Japan has the unique advantage of one set of laws, regulations, and cultural practices as befits a single nation-state. Therefore, the ability of European mobile phone operators to change the value proposition of the wireless Internet in terms of price, quality and service must wait until the macro European political environment becomes clearer.

Actionable segmentation

Here is the segmentation question asked of probable Japanese and European mobile phone customers by local market researchers: Do you seek performance or do you seek technology? IMode customers in Japan want performance so they can download *manga* cartoons. GSM customers in Europe want technology so they can do their purchase and bank transactions anytime and anywhere within Europe. Analog, TDMA and CDMA customers in the US don't know enough about the new mobile phones to make an informed decision about what they actually want in these phones. Yet frequent flyers in Europe and the US want both performance and technology at 31,000 feet. Marketers have learned these two crucial facts from both hard demographic data and soft value-based data. Thus the wireless telecom firms use actionable segmentation to create new market space.

GAME THEORY IS AT THE CENTER OF 3G LICENSING

Game theory deals with the fact that when there are just a few players, all of them have to worry about the response of their opponents. Rivals don't know much at all about what the others have planned to do. Also rivals had access to different information. Good managers assign probabilities to the possible moves of the players and the outcomes.

Deutsche Telekom paid a high price for VoiceStream, a whopping $21,639 per subscriber, because it assumed other European or Japanese telecom firms might want VoiceStream, too. The price Deutsche Telekom paid for VoiceStream is five times as much as Vodafone paid for AirTouch, the former Pacific Bell wireless subsidiary, and two times greater than what Vodafone paid for Mannesmann (Germany). Did Deutsche Telekom overpay? Time will tell, but not until 2007 at the earliest. And this date is too far in the future to make any accurate predictions about sales revenue, cash flow, and returns on investment.

We do know the following: Americans will need a lot of convincing to switch from landlines, PCs and voice-only mobile phones to a more advanced wireless Internet phone system. For many in the US it is not readily apparent why they should switch from their known telephone products to the unknown of 2.5G or 3G. Both Deutsche Telekom and VoiceStream assume Americans will change their private behavior concerning smart wireless phones. There is a high probability that Americans will fall in love with these smart phones, and this outcome will be good for all wireless firms.

Auctions

The UK, the Netherlands and Germany are offering licenses for their spectrum to the highest bidders – that is, those with the keenest prices, best services, and lowest costs. The UK did one thing better than the Dutch and Germans; the British left one 3G license open to an outsider rather than limiting competition to only current 2G providers; this drove up bid prices for the licenses. Initially, the Dutch and German auctions give too much spectrum to the eventual winners, or they give away some piece of the spectrum for very little hard cash. The Dutch may have no choice, because the Netherlands is a small market.

However, Germany is a large market. Thus the government decided to revise its rules while the mid-summer 2000 auction was taking place. Each surviving bidder in the German auction had to add ten percent to its bid until the final bidders were chosen. In early August 2000 after 126 rounds of bidding for a German wireless license, Germany's fifth largest mobile phone operator, Debitel, pulled out of the auction for high-speed 3G mobile phone licenses. The price simply got too high. If Debitel had stayed in, it would have had to give up its strategy of renting capacity and build its own network from scratch. The price was too high for the firm and its backer, Swisscom.

After the German licenses had been awarded, Hutchison Whampoa also pulled out. The bid price was so high for this Hong Kong-based firm that it could not see how it would make money within the next five–ten years after the 3G infrastructure had been put in place and used by many millions of Germans. Hutchison Whampoa left its Dutch partner, KPN, and others to come up with the difference between what was bid for the German license and the amount not paid by Hutchison Whampoa.

Sunk costs

The costs of the licenses are essentially sunk costs. This cost should not affect future marginal decisions. These are:

- *How to extend a wireless network.* Does the telecom firm take on partners, acquire other firms, or build greenfield investments from scratch?
- *What prices to charge customers.* Does the telecom firm charge one rate to roam the world? Does it charge multiple rates based on geographic proximity to the caller or distance from the caller? Thus the cost of the licenses is unrelated to future revenues and costs.

Deutsche Telekom got it right when it paid its rather high price to extend its network to the crucial USA market. Deutsche Telekom had to be in the US or lose its place in the world telecom market. Also if Deutsche Telekom goes through with its one rate plan for American customers, then it will have gotten its pricing model right too. Both intangible attributes are crucial to Deutsche Telekom's acquisition of VoiceStream and the former's long-term success in Europe, North America and the rest of the world.

M-COMMERCE TRANSACTIONS

The whims of consumers, especially American consumers who are the eighth wonder of the world, can wreak havoc on forecasts, market share calculations, acquisitions, 4 Ps marketing strategies, bids for licenses, and the successes or failures of the most powerful wired and wireless telecom firms. Older mobile phones were bigger, clumsy and cost a lot when you roamed outside your base territory. The new wireless Internet phones will let you call anyone, anywhere, anytime whenever you want to call them for talk, data and products.

All of us are in the mad scramble to transform the telephone and make it more attuned to the spirit of the marketplace. In this new market, groups are narrower and defined by interests, and the ultimate interest is:

- kids – needing to talk with friends;
- young adults – needing to talk with family, and get data from associates; and
- business executives – needing to manage a business anytime, anywhere, and talk with family and friends.

The crucial point about these target groups is they always get what they want, or at least get what they think they want.

Wireless Web with strings attached

The reality in 2001 is that today's wireless Internet devices still are similar to those that have existed in the past since at least 1995. You have to have patience. And you must be willing to spend money on the hardware and the connection time. Even so the current array of Web-connected cellular phones and personal digital assistants presents frustrating limitations.

The promise for the year 2002 is that cell phones and PDAs will become one unit with touch screens, faster connections, and, perhaps, lower prices. Tapping into the Internet with handheld devices is slow and tedious, but the future holds promise.

Here is the rule of reason on the state of the wireless Web. Buy the new gadget first, ask questions later. Heed its siren call because the temptations multiply for people with handheld devices each time they use these new smart m-commerce devices.

More potency from wireless still in the wings

Will m-commerce eventually change how consumers use the telephone? Yes. What else will change? The world will intrude even more on the life of customers because the technology is now available to connect anyone, anytime, anywhere. The smart wireless device is ideally suited for the global, largely American lifestyle as it is currently operating in the world, especially, the idea that consumer choice must be exalted to the highest level. That's the promise for the year 2003.

MONEY-MAKING DEALS

Let's answer the promotion marketing questions with our current information on world-changing products:

Market space for sale

■ Is Web-based information anytime, anywhere a valuable asset? Yes for American telecom executives who must acquire spectrum (channels 60-69) from US broadcasters. Yes for European telecom executives who are telling venture capitalists to look at Europe first. Bids there on unencumbered spectrum licenses have been and continue to be accepted by the EU national governments. During 2001 European-owned telecom firms together with Japanese- and US-owned telecom firms are ready to turn valuable assets into value-creating, income-producing UMTS property.

Wired telecom firms share conventional wisdom about who their customers are, what they value, and the value proposition of product offerings. For the last 15 years, since the Modified Final Judgment went into effect and deregulation took hold in the US, Europe and elsewhere, these telecom firms competed solely on the basis of incremental improvements in quality or cost or both.

Reconfigure value chain

Those wired telecom firms who push value innovation study substitute industries to reconfigure their value chains. For example, AT&T buys cable companies because it doesn't own "the last mile" into the house or office through which the Baby Bells lay slower ISDN or faster DSL lines. Implicitly, buyers of telecom services weigh the costs and benefits of substitutes; sellers need to get into the minds of customers and find out how the latter make trade-offs among substitute products. If sellers change technology and products, promotional campaigns, and prices, buyers begin to weigh their options once again.

Transform latent demand into real

Here is the time when innovative sellers create a new value proposition, such as, an innovation in product positioning, after market service, or new uses for existing products. The task facing innovative wireless telecom marketers is to transform latent demand into real demand, charge prices higher than marginal cost, and make money on a long-term basis. At the moment, no wireless firm has had the success of Home Depot, Federal Express, Starbucks and Enron in creating new market space for customers of m-commerce.

Product marketing

At the moment, no one knows what these portable devices might look like, what they can do initially, and what consumers will be willing to pay for the services they offer. Neither the telecom firms nor the equipment manufacturers have the answers. However, they do not believe they can afford to miss out on the 3G opportunity nationally and across Europe. Thus when France Telecom's British subsidiary dropped out of the bidding for a UK wireless license at £4 billion, the parent firm had to go after the fact and spend £41 billion to purchase Orange, the former Vodafone subsidiary. France Telecom paid £3,500 per head for each of Orange's customers, less than Deutsche Telekom paid for VoiceStream's customers, but still high.

Bids and licenses

Europe creates value in three ways. First, each government provides the bidders with some information about the process, and the information changes with each round of bidding. Second, the bidders provide information about the products and services they will provide the national and pan-European market once their bids are accepted. Third, when 3G is deployed, the telecom firms offer different portable devices to their customers. Thus ideas become content, content becomes transaction information, transactions become products, products become infrastructure, and place becomes promotion. These are new ways to think about creating economic value and making money.

Market opportunities

Even with the bids completed, telecom firms must learn how to identify opportunities. Is Deutsche Telekom's acquisition of VoiceStream's GSM business in the US an opportunity? Is Siemens' deal for CDMA in the US an opportunity? Is France Telecom's purchase of Orange's GSM business in the UK an opportunity? Perhaps. Even if these are opportunities, telecom firms must learn how to realize a profit potential from emerging trends and then sustain their margins over long periods of time. Firms that are successful in establishing a 3G wireless presence will change their value proposition for good. The once ubiquitous payphone and other wired phones appear vulnerable to smart wireless devices.

These probable benefits will translate into added value delivered to customers; because wireless Internet phones will satisfy customers more effectively while providing the services more efficiently. The wireless phone is a window into selling other information-based services, too at near zero variable cost per unit. Why? Once the consumer is loyal to one context, the potential for related transactions is almost unlimited. The successful telecom firm must manage information effectively and create new market space for content.

Understand user interface

- How has NTT DoCoMo locked in its Japanese customers?
- Why has iMode's short messaging services (SMS) moved from being a fad to a fashion statement for Japanese kids and young adults, and a necessity for the business persons and foreign-born expatriates who live in Japan?
- Will these long-term relationships open up new audiences in Europe too?

"In Japan you get the train schedule with two clicks," says Andrew Seybold, an American wireless expert who makes periodic trips to Japan to see what marketing techniques can be adapted to the US and Europe. "When I try to find a plane flight on a US cell phone, I have to go through seven menu levels before I can enter the flight number."

As the Japanese head onto the Internet in droves, they are doing so without wires. No analog. No ISDN. No DSL. No fast cable modems. No satellite connections. It's all wireless.

About 32 million Japanese, or one in every four uses the Internet, and half of them, a little over 16 million, gain access to the Internet through wireless phones. Also 13 million Japanese use the wireless connection provided by iMode cellular phones of NTT DoCoMo. For most Japanese teenagers their iMode phone is their only phone, and it is a substitute for going to the 7-Eleven convenience store to make a phone call. The prices for iMode wireless phones and for service are at par with wired phones from NTT. Today, these phones can provide both voice and data communications, and the newest PHS phones transmit data as fast as the wired, ISDN digital lines in Japan. Moreover, 2G technology is taking over iMode and providing the Japanese with location-awareness commercial transaction services for local business executives.

The revolution comes in 2001. NTT DoCoMo will offer five different types of wireless Internet access devices that combine the iMode phones, pagers, PDAs and the computer. Since most Japanese do not have separate living rooms or offices in their houses, their homes remain unwired and now it is too costly to start wiring them. Also most Japanese spend less time at home and more time at work or in their rice paddies or both. They commute longer distances and are more mobile than Europeans.

Japan's success story with iMode and wireless Internet means that as these teenagers become young adults and the latter become business executives they, and perhaps their peers elsewhere in East Asia, will be the first generation in the world to function completely in the wireless world. This could be an enormous competitive advantage for NTT DoCoMo over European- and US-owned wireless firms as the industrial world rethinks the technological and emotional orientation of the telecommunications industry. Japan is the prototype national market for the new economy at work in m-commerce and the wireless Internet.

No finish line for telecom firms

- Which global telecom brands dominate m-commerce in 2001?
- Will they dominate the wireless Internet in 2003 and 2005?
- What are the actual consumer purchases among TDMA, WAP, iMode and CDMA?
- Did customers get their information from print or TV media, news articles, or word-of-mouth?
- Does m-commerce lend itself to single-source data as the means to measure the effectiveness of advertising, promotion and integrated marketing communications?

Market creation and market re-creation are the central strategic challenges facing wireless telecom marketers in the next few years. The lesson is that there is no finish line. Competitors will imitate, play catch up to try to get ahead, and keep running the race. Thus wireless marketers will create new market space by doing one or more of the following:

4 Ps marketing strategy[5]

- Apply product marketing techniques from a substitute industry, such as wired telecom or the Internet, or from another country, such as Japan, to the new, emerging industry called 3G m-commerce in Europe and the US.
- Choose among promotion marketing techniques, such as brand marketing, to distinguish among GSM, CDMA and other digital standards.
- Select price marketing techniques, such as one rate and microbilling, to jump start GSM in the US and promote it over CDMA.
- Use place marketing techniques to insure content becomes information, information becomes products, products become location awareness, and place becomes promotion.

■ Create target market groups out of broader market segments, and sell wireless devices that cater for voice only anytime (for high school teenagers), and voice, data and transaction capabilities anywhere (for frequent-flyer business executives).

■ Teach early adapters among kids and young adults and probable business customers how to use the new smart wireless devices under the mantra of the *new* marketing concept.

■ Rethink the functional and emotional orientation of the industry, its firms and its potential customers.

■ Try to shape external trends, such as establishing UMTS as the international standard.

■ Collect single-source data to test these marketing and competitive ideas in one market within the US or Europe. If the campaigns are not capturing incremental sales, change them to reflect the concerns of customers in local, regional and national markets.

■ Compare how, for example, Enron, Cisco, The Body Shop, Starbucks, Lexus, Walkman, and Home Depot created new market space and stayed ahead by never crossing the final finish line.

Correlate information on actual consumer purchases of smart wireless devices and m-commerce Internet services in Japan, the UK, Europe and the US. Use single-source data in lead markets, such as Akihabara, Tokyo's electronics district, before rolling out new and different smart devices. What works well in Tokyo will work just as well in Los Angeles, New York and Chicago, and in London, Frankfurt and Helsinki, especially for teenagers and young adults, and the business executives. Marketers know this from their analysis of hard and soft data as they carry out actionable segmentation to create new market space.

Power selling on the cheap

■ Is there a set of best practices for creating new market space for m-commerce or the wireless Internet?

▓ Will wireless Internet telecom firms live up to the central strategic marketing challenge facing m-commerce, and create and re-create new Web-enabled markets?

▓ How well are the airlines doing with the wireless Internet?

▓ Will the wireless investors continue to make rational investments in a world dominated by irrational, increasingly irrelevant wired telecom firms?

Power selling is similar to a tag-team race:

1   The power firms perfect their selling and marketing strategies, and collect single-source data to reflect real consumer choice in wireless Internet connections.

2   These power sellers achieve industry levels of performance quickly, and then surpass them with a good user interface, great one-rate prices and excellent promotion information. For example, the Hong Kong users of iMode can race cars on their wireless phones, the Miracle Grand Prix.

3   Power firms insist suppliers, managers, and customers buy into the former's value proposition – that is, location awareness of commercial services, and voice and data communications.

4   Power wireless telecom firms push for explosive growth in the expansion phase of the product life cycle.

NTT DoCoMo's iMode is the world's first mobile Net service to offer a constant on-line connection and enticing content. This is power selling at its best.

Britain's Vodafone (acquiring Germany's Mannesmann), France Telecom (acquiring Britain's Orange), and Germany's Deutsche Telekom (acquiring America's VoiceStream) have made the acquisitions model the current standard for building up the wireless industry. NTT DoCoMo thinks this is an expensive way to create a new business model for the wireless industry.

Instead, NTT DoCoMo is taking a minority position in Hutchison Telecom (Hong Kong), KPN Mobile (the Netherlands), and 3G UK Holdings (UK). More deals are on the horizon for NTT DoCoMo. The Japanese firm plans to sell mobile content and applications to its partners, such as city guides, news, and local advertising. Its mobile handsets are the world's smallest and the most sophisticated. In 2001, DoCoMo will roll out W-CDMA, one possible international 3G UMTS standard, in Japan and Europe and, with its content, NTT DoCoMo will be hard to beat in the race to dominate the wireless Internet or m-commerce.

BRAND MANAGEMENT[6]

Originally, brands were simply a means of differentiating one product from another, Dial from Dove soap. Then, some of them acquired a more aspirational function: teenagers wore Nikes in the hope of conveying they were great sports personalities; executives flew business class, joined frequent-flyer clubs, and entertained in fee-based air lounges with the intention of suggesting that they were affluent decision-makers; and computer geeks became Apple or IBM clone members to show they had the most up-to-date information technology.

Now people want to be different. They adopt brands that reflect their values and self-image. In some cases, they move away from the mass market, from Coke to Royal Crown, Dr Pepper, and Mountain Dew.

The first wireless brands carried the names of their wired parent firms, such as AT&T. Others had different names, such as CellularOne, and were used to differentiate them from their wired parent firm, SBC Communications. Then came the alphabet soup of new names for start-ups, such as VoiceStream. Soon the US will see brand names, such as NTT DoCoMo, Deutsche Telekom, Vodafone AirTouch, and many more. All these brand names for mobile phones are simply means of differentiating one cell phone from another. These brands are neither aspirational nor do they reflect the self-image and values of users. In short, marketers are back to where they began with brand management many years ago, and this type of brand strategy is showing its age with the advent of m-commerce.

Rival mobile phones differ so little that it is difficult to promote their brand names. Yet there are so many brands that customers face complexity and stress in decision-making. This is happening just at the time when the costs of new acquisitions for Vodafone, Deutsche Telekom, and France Telecom are so high that they need brand name differentiation to charge users prices a great deal higher than marginal costs. Otherwise, these firms will not be able to pay back the debt they incurred for their acquisitions or make money on operations. Thus brand management for m-commerce and the wireless Internet needs a marketing reorientation that uses information to create value and inform customers about the product, its content, and after market service. What to do?

Value proposition

1   Match information, products and content to the actual needs of customers. They want tangible product benefits, such as, location awareness, voice and data communications, and transaction capabilities. Also they want intangible product benefits, such as an international digital standard, microbilling, one rate pricing, packet-based switching, and skill at not paying too much for the new wireless licenses (or game theory).

2   Offer a unique value proposition. Here are the questions that must be answered about the value proposition: do wired firms have the skills and talent to manage wireless firms? Are the former's products equal to the task facing the latter? Do wired firms have the right set of customers; can they capture a new set of customers who favor wireless m-commerce? Can wired firms offer wireless telephones that can be packaged and delivered in an innovative way so that customers, such as, the high value-added frequent flyers, will respond to this added value by paying higher prices.

3   Provide early adapters and loyal customers with targeted information about the products, their prices, and the firm's after-market services. Most of this is best done via the Internet rather than through the traditional media. Information about products and services, and their cost and price data tend to become transparent over the Web.

Without brand recognition none of the current wired and future wireless telecom brand names will stick in the minds of customers. Thus no new market space will be created by branding wireless products. Instead, the products will have to sell themselves with different functions and, perhaps, different colors rather than with the values and self-image of users.

New market space for m-commerce will come from wireless Internet technology – that is, the choice between GSM, CDMA or iMode, 3G or something else. Europe and Japan will lead with their new technologies. If the US resolves its technology issues, then a lot more effort will be spent on marketing topics, such as branding, media buys, advertising copy, etc. Promotion marketing won't be an equal partner in the 4 Ps marketing strategy for smart wireless devices until the US is fully engaged in 3G m-commerce.

In one case example, some time before 2003 virtually all airlines that serve business travelers and maintain frequent-flyer information will migrate to real time because these customers are demanding Web-enabled enhanced services. Such new market space will be as important as the introduction of frequent-flyer clubs, business-class seating and service, individual TV in the seats, upgraded food offerings and the like. The airlines will offer location awareness together with voice and data communications, and transaction capabilities. No business traveler will be without 24/7 connections – that is, unless he or she turns off the phone.

THE GAME'S WINNER[7]

NTT DoCoMo developed the following business model for iMode:[8]

- Customers must experience something fresh every minute, every hour, every day from iMode mobile phones.
- Customers should get more than short messaging services (SMS) as their wireless Internet contextual experiences deepen with text, data, and transactions from iMode.
- Customers should be encouraged to repeat their visits time-and-time again through their iMode cell phones.
- Customers should be able to see the benefits, hold the content in their hands, and plan the long-term use of iMode in their daily lives.

This is a positive feedback model in which good content attract users; better users attract higher-quality content; and so on throughout iMode's value chain. DoCoMo's success is a marketing story in which the firm has added value to the wireless industry, to itself, and to its customers.

Real options

NTT DoCoMo began with the notion of embedded flexibility – that is, it had no obligation to make future investments. But it did make more investments. Subscribers signed up at the rate of one million every two months, and content providers signed up even faster to now number over 10,000. At each investment stage, marketing practitioners of real options assumed a 50 percent standard deviation. This means the value of positive cash flows from an investment by DoCoMo will almost double, or the value of these cash flows in fact will fall by one-half in each of the years until all investments are made in 2G to 2.5G, and in 3G. Although DoCoMo may have to forego alternative investments, the option to go ahead with iMode offers higher returns than the option to not go ahead.

Industry leader

Today, NTT DoCoMo is the pacesetter and is far ahead on the learning curve of the wireless Internet. It is the industry standard, the leader, the first mover, and the key partner of US-based Verio, Hutchison Whampoa, KPN Mobile, and AOL. If DoCoMo fails in making the transition to 3G, then investors will make different calculations about Vodafone AirTouch, Deutsche Telekom VoiceStream, and other pending wireless deals.

According to our real options analysis, DoCoMo's downside risk of failure is low and the possibility of its success is high. In summary, NTT DoCoMo must continue to act as an advertising agency to promote the mobile Internet and communicate to customers the better value of iMode versus WAP. This is how DoCoMo creates and re-creates market space.

CONCLUSIONS

How to conquer the wireless world? Apply traditional promotion marketing strategies to m-commerce, especially to show the relative strengths and weaknesses of GSM and iMode. Here is a checklist of things to do:

- Put Web-based content out in the market anytime, anywhere with 3G-enhanced mobile or cell phones.
- Build market share with a 4 Ps marketing strategy together with a single-source data marketing research strategy that is carefully adapted to building up brand name recognition.
- Offer customers crucial salient intangible product attributes, such as one international 3G digital standard, one rate pricing plans, packet switching technology, and game theory analysis.
- Create value with new market space, and power selling and marketing, and be investors who are crazy like a fox.

Now let's look at how to price value creation and new market space in the emerging wireless world both at home and abroad.

CHAPTER 3

Pricing M-Commerce Services

EXECUTIVE SUMMARY

MARKETERS OFFER BOTH COMMODITY and higher value-added prices as marketing managers divide m-commerce customers into those who do virtually everything on-line and those who prefer personal services from telecom, content, and financial service providers. Also marketers offer the lowest prices for basic text content, higher prices for improved tangible and intangible product qualities on digital handheld information appliances, and the highest prices for advanced 3G wireless Internet service. The choice marketers make among prices, levels of quality, and services is the foundation upon which they implement a 4 Ps marketing strategy, reconfigure the value chain, and create and re-create new market space. Here's what they must do to get the pricing right:

- Re-compute the ability of European telecom firms to pay back the excessive cost of bids for UMTS licenses in Europe.
- Quit telecom partnerships and abandon UMTS licenses as did Hong Kong-based Hutchison Whampoa in Germany and Blu in Italy.
- Forecast pricing difficulties for Vodafone, Deutsche Telekom, Royal KPN, and France Telecom because of the high cost of constructing a continent-wide 3G infrastructure for dual-band WAP and iMode mobile phones.
- Organize alliances and partnerships with successful non-European firms, such as NTT DoCoMo, to help overcome competitive product marketing, promotion and advertising, and pricing challenges.
- Market 2G and 2.5G mobile Internet to early adopters in the US, for the purpose of creating a revenue stream to pay off European 3G debts.
- Charge m-commerce customers for Web-based content, as does DoCoMo, rather than giving it away as is the current practice for users of wired PCs.

▓   Carry out a *new* 4 Ps marketing strategy that offers marketers alternative channels of distribution, especially for on-line financial services.

Capture revenue through price marketing deals

Are the deals priced right? Are marketers now able to distinguish between iMode as CRM (customer relationship management) handheld devices versus GSM as commodity mobile phones? Can GSM overcome the slowdown in the expansion phase of the product life cycle for simpler devices? Can iMode create a new product life cycle for itself or together with GSM in the dual-protocol world of UMTS? What do corporate users want from m-commerce and how much are they willing to pay for linking up their customers to new ordering and payments systems? Can wireless telecom providers and their content provider partners make money from m-commerce? Also do the deals deliver appropriate financial results, especially in terms of positive cash flows and earnings from sales? Do the following price marketing deals create and deliver value?

▓   Add the three-part relationship of price, quality, and service to the alliances and partnerships among European, Japanese and Hong Kong telecom firms. If these deals are priced correctly, then they will answer important marketing questions and deliver crucial financial results. The crucial link to success in m-commerce is getting the pricing right; because the fees for licensing spectrum and the costs of building 3G infrastructure are higher than the wired telecom firms can afford. If customers view the quality and service of m-commerce as offering enhanced CRM, then they will pay for m-Internet banking and other m-financial services.

▓   Offer customers a range of prices from higher-priced deals to commodity-based mobile phone deals. Also the crucial link to success is distinguishing which m-commerce content is best suited for the iMode model of paying for it every time the content is downloaded on mobile phones. Without customers accepting this change in how content is used and paid for through m-commerce, wireless telecom and content providers will burn cash too fast, not deliver positive cash flow quickly, and be unable to translate sales into earnings.

▨ Establish alternative channels of distribution for m-commerce users among bankers, stock brokers, hotels, airlines, and many others in the B2B and B2C Internet business world. Right now only Japan is a success with m-commerce. Europe faces high licensing and infrastructure costs, and lower than expected revenues. Europe's break-even point is nowhere in sight for any reasonable short-term and medium-term forecast. Of course, the US is not at the starting gate in the race to grow sales and throw off revenue for m-commerce. Japan will not be able to subsidize the introduction of m-commerce both in Europe and the US.

▨ Increase the brand equity for mobile phones, m-commerce, and the wireless Internet among the young, affluent, urban-based customers who want m-banking and all other financial services on-line. Assemble hard demographic data, and soft values and lifestyle information about the personal preferences of Gen-Y or the Net Generation for the products and services from miniature information devices, m-commerce content, and the mobile Internet. The cultural characteristics of Japanese m-commerce customers are in part similar to those in Europe and the US, but they are also very different. Marketers must recognize these differences and use them to roll out an effective 4 Ps marketing strategy for Europe and another for the US.

Recommendation

Wireless telecom marketers are making decisions about how to price new handheld devices, m-commerce content, and wireless Internet connections. In 1999–2000, marketers packaged coolness as the most important intangible product attribute of m-commerce business. The ads were great. Yet the nagging question remains: Was the boom in m-commerce a one-time event? Will its use slow to more normal telephone levels? We saw the boom in the use of the Internet between 1995 and 1998, and the boom in e-commerce between 1998 and 2000. Then both the Internet and e-commerce ran into diminishing use by customers and diminishing returns in the economics of the network.[1]

Some marketers will tell you that the products weren't just right. Others will say the promotion and advertising didn't convey the value of the Internet, e-commerce, and, most recently, m-commerce. My view is that marketers failed to get the pricing right. If marketers do their job correctly, their price marketing decisions drive product development, promotion and advertising, and place marketing. This chapter is about how to get the pricing right.

Here is the marketing assignment for wireless marketers:

- Segment digital customers in terms of disposable personal income or how much they actually have for m-commerce after they pay all their permanent monthly bills.
- Target high net worth individuals for more expensive, dual-protocol iMode and GSM miniature CRM handheld information appliances, the mass affluents for less expensive separate mobile phones and PDAs, and target the middle class for simpler GSM mobile devices.
- Position high levels of functionality in m-commerce devices with high levels of disposable personal income. Charge higher prices. Match middle ranges of functionality with middle levels of DPI. Charge medium prices. Position lower levels of functionality with lower levels of DPI. Charge lower prices.

Thus marketers must deal with the serious pricing difficulties ahead for the wired European telecom firms as they seek to transform themselves into wireless telecom firms. Will these firms follow the pricing practices of DoCoMo and make money, or will they fail to follow DoCoMo and lose money? Let's see what wired and wireless firms are doing so far and show what they must do to succeed in the future.

INTRODUCTION

Here's our price marketing strategy:

- Recoup the licensing fees and investment costs paid by wireless telecom providers for the mobile Internet from the operating revenue paid by bankers for m-commerce financial services. Help these users with "deep pockets" create an alternative channel of distribution for on-line financial transactions, and capture high levels of revenue from customers with the highest DPI possible.

- Consider the investments of wireless firms in 3G infrastructure as sunk costs, especially if the commitment to m-Internet banking and its higher prices lag behind the introduction of fun things for the consumer at lower prices on the Internet. Use real options analysis to decide whether to invest in m-Internet banking or consumer m-commerce content, or both.

- Invest in value relationships for wireless telecom in m-banking and m-commerce. Price on-line services to cover operational costs. Offer penetration prices to drive down the cost curve and build up market share. Try as many price, quality, and service relationships as possible. Fast forward the development of cars equipped with wireless technology that offers boosts in horsepower to climb mountains, notifications for maintenance of engines, and, of course, the location of accidents for ambulances, stalled vehicles for repair trucks, and synchronized traffic lights for police and fire services.

- Reconfigure the value chain for wireless, wired and all other competitors in the telecommunications industry, and reconfigure the value chain for traditional bankers as the latter add an alternative, m-commerce channel for on-line financial services.

PROMISING INVESTMENTS

What do dumb investors and 'crazy like a fox' investors agree on?

The smart investors want to make wireless investments in promising carriers. For example, Vodafone has little in the way of fixed, wired assets. The firm does not have the bureaucratic baggage of those European telecom firms that once were the postal, telephone and telegram monopolies, such as Deutsche Telekom, France Telecom, and British Telecommunications.

Instead, Vodafone starts from a more efficient, focused and large base of wireless subscribers. Then add its network of content and innovation engines – or Vizzavi, which is a global mobile portal joint venture with France's Vivendi

– and Vodafone's users have a large international music portfolio, a film library and an Internet games portal. Vodafone's goal is to provide these services to customers in a consistent format across Europe, across different platforms, including mobile handsets, PCs, TVs, and PDAs, so that users can get the type of content desired and in the desired format.

Wireless telecom is about creating and delivering value through product content and marketing innovation, and it's the gift marketers offer firms, users and investors in this new age of global telecommunications. Teach them about wireless, show them how to use it, and they will buy mobile phones, wireless Internet connections, and multiple types of content. Wireless telecom is the test case of how the *new* marketing concept takes hold and comes to dominate an industry. Let's finish this section by exploring several new value propositions and show how marketers price them within the framework of m-commerce.

BUSINESS OF M-COMMERCE

Since the cell phone first appeared about a decade ago, users have wanted more services than the telecom firms could provide. Within the last two years, American customers have begun to demand better voice communications – i.e., clear and continuous voice connections, and an end to roaming charges, and different and incompatible standards. Americans see what is available in Europe (for example, one rate, WAP, and electronic wallets) and want the same or better; also they see what is available in Japan (*manga* cartoons, iMode, and short messaging services) and want more of these things, too. Americans are willing to pay for these new toys because they are becoming the necessities of a good life.

Teenagers, university students, and many business persons in the US view analogue phones as necessities. All of them would like to upgrade their cell phones without paying substantial additional fees. However, American customers are two–four years away from having a decent wireless service in the US. The challenge for wireless telecom firms is to guess accurately what services customers really want. In 2001, "Companies are in a funk," says Tim

O'Neill, a senior wireless services analyst at the investment bank Wit Soundview. They "have moved from disappointment to confusion."[2]

Although the American-owned telecom companies have created a domestic market for their newest products, they have left a good part of the demand unfulfilled. Instead, the firms have squabbled over standards (TDMA versus CDMA, and the latter versus GSM). Also they have continued to price their service based on time and distance within the calling area covered, and some still insist on roaming charges to connect to other providers elsewhere in the US. Moreover, US wireless carriers insist that those who receive a cell phone call pay for the privilege of having it connected to their phone rather than charging cell phone users only for the outgoing calls they make to others.

These poor marketing practices limit the ability of US-owned wireless telecom firms from converting more latent demand to real demand. Time will tell whether European- and Japanese-owned wireless firms will prosper from their opportunities in the US, put together a better set of marketing practices, and win a significant share of the American market.

WHAT DO I GET FROM BEHAVIORAL FINANCE?

Users of cell phones – that is, when there are payphones or other wired phones available – may be making an irrational decision about how they spend their money. They are overvaluing the value of time for almost instantaneous connections with family, friends and business associates; and undervaluing the time in line while waiting for a pay phone. Also their lifestyle demands they be hip. They must carry a cell phone attached to their belts or in their purses, and with a pulse vibrator know right away someone is calling or has left a message.

Combine these values and lifestyles (or value-based segmentation) with the data about teenagers and young adults who will become business executives (or demographic segmentation), and marketers have sufficient potential customers for actionable segmentation. Both sets of data are the mother's milk of successful marketing campaigns.

Consistent illogical thinking

The shift from wired to wireless is both psychological and emotional. Wireless Internet users can use their PCs that are connected to wired phone lines to do the same things – that is, send data and do transactions. Yet they will pay more for wireless service. This is illogical and irrational because alternative installed wired capability is already widely available in the US.

Telecom firms are no less susceptible to these human foibles. They will spend just under $100 billion to acquire licenses for wireless service in the UK and Germany; even though the market tells them they cannot charge customers enough in user fees to recover their initial investments over any forecasting period useful to marketers and financial managers. Also when one of their own from Hong Kong, Hutchison Whampoa, pulls out of the German deal because the price is too high, the others don't recognize the logical investment errors they are making by sticking with the bid price of the final round. Deutsche Telekom, Vodafone and others will hold on to their losing investments in the German wireless market because, at some point in the future, they might recoup their losses.

None of these decisions by wireless users and wireless telecom firms makes good investment sense. Both groups have excessive confidence in their ability to make good decisions. Yet neither group wants to have buyer's regret about making bad decisions. Users will feel foolish giving up their cell phones after they have told friends and family they are hip, new age adults. Wireless telecom executives know they are plain stupid to invest their shareholders' money without any substantial return on investment within the next two–five years. But they do. These investment actions contribute to the volatility in the wireless market.

Both groups of investors are reacting to a narrow range of concepts that represent complex choices. These include novelty, new, substitutes, instantaneous voice and data connections, transaction capabilities, and so on. Investors are anchored in the past success of analogue and primitive digital phones. However, they are not reassessing new information about the cost of more advanced digital connections, and the high expense of introducing 3G digital wireless phones for fun and games, and for universal m-banking. *The New New*

Thing may fall victim to irrational judgments, but we won't know this until a great deal of money has been lost ten years down the road.[3]

Unexpected and costly results

All the wireless telecom firms are advertising cell phones at incredibly low prices so long as users buy an 18-month contract for service. This is bundled pricing. The marketing strategy of the telecom firms is to hook users into a specific wireless technology, such as Sprint PCS, Verizon CDMA, or Voice-Stream GSM, with a tri-mode cell phone that offers connections to older analogue phones. This "deal" is their value proposition. They call their pricing strategy "value pricing," a synonym for low pricing.[4]

Unfortunately, the real essence of value is the tradeoff between the benefits users receive from wireless telecom services and the price they pay for it.[5] This is the real work of marketers. Yet not much work is going on in creating these tradeoffs in the American wireless industry. Users are disappointed with their current cell phones because they cannot pay their mortgages, transfer money between their savings and checking accounts, and do other on-line financial services. Today, users are still confused with the profusion of offers and don't know whether they are getting good or bad deals.

Value management

The task facing wireless Internet firms is to position their cell phones and service packages against the offerings of their competitors, and then set the right price premium over, or discount under them. This is the theory behind value management. Unfortunately, wireless firms are making two mistakes. In the German auction case, the six winners already bid just over $46 billion, and this is the total for the licenses alone. Then they each have to invest about $4 billion additional to build their own 3G network, make it operational, and convince users to use it as their primary telephone and e-banking service. Moreover, they have to see what the reactions are from competitors and customers, the effect on total industry profitability, and on the transfer of surplus from users to telecom suppliers.

Their customers do not buy solely on low price. Instead, they buy on the basis of customer value, or the difference between the perceived benefits the firm gives customers minus the perceived price it charges. The greater the difference, the higher the value to customers, and the greater likelihood that users will choose one wireless service over another. Therefore, wireless telecom firms must try to minimize costly positioning errors or lose out in the race to be the top competitor in value management.

Positioning GSM in the US

VoiceStream Wireless is the ninth largest wireless firm in the US. It uses the European-based GSM digital standard. In the year 2000, Deutsche Telekom agreed to purchase VoiceStream, and at the same time the latter agreed to purchase PowerTel, a smaller American-owned GSM provider in the southern part of the US, and roll it into its previous purchases of Omnipoint Communications and Aerial Communications.[6] Together, these US firms under the VoiceStream umbrella are delivering high levels of technological performance at reasonable cost to wireless users in the US; when they are a part of Deutsche Telekom, they will have the resources to expand their wireless footprint and deepen their services to all users. American customers can call 70 countries with their US telephone number and be charged one rate no matter where the call came from and where it is going. If American customers accept GSM as their digital standard and the one rate pricing plan, then Deutsche Telekom-VoiceStream will gain market share and their competitors, such as AT&T Wireless, Verizon and Sprint, will lose market share.

Are one-rate connections to 70 countries the most important customer-perceived benefit? Or do cell phone users prefer their existing technologies because of familiarity and cost? Here are some crucial points about positioning value for users:

■ Gain a clear understanding of the real attributes driving customer choice and their relative importance.

- Do remember that intangible (or softer) benefits (e.g., no roaming charges that must be paid to rival cell phone companies) are as important as tangible product attributes in customer decision-making.
- Rely on customer feedback about what is crucial and what is not among all the product-service-quality attributes.

Tradeoffs

These then are the tradeoffs. Users want the benefits they are promised, and they want them at a price they can afford. The positioning strategy can fail when the price is low and the volume of sales is low too; or it can fail when the price is high and the volume of sales is low.[7] In both cases, no customer imperative exists for choosing one wireless product over another. These two possible failures in positioning leave the wireless market open to competitors.

In the case of the US wireless industry, the entry of foreign-owned telecom firms is a dynamic event that changes the tradeoffs between benefits and prices. Vodafone's acquisition of Pacific Bell's AirTouch wireless subsidiary brought the first major non-US GSM competitor into the California market. Wisely VoiceStream has stayed away from that market. Both AirTouch and VoiceStream have fine-tuned the benefits they offer at prices low enough to induce users to buy the GSM phones and the bundle of services.

No doubt wireless customers will continue to buy minutes, time and services from both companies. This is something hip to do. Also this decision is smart because it connects American users to Europe and other parts of the world. Finally, this decision is one of many these customers will make once the number of American users of wireless phones shifts from 33 percent to over 50 percent. Although there is a bit of irrationality in the decision to replace wired with wireless phones, in this case, the age of m-commerce is upon all of us. We go with the flow or we get pushed back across the technological divide. Those who don't adopt new technology will remain behind for many years in the future. Behavioral finance teaches us that the irrationality of users is a gold mine for the wireless telecom firms.

VALUE-BASED MARKETING DECISIONS

Here are value-based decisions made by those carriers that think they need
3G, high-speed service to support their wireless Internet customers:

What is the context of a decision?

Do we need 3G? This is the question that the European telecom firms should
have asked before they bid almost $100 billion on the UK and Germany li-
censes. Current European technology is 2G; it has a maximum throughput of
9.6 kilobits per second, too slow for packet switching, but OK for Europe with
its dependence on circuit switching for its WAP cell phones.

On the other hand, current Japanese technology is 2.5G; it delivers 100
kbps; 2.5G offers packet switching to make iMode work and is fast enough to
provide high-speed broadband connections. 2.5G packet switching networks
are always on for users.[8]

Why 3G? Japan will roll it out in 2001. Therefore, Europe must do the
same by 2003. 3G supports speeds of up to two megabits per second, provides
very high-speed broadband connections, and permits packet switching for all
types of transactions, especially m-Internet banking. This is the crucial piece
of information that makes all wireless telecom firms spend outrageous amounts
of money for their 3G infrastructure.

The UMTS licenses (Universal Mobile Telecommunications System) or
the "Unlimited Money To Spend" for 3G worry financial investors. They are
less impressed with the potential to surf the Net, deal in shares, listen to sports,
or watch television on mobile phones; and these investors are more concerned
with revenues today, tomorrow, and in the future. Thus in the first few weeks
after the licenses were granted, the share and bond prices of the telecom firms
dropped sharply. Also Royal KPN of the Netherlands reported losses. The content of an investment decision is to see whether their instincts about the future
of wireless telecom are confirmed by others through the beauty contests or the
bidding process for 3G wireless licenses. Even with the best set of partners,
one or more of them may have second thoughts and pull out once the bidding
process is over.

What is the object of a decision?

When wireless firms deploy capital into building a network for providing tele-com services, these assets are sunk because they are expended before any op-erating revenues can be derived from users. Carriers must have network facili-ties first before they provide telecom services.

Sunk costs come in two varieties. The first are capital leases, or the pur-chase of capacity from other carriers. These leases are made under indefea-sible right of use (IRU) terms;[9] the channel is dedicated to the leasing carrier irrespective of the capacity restraints on other channels of the fiber. If telecom firms use leases, carriers can extend their networks without having to assume the up-front costs of construction.

The second are investments in long haul, local, and switching facilities, be they over fiber, copper, satellite, or wireless mediums. Carriers own their own networks. The object of an investment decision by carriers is to borrow from the bond market, pay down debt, convert debt to equity, and raise more capital by issuing additional equity stock from treasury stock or IPOs. Even with the best financing possible, the new investments in wireless may prove to be a sunk cost and never recovered from operating fees.

What is the impact of a decision?

These carriers try to price their services to get a return on invested capital or pay down their debt. Unfortunately, more debt means poorer credit quality, and a lower rating in the bond market and drop in share price in the stock market. The impact of an investment decision has ripple effects far beyond the bidding process in one country and if the investment gets too expensive, one or more of the bidders in a partnership may pull out altogether.

Also the carriers attempt to price their services so they can acquire the built-out networks of others to increase the value of assets more quickly. Enron builds broadband networks and then sells them to telecom firms. The problem for the buyers is that the impact of an investment decision is such that some telecom firms could have a concentration of risk problem. So much of their as-sets are new wireless services within their own home country of the European

Union, or in Japan or the US. These telecom firms have failed to diversify adequately overseas.

Moreover, the carriers try to price their services to grow revenue. At the moment, these telecom firms find no better use for their capital employed; if they do find a better investment, they should be willing to sell these telecom assets because a better opportunity for these funds has arisen. Of course, most of them won't sell their leases or their networks, and newcomers will come in to challenge them with more creative uses for capital assets. Enron has come in and established built-out networks and then sold them to gas and electrical firms in the power industry and to telecommunications firms who will pay any price for broadband capacity.[10] The impact of an investment decision is to open the flood gates to many new players in the wireless telecom industry.

Decision opportunities by unpredictable outliers

"We have to be more creative about getting into the market. To throw money around is not the way to do it,"[11] says Canning Fox, the group managing director of Hutchison Whampoa. This Hong Kong firm holds to the same investment philosophy as does Enron: invest, buy, and sell assets when management finds a better use for capital employed.[12] In 2000, Hutchison made money by selling Orange to Vodafone. Then Hutchison bid successfully for a UK 3G license. After that it sold its position in Germany's Mannesmann to the new parent, UK's Vodafone. Later on Hutchison went into partnership with Royal KPN of the Netherlands and NTT DoCoMo of Japan to bid for a German 3G wireless license. Although the alliance was a successful bidder, Hutchison pulled out and gave up its coveted license to offer advanced mobile services in Germany. The price of the bid for a foreign firm without an established network already in Germany was simply too high.

Could Hutchison buy back its share of the German license from its partners? Yes. Would Hutchison buy it back at a reasonable price? "Each asset is valuable as long as you get it at the right price," says Canning Fox. "We haven't lost anything from Germany. I won't say we've gained, but we haven't lost."[13]

Hutchison's chairman, Li Ka-shing, is known for sniffing out good deals and steering clear of bad ones.[14] The price for the three partners of the German license was $7 billion, and Hutchison thought this was too expensive. Also Hutchison refuses to fall in love with built-out networks, broadband m-Internet banking, wireless Internet connections, and consumer-based m-commerce. Hutchison invested in Vodafone's AirTouch and made money. Also Hutchison invested in VoiceStream Wireless and will make money when the Deutsche Telekom acquisition goes through in 2001. Both deals and the new bid for a 3G license in Italy show Hutchison's commitment to GSM digital standard.

Hutchison's decision to pull out of its successful bid for the 3G German license says two important things to investors. First, even the most promising technologies have their price limits. The high price of the German license is not cost effective. Hutchison has no pre-existing network in Germany.[15] Also there were a large number of new entrants into the bidding process for 3G German licenses. All of them would have to build their networks from scratch. Thus greater competition in Germany's future wireless market means lower margins for new entrants, and the returns on capital employed become more uncertain for Hutchison.

Second, Hutchison now becomes the hunter rather than the hunted for built-out networks, assets built on debt capital, users for fun and games, and rapid data communications. When these wireless telecom assets go down in value Hutchison might buy them at more reasonable prices.

Reconfiguring the value chain

Who are the hunters among European telecom firms?[16] Deutsche Telekom, France Telecom, British Telecom, and Vodafone are the crucial hunters in the wireless telecom business. Royal KPN is more in the hunter camp than is Telecom Italia. Telefonica of Spain is more of a fringe player in Europe. The others in Finland, Norway and elsewhere are too small to be hunters and will be taken over by the hunters.

Only Bell South, Bell Atlantic and SBC Communications among American telecom firms have some strength to participate in the on-going auctions for 3G UMTS licenses within Europe. AT&T tried to get into Europe in the

1990s and failed; now Ma Bell is among the prey for the likes of British Tele-communications or Anglo-American Vodafone (a partner with Bell Atlantic).

Of course, NTT DoCoMo, with its penchant for minority partnerships with both European and American firms, should be watched too as a potential buyer of cheap American telecom assets.

Transforming firms, industries and markets

Transforming "old-economy" wired telecom firms requires good investment skills, such as those shown by Enron and Hutchison Whampoa. Buying built-out networks at a good price is a good investment strategy. Selling assets when they become too pricey is an even better investment strategy. Once competitors become aware that the firm buys *and sells* assets based on the return on capital employed model, others will try the same strategy. Therefore, the hunter must take into account what its competitors will do and turn their static strategy into a dynamic strategy.[17] To do this, all telecom firms need to benchmark themselves every two years against Enron and Hutchison Whampoa.

Also transforming these "old-economy" wired telecom firms demands growth in the number of users and the number of services used by customers, such as those provided by NTT DoCoMo and Sonera of Finland. To do these two things requires a redesign of the firm's marketing strategy on how to attract better paying customers and how to attract more higher-paying suppliers of email services, sports news, financial markets, and *manga* cartoons. Wired telecom firms that are becoming wireless telecom firms must understand what world class is, and then go and achieve it.

Moreover, transforming these "old-economy" companies requires a more rapid introduction of new innovations in technology and marketing, such as the introduction of GSM into the US by Vodafone AirTouch and Deutsche Telekom AirStream Wireless. To do this depends on new ideas in the use of software to improve existing 2G in Europe and 2.5G in Japan, and the introduction of more advanced software for the future 3G networks.

Of course, the transformation in the wireless industry is far from complete. No one knows how many firms will be left standing within the industry after the hunters capture their prey. No one knows whether the industry will have one or more strategic groups clearly separate from one another, or whether the mobility barriers within the industry will be breached by existing and new firms competing against one another. And no one knows what the potential for sales and revenue growth are buried within the wireless market.

ACTIONABLE SEGMENTATION

Here is the segmentation question asked by market researchers of probable m-Internet banking customers: do you want your m-bank to operate like a technology company that works in banking, or do you want your m-bank to operate like an established bank that works with technology? M-banking customers in Finland, Sweden and Estonia want their m-bank to be excellent in technology so they can obtain and pay down their mortgages, borrow from their money market accounts, purchase stocks, parking slots, and cola drinks, and do all other financial transactions without going to the bank itself. These m-banking customers live within a different culture, practice a different financial life, and respond to different promotion and advertising themes. Their values and lifestyle are the new economy writ large.

Excellent technology companies that are banks and work to dominate m-banking have deep pockets. They have elbowed themselves into the lucrative business of taking deposits, lending funds, and making money on the spread in interest rates. Their bank is their brand name and it transfers easily to the m-banking unit. These banks have asserted in their print and TV ads that they are crucial players in the new economy because they offer all their financial services through an m-banking unit.

Promotion marketing

M-banking advertising spots in the US say: "The Pacific Ocean stopped the westward movement of Americans but not their minds ...The Internet should be viewed more substantially for banking ... because there's still so much more to be done ... We don't want to be Bank of America ... We were part of the new economy before it was hip ... Thanks old economy ... We'll take it from here."[18]

Image building is crucial to m-banking. This brand advertising is designed to attract more loyal customers and, more importantly, new types of employees. The parent bank of m-banking units wants to create a different corporate culture, one that is hip, cool and rocks with the times. This will be the definitive culture of the bank in 2001 and beyond.

After establishing brand awareness, the e-banks must establish brand relevance. Can the new economy m-banks do everything the old economy banks did, and more? Can the m-banks take care of IPOs, M&A transactions, the brokerage business, and all the personal financial transactions required by the busy executives of high-tech start-up firms? Check out Robertson Stephens in San Francisco, its parent Fleet-Boston Financial, and the former's local partners, Montgomery Securities, Hambrecht & Quist and Alex. Brown. Their promotion and advertising campaigns stress their new economy differences from their larger, old economy competitors.

Shrinking profit margins

Hear what the old economy bank professionals say about m-banking: "Online banking is the invasion of the body snatchers," says Huw van Steenis, banking analyst with J.P. Morgan, the investment bank. "Fending it off could knock $6.7 billion a year off the profits of leading European banks alone."[19]

He believes banks will have to reduce their retail banking costs by almost one-fifth over three years if they are to compete against Internet upstarts. In the short run, profit margins will shrink in the UK and Ireland where margins are above the European average.

Jose Luis de Mora of Merrill Lynch takes another view. "Both established banks and e-banks [will] converge towards ... clicks and mortar."[20] He believes the winners will be those that offer customers all the channels, adjusting the price of services on each to reflect costs.

In the US, pure on-line banks such as Wingspan grow slowly, despite large marketing budgets. And brokers, such as Charles Schwab find customers prefer to open their accounts at branch offices even when they plan to trade on-line.

Customer preferences

Some customers switch their accounts from traditional branch banks to on-line banks because the latter offer slightly higher interest rates. When the former offer price cuts, customers stop switching. This switch back and forth between two bank channels because of price marketing is a temporary phenomenon. Within the next five years, says Matthew Barrett, chief executive officer of Barclays, the established UK lender with more than one million on-line customers, which makes it one of the largest on-line banks in the world, "There will only be companies that have learned how to change their business model and survived and those that have fallen by the wayside."[21]

Cash is small potatoes for banks because most transactions occur digitally with credit cards and through computer networks. Banks both process information and manage money. Virtual or m-banks contract out data processing, use interactive software to provide personalized service, and back their business up with call centers in low-cost areas of the world. These on-line banks offer daily sweeps of accounts to reduce interest rate charges on loans, and offset debts against money in checking and savings accounts.

Price marketing

When established banks set up m-banks, the prices charged by banks for various financial products services become transparent. If the interest rates are too low, on-line customers will take their business to m-bank competitors. Many bank products will be turned into commodities, such as home mortgages, stock brokering, and even savings accounts. Smart established banks will fight back before they lose too much business to on-line banks.

Customers trust established banks. The former recognize the brand names of the latter. Customers may not like banks, but they don't think they are dishonest as they believe some on-line service providers may be. The vast majority of customers stay with their established bank, but they do expect to be offered an on-line opportunity to use their accounts on the Internet.

Banks have a lot of information about their customers. Unfortunately, the banks have organized this information based on products rather than customers. The established banks know customers have checking and savings accounts, mortgages and other outstanding debts, and credit and debit cards, but the banks don't know which customers have all of these accounts and which have only some of these accounts and which customers have just one of these accounts. The established banks have to modernize their information technology systems before they can be effective competitors in on-line m-banking.

On-line m-banks

Without an established brand-name bank leading the way, an all-purpose, on-line independent e-bank will have a hard time surviving. For example, Compu-Bank, the first on-line bank to receive a charter, has established a partnership with General Electric. Also all of the nation's top 25 retail banks now allow customers to gain access to their accounts on the Web and most have added on-line bill paying capacity. Citigroup is providing America Online's 23 million users an on-line payments system, and Wells Fargo is doing the same for eBay's customers. Netbank has partnered with Fidelity Investments, Telebank with E*Trade, and USA Bancshares with Palm Pilot.[22]

Even with all of this churning the m-bank market, less than one percent of on-line customers consider the e-bank their primary bank. Still the on-line banks keep trying. Wilmington Savings Fund Society launched everbank.com in early 2000.[23] It uses direct marketing and affinity relationships to pull in its young, affluent, predominately urban Gen-Y customers. Also the bank has an exclusive contract to offer financial products on Bloomberg News Web site. Customers can make deposits at 15,000 ATMs. Moreover, NationalInterbank.com accepts deposits at the 3,600 offices of Mailboxes Etc.

The demographic numbers are still small for on-line m-banking. However, this alternative channel for banking appeals to the young, the educated, the affluent, the urban Net Generation person. Therefore, there is an opportunity to do some form of actionable segmentation for m-banking. Until those currently aged 16–26 become important business executives, sometime in their mid- to late thirties or early forties, their values, preferences and lifestyle choices for financial services will keep m-banking as the smaller alternative channel for banking. Within the decade this will begin to change.

HUMAN TOUCH OF CALL CENTER CRUCIAL TO E-BANKING

One of the crucial problems for on-line banking is building loyalty among the young, affluent, urban-based Gen-Y customers and keeping this relationship strong and committed as these consumers grow into middle-aged, highly affluent, urban-based parents and business executives. Successful m-banks offer multimedia communications links in the form of email, web chat, video conferencing as well as the traditional voice communications over the telephone. M-banks have made substantial productivity gains at their call centers with automatic call distribution and interactive voice response to automate the mechanics of handling customers' calls. Now on-line banks also use call centers to handle queries and track customer transactions across multiple channels of product information. As established banks gain confidence with the technology used by their m-banking divisions, banks will take separate product information, group it differently, and come up with better profiles of their customers. In this way, call centers will generate more revenue for established banks, and if they are smart keep a human touch, too.

Customer relationship management

When established banks or their m-banking units or both set up a Web site, it must be able to handle the hits 24/7 anytime, anywhere. Sites that are taken off-line repeatedly force customers to other sites or back to established branch banks. Cahoot, the Internet banking arm of Abbey National, a leading UK bank, launched its Web site in the second quarter of 2000.[24] It could not handle the hits and went off-line time and again. Cahoot was designed as a low-cost Internet-only channel for routine business – for example, opening an account; however, when the site went down, no telephone number was placed on the site for potential customers to call and sign up for an account through a personal banking representative. Fiserv, a US information technology company, supplied the initial Web site and has had to help Cahoot do a better job with its potential customers.

CMG, an Anglo-Dutch IT services group, works on unifying voice telephone calls, interactive voice response, fax, email and Internet interactions into a single system. CMG develops IT solutions for banks that instantly switch between voice messages, handling a live call, reading email or sending a text message to the mobile phones of m-bank customers. This multi-channel strategy enhances the capability of m-banks to build and keep customer loyalty. This is the year 2001 way to do the best job possible in (CRM) customer relationship management.

Outsourcing

Dimension Data (which owns Merchants, a UK call-center outsourcing business) runs customer service operations for businesses that do not want to own their own call centers.[25] Virgin Mobile, the fifth largest cellular provider in the UK, lets Merchants run its 300-seat call center on a "build-operate-transfer" (BOT) model that allows Virgin to take over the operational management of the call center over three years, if it chooses. Outsourcing is the new economy writ large for both m-banks and mobile Internet telecom firms. Today, call centers for mobile telecom, m-banking, and utility customers are designed to receive inbound and provide outbound communications through voice, email, fax and Internet Web sites. These interactive interactions will lower costs, reduce prices, raise margins, and increase profits for all m-businesses.

M-COMMERCE TRANSACTIONS

Time has come to test the whims of American consumers for virtual banking and insurance. Citigroup (or the merger of Travelers Group, an insurance firm, with the bank, Citicorp) has had some success in getting its customers do their banking on-line and also use the m-banking facilities to buy insurance products.

Returns on capital employed

The problem for both American and non-US banks as they seek a presence in the US is that they tie up a lot of capital for generally sluggish returns. They are doing the opposite of what Enron and Hutchison Whampoa recommend for good financial management. They could decide to employ their capital else-where and earn a greater return on their investment. Also they face competition from insurance firms. State Farm Mutual Automobile Insurance Company, the biggest American insurer of cars and homes, is offering a wide range of financial products and services on-line and through its agents. MetLife, one of America's largest life insurers, bought a small New Jersey bank, Grand Bank, that will offer banking and insurance products and services on-line. All banks have their work cut out for themselves to make good money from on-line financial services.

Obsolete business definition of retail banks

Established retail banking is obsolete. M-banking as the only channel for financial transactions is not a winner. Thus established retail banking with two channels, one for bricks-and-mortar and the other for on-line banking, is the new definition of retail banking. Will American customers buy into this new definition of retail banking? Yes, over time.

Here is the marketing strategy that established banks must follow to convince customers of the efficacy of their new approach to retail banking. First, the value chain of the dual-channel established banks must include all the information that flows within the bank and between the bank and its co-respondent banks, mortgage brokers, stock brokers, and its existing or potential customers.[26] Second, both banks and customers must recognize that brand identity, process coordination, customer loyalty, employee loyalty, and switching costs all depend on various kinds of product and consumer information. Third, since some of this information is proprietary and some is in the public domain, especially the brand name of established banks, customers should push banks to be more open in providing information to the market.

In today's world, the Internet connects everyone and makes most information, especially on prices, transparent. Bank customers now can access information and make transactions in a variety of new ways, all without the need of using established banks, their branches, and even their captive on-line banking units.

Therefore, established banks with broad product lines will lose ground to financial service specialists who can dis-aggregate bank-type products and services, and offer them at substantially lower price points than the vertically integrated established banks. The latter's carefully manicured cross-selling of financial products and services will be deconstructed, thrashed and thrown away. Margins, prices and profits of the established banks will fall – that is, unless they do a great job in repositioning themselves into virtual, on-line m-banking. These established banks must unbundle all aspects of their physical value chain for the sake of delivering information anytime, anywhere to the 24/7 targeted market segment.

Today, 75 percent of the profits for established banks with a virtual banking unit comes from the ten percent of customers who are young, affluent, computer savvy, urban-based and use personal-financial software. They are known as Gen-Y, or the Net Generation. Tomorrow, more profits will come from this target market segment as their numbers grow in demographic terms, and as their m-banking values and on-line lifestyles come to dominate folks in their thirties, (or Gen-X), and their parents (or the baby boomers). Thus a good case can be made for an m-banking marketing strategy that is based on demographic and value-based segmentation, or actionable segmentation.

MONEY-MAKING DEALS

Let's answer the price marketing questions with our current information on world-changing products and services:

Auction pricing

■ *Is it time to focus less on wireless technology and more on the business of marketing m-commerce to established bankers?*

Yes for the European-owned telecom firms that bid just a bit under $100 billion for wireless licenses in the UK and Germany, and spent over $50 billion to acquire US-based wireless telecom firms.

■ *Did these firms pay too much for their licenses and foreign direct investments?*

Yes.

■ *Will they be able to recoup their initial investments from operating revenue within any reasonable forecasting period?*

No.

Deutsche Telekom has been bitten with the wireless technology bug. It was willing to put up $7 billion for its German wireless license, $40 billion for VoiceStream Wireless, and another $5 billion for PowerTel. Then it has to spend an additional $4 billion up front to build its 3G UMTS wireless network between 2001 and 2003 before it sees any revenue from operations. The shares of Deutsche Telekom's stock tumbled and its bond ratings slipped as investors reevaluated the firm's ability to make money within one, three or five years. Deutsche Telekom is suffering current financial pain with the hope that its investments will pay off with future gains. In summary, Deutsche Telekom's goal is to derive about 25 percent of its sales revenue from outside its home market of Germany.

Deutsche Telekom can make these very long-term investments because 58 percent of its shares are owned by the German government, and the latter doesn't require what investors want – growth in current earnings, relatively low price-earnings ratio, some yield through dividend payments, and a spectacular increase in share price within six months to a year.

However, American users of GSM wireless technology through Deutsche Telekom and its US subsidiaries will compare prices with those of the wireless telecom firms that offer CDMA and PCS service. Deutsche Telekom and Voice-Stream Wireless will have very little control over their prices in the American market. Deutsche Telekom could be short of revenue to pay down its debt to creditors, offer dividend income to shareholders, and throw off profits to investors. If Deutsche Telekom were a privately-owned firm, such as AT&T, rather than a partially-owned state enterprise of the German government, Deutsche

Telekom could be put in play by investors as they look to Hutchison Whampoa and other successful hunters to buy Deutsche Telekom's assets on the cheap.

Some control over roll-out of 3G wireless service

- *Should the wireless telecom firms consider their investments in 3G infrastructure sunk costs?*
  Yes definitely within the first decade of doing m-commerce business, especially if commitment to m-banking lags far behind the introduction of fun things from the Internet.
- *Can they use real options eventually to make money in the new market space they are creating for wireless telecom technology?*
  Yes in the longer run.

After the $7 billion bid price for the German license is paid to the German government, Deutsche Telekom does not have to invest all the $4 billion to make its 3G wireless network operational immediately. Deutsche Telekom can spend a little each year. The firm can cap its network without making it operational until market forces in Germany, elsewhere in Europe, and in America demand a fully developed 3G wireless network. This is the essence of a real options strategy applied to investing in new technology and opening up new markets. Enron pioneered this approach when it found oil and natural gas, spent the minimum amount of money to cap the field, and waited until the price of crude oil in the world market was high enough for Enron to make a lot of money. Pfizer did the same thing when it sought FDA approval for new ethical drugs and then waited until the price was right in the pharmaceutical market to introduce the new drugs. Deutsche Telekom, other wireless telecom firms, and even established banks with an m-banking unit could do the same.

Sometimes the consumer market is not ready for a new innovation. Sometimes the market segment is not large enough to make it financially attractive for firms to roll out their new technology and spend money on marketing new services. And sometimes the targeted group does not have sufficient income or time to learn how to use the new technology. All of these contingencies can stall the introduction of a technology and the willingness of corporate decision makers to spend money on promotion and advertising.

Naturally, all they have spent before the introduction of the new products and services is sunk cost. It has been spent. It's gone. If the new technology is a bust, the investments will never be recouped. If the new technology is marginally successful, a little of the original investments may be recouped. If the new technology is a great success, then some of the original investments could be recouped. But don't count on it. The task is to forget sunk costs, and to make enough in sales revenues to cover operational expenses and throw off some profits.

More control over the value proposition

* *What is the value proposition for wireless telecom in m-banking? Can the wireless firms price their on-line services to cover operational costs?*
  Yes.
* *Should they offer penetration prices, drive themselves down the cost curve, and build up market share?*
  Yes they should try many price, quality, and service attributes.

The value proposition for wireless telecom firms is twofold. First, they must put up the 3G network and not try to recoup their sunk costs. Second, they must tie their wireless services to those coming from other industries, such as e-banks, stock brokerages, news services and many more. M-commerce firms must do a good job on customer relationship management (or CRM) with these banks and other companies that depend on on-line services. Managers of wireless firms must ask whether their m-commerce business activities are effective – that is, they do the job demanded – and they must ask whether they are being carried out effectively, too. Both give the wireless Internet firms more control over the value proposition.

M-commerce firms need the ability to apply analytical tools to databases and run applications that utilize this information. This is the heart of checking whether the business applications that deliver the value proposition to users are being carried out effectively: first, by those telecom firms that lease access to or build 3G networks; second, their established banks that use outsourcing or set up their own alternative channel for m-banking; and third, the whole potpourri of traditional firms that seek an m-commerce solution to slow sales and lagging profits worldwide.

The wireless firms must bring non-transactional intangible data into the analytical framework, and build a more complete picture of the business. The task is to improve customer satisfaction, optimize returns on investments, maximize shareholder value, and manage risk.

Shrinking financial margins

■ *Will the wireless telecom firms reconfigure the value chain of wireless, wired and all other competitors in the telecommunications industry? Will these m-commerce firms reconfigure the value chain of established bankers as the latter add an alternative channel for on-line financial services?*

Yes. How they do it and what will be the results are unknown at this time. However, if wireless telecom firms fail, they will become competitors in a commodity business while others who can apply appropriate technology to e-banking increase margins, raise prices and grow revenues.

Both telecom firms, established banks, and other traditional companies will have to reconfigure their value chains to include m-commerce because margins are shrinking and costs are rising. Their industries are those faced with deregulation, increasingly sophisticated customers, and competitors from other industries who know how to create new market space. These new m-commerce firms need to know which activities are the real cost drivers, determine whether all overhead costs are really necessary, and specify which non-value-added activities can be replaced with activities that do add value for customers.

LIVING AND WORKING WITH THE WIRELESS WEB

"On-the-go" people want information when they want it and where they want it, without restrictions. These younger managers want information, contacts, and other data that are consistent among their laptop PCs, PDAs and cell phones. Also these affluent younger people want an end to one-way short messages and the complete ability to use two-way short messages (or SMA text between phones). Unlike PC-based email, however, mobile messaging is short, filtered, generally without attachments, and can be further customized based on the user's location at a given time. Moreover, these urban-based young people want content rendering, or specialized software that converts a PC-based Web site to work on a PDA, cell phone or other handheld device. Finally, these Gen-Y folks want m-commerce, which enables them to buy from any handheld device, at any place, at any time.

All of these technologies have become "must-haves." They are user-friendly, convenient and have a very short learning curve. These are the killer apps of the wireless world.

European customers rely on their mobile phones for critical, personalized information and applications that are time- and location-sensitive. This is information they must have while on the go, and is a major contrast to the search/surfing model of how American customers use the Internet interface of desktop PCs. Will Internet-tethered users in the US adopt the untethered Internet approach of Europe and Japan? Vodafone, Deutsche Telekom and NTT DoCoMo are betting that American users will switch to the mobile wireless world once these foreign firms install the 3G packet switching infrastructure by 2005 in the US. If they are correct, the US still will be three years behind Japan and two years behind Europe in implementing 3G m-commerce and, given the rapid changes in wireless telecom technology, the US may never catch up or get ahead of its overseas rivals.

Getting killed by customers

The European and Japanese wireless firms will treat their American customers like kings. They need market share in the US to claim they are really international telecom firms. Also they need these payments from American users to take profits out of the US to upgrade facilities in the UK, Germany and Japan, and pay down the huge debt some of them incurred in their bids for licenses in the UK, Germany, Switzerland, France and elsewhere in Europe.

When you treat customers like kings, they quickly turn out to be tyrants. Never in our lifetime will foreign-owned wireless firms so gleefully abase themselves by throwing in almost free mobile phones and hundreds of free minutes, catering for every whim about no-charge roaming privileges, and burning up millions of dollars in pursuit of that elusive thing called "loyalty." This will make for some very happy wireless customers and for some very sick wireless telecom firms.

The basic problem is simple: all wireless customers are not created equal. Good customers in California, in which Vodafone AirTouch has its footprint, use their mobile phones beyond the free minutes and spend a lot of money over a long period of time. Bad customers in Mesa, Arizona, in which VoiceStream Wireless, has one of its footprints, use their wireless phones sparingly and are freeloaders who aren't worth what it costs to serve them. To make money, VoiceStream has to dodge the bad customers or force the good ones to subsidize freeloaders. In the haze of the new economy, Deutsche Telekom thought the important piece of information was how many customers Voice-Stream Wireless had, and not how much they cost to serve them in many of the non-wired parts of the US. VoiceStream, PowerTel and others spoiled their customers rotten, and found one of the European hunters who is willing to spend big bucks to pay for the endless goodies given to freeloaders. Similar to many foreign direct investments in the past, US firms took them in with what looked like a good deal, cleaned their pockets out, and left them to pay down the debt incurred by making these investments in the US.

The prayer is a long mournful chant: the wireless firms will spend a lot of money up front to build their 3G networks. Also they will advertise to convince customers to try them out. Then they invoke the gods of wireless telecom. These firms want the investment to pay off each and every time after the first wireless telephone call so the firms start to make money on each and every subsequent wireless telephone call. Marketers are especially interested in the "post-the-first-purchase decision" made by users of wireless telecom services. They have found out that each time a customer makes a wireless phone call, the wireless firm loses money. And the more customers it has, the more money it loses. These wireless telecom firms are a charity.

New economy mantra

NTT DoCoMo got it right in Japan. Users pay a monthly fee for access to packet switching, a time-of-use fee for incoming and outgoing wireless calls, and a fee for each Internet service they download on their mobile phones. NTT DoCoMo knew better than to take every customer who applied for wireless service, and ruthlessly fired customers who were not spending between $75 and $155 per month for W-CDMA wireless service. Fire our bad, under performing customers should be the mantra of the new economy. This is tough love applied to the wireless Internet.

Unless the foreign-owned wireless telecom firms build up their market share rapidly, they won't enjoy the benefits of network economics. The costs of servicing 20 million customers is almost the same as servicing ten million customers. Each new customer represents pure profit once the network is fully built.

Right now the foreign-owned wireless firms are dying for more American customers. Until the network is fully operational – and it may never have enough US users – these European-owned wireless firms may just die from their American customers. This is the soft underbelly of the m-commerce business that could kill the potential wireless boom during the next five–ten years.

CONCLUSIONS

How to conquer the wireless world? Apply traditional price marketing strategies to m-commerce, especially to show how investors view investments in wireless telecom and m-banking. Here is a checklist of things to do:

- Put Web-based m-banking financial services out in the market anytime, anywhere with 3G-enhanced mobile or cell phones.
- Build market share with a 4 Ps marketing strategy that is carefully adapted to making money from wireless operations.
- Offer customers price, quality, and service attributes as the value proposition for early adapters among the Gen-Y or Net Generation.

- Create value by reconfiguring the value chain for wireless m-banking and on-line financial services, the crucial target of opportunity for high priced services from m-commerce, and offer promising investments to smart investors.

Next let's look at how marketers use segmentation strategies in the emerging wireless world both at home and abroad.

Value Delivery

CHAPTER 4

Segmenting International Markets

EXECUTIVE SUMMARY

MARKETERS DIVIDE LIKE GROUPS OF PEOPLE across national frontiers into those who have the income, are the correct age, live in the right neighborhoods, and belong to modernizing ethnic groups as candidates for the purchase of miniature information appliances, 3G telecom services, and interactive Internet content.

Also marketing managers look for the following demographic, and values and lifestyle characteristics among like groups of people:

- citizens of countries, and residents of regions and cities with fast 2.5 and 3G digital connections;
- individuals with high net worth and with high levels of disposable personal income or DPI;
- age-cohort groups with high numbers of Gen-Y (twenty-somethings) and Gen-X (thirty-somethings);
- info-tech geeks whose personal values include work and play in virtual worlds;
- computer jocks whose lifestyles include the use of PCs, PDAs, and mobile phones at the office and when they work at home, and also when they send email and chat with friends and family; and
- global "netrepreneurs" who work, bank, trade stocks, and live in the Internet environment.

Moreover, marketers put these group characteristics together and obtain actionable segments in Japan, Europe, the US, China, and elsewhere in the world. Here's what they must do to acquire m-commerce customers:

■ Determine whether the growth rate for m-commerce is increasing at an increasing rate or increasing at a decreasing rate, and then disaggregate the two growth rates by the six group characteristics listed above.

■ Decide whether to offer luxury, medium-level, or commodity prices, or all three, to segments of customers with different levels of net worth and DPI.

■ Select teenagers, twenty-something netrepreneurs, or thirty-something business executives, or all three, for segments of customers whose values about the use of m-commerce, the Internet, and the traditional PC differ because of lifestyle differences.

■ Seek out early adapters among professional business women, senior executives, "Bit Valley" technophiles, and "Supli" teenage women as early sources of revenue.

■ Accept the hard bargains demanded by the early adapters on the price of mobile phones, m-commerce content, and wireless Internet connections.

■ Give actionable segments (i.e., those with income and the most appropriate lifestyle) of the m-commerce services these customers wish to have at all times and in all places.

■ Carry out the *new* 4 Ps marketing strategy that offers marketers the option to segment m-commerce customers into those who have the DPI and the personal willingness to pay for m-commerce content that they once got free of charge, and those who have the DPI but are unwilling to pay for "free" content.

Invest in payers, and drop non-payers

Are the payers in Japan substantially different in lifestyle experiences than the potential set of non-payers in the US? Is the near universal absence of PCs from offices and homes in Japan and the lack of experience with PC-based free Internet content the reason why the Japanese are so willing to pay for the Internet content provided by iMode mobile phones? Is the habit of living with one's parents among unmarried twenty-somethings the reason Japanese men spend their DPI on late-night socializing and golf, and Japanese women spend their DPI on expensive perfumes, luxury bags, and exotic travel, and now both are spending their DPI on short messaging services, Internet content, and m-commerce transactions through their iMode phones? Are these actionable segments in Japan useful indicators of what is possible in Europe, the US, and China? How do marketers deliver value to those actionable segments that cross national frontiers and tie themselves together in a global m-commerce lifestyle?

- Add new experiences to the global lifestyle of mobile Internet customers. The iMode brand gives Japanese users a robust wireless experience, and now this experience with "always on" mobile technology is the only brand for the Japanese. Thirteen million Japanese customers in 2000 cannot be wrong, and more will sign up by May 2001 when 3G becomes the standard for wireless telecom connections throughout the country. Within a year, Europeans will ask the iMode brand to give them a similar experience, and within three years Americans will ask the same of the iMode brand.

- Offer W-CDMA technology and the iMode brand name to KPN Mobile, other European telecom firms, Bell South-SBC partnership, and other American telecom companies. Should these alliances and licensing deals happen with the same success as they did in Japan, then iMode's wireless experience will become the brand for Europeans, Americans, and others, especially the Chinese in Taiwan, Hong Kong, and mainland China.

- Establish "high loiter" areas for wireless Ethernet networks in airline clubs set aside for frequent flyers, in the lobbies of five-star hotels, within business and professional offices, across university campuses, and coffee houses. The technology is available for Japanese iMode users at ANA and JAL clubs, the Nikko, Imperial, Palace, and Shiba Park hotels, at the Tokyo Tower area offices, and at coffee and tea houses in the Ginza, Shibuya, and other neighborhoods. For American PC users, the technology is available at the Red Carpet Clubs of United Airlines, the Hyatt Regency, and at Starbucks. These are self-assembling networks with no one telecom and content provider in control of the mobile Internet experience. Instead, in the US the upwardly mobile middle class among Gen-Y and Gen-X age groups, especially those who travel for work or have leisure time or both, is the force behind the self-assembly of wireless Ethernet networks.

▦ Increase the staging of experiences for 3G users, and let iMode differentiate its products and services by deepening its brand equity among Japanese users, creating brand relevance for Europeans and Chinese, and establishing brand awareness among Americans. Let the iMode or "anywhere" brand enhance the global wireless lifestyle of all nationalities.

Recommendation

▦ *Will others join the race to experience iMode mobile phones, or will the Japanese national segment be the only one to use the iMode brand? Will the experience become the brand elsewhere in the world?*
Frame the questions in another way:

▦ *Will a local Japanese mobile Internet technology face strong negative reactions from Europeans, Chinese and Americans about becoming a global wireless Internet standard? Will other wireless experiences, such as GSM and Sprint PCS, become the preferred brands everywhere outside Japan?*
Frame the questions a third away:

▦ *Is iMode a global brand in step with the cross-cultural similarities between Japan and the rest of the world? Or is iMode a local brand with too many cultural differences that pertain only to Japan and its national culture?*
The answer is not easy to give. The Japanese live within their own national culture, or *nihonjin*, "We Japanese." The iMode brand may be seen as peculiarly Japanese with those funny *manga* cartoons, Pokémon characters, and kiss icons. This strong tie to the *nihonjin* culture of the Japanese tends to dominate the theater, board games, movies, and many other forms of entertainment in Japan. However, in popular music and baseball, the We Japanese culture shares itself with the global, largely American lifestyle; the former adapts its all girl (rather than all boy) bands to the whims of Japanese teenage girls, and its sports teams to the needs of winners and losers not losing face on the baseball diamond. With a few changes in the visuals on the "hard deck" or screen, the iMode brand can be seen as a weak tie to the *nihonjin* culture, or a cultural artifact that can be transformed into something suitable for European and American tastes. Thus if DoCoMo wants to be a worldwide technology, it must use its partnerships with AOL

Japan, KPN Mobile, and others to become an effective competitor outside Japan.

Here is the marketing assignment for wireless marketers:

- Segment digital customers into those who will pay for content similar to the Japanese and, perhaps, the Chinese in Hong Kong, Taiwan, mainland China, and throughout South East Asia, and those who will not pay for content, at least in the short run, in Australia, Europe and the US.
- Target digital customers among the age groups who are info-tech savvy and who need mobile phones, m-commerce and the wireless Internet in their daily working and personal lives. Examples include: new job seekers among young twenty-something unmarried salarymen and office ladies in Japan, and freshly-minted bureaucrats and junior executives in China's larger cities. Others include small appliance and computer manufacturers who have gone around the large, family-owned conglomerates in Korea and who now sell finished fans, air conditioners, PCs, and PDAs to Japan, China, the US and Europe. And foreign export traders in Australia who sell minerals to Japan, technology to South East Asia, and lamb and wine to Europe, the US and Canada.
- Position iMode mobile phones as the preferred choice of smart customers throughout East Asia and Australia, dual-protocol iMode and GSM phones as a second-best product in Europe, and hold off decisions about whether iMode or iMode in combination with another technology should be introduced in the US as wireless Ethernet networks in airport lounges, hotels, and other "high-loiter" areas.

Thus get ready for wireless marketers to use all their powers of segmentation as they roll out iMode across the globe, and as they deal with competition from other technologies now in place in several major markets of the world. Between now and 2005, national markets in East Asia, Europe and North America will call for different segmentation strategies because each has a different set of wireless legacy systems in place. Telecom and content providers will take a few years to agree on how to roll out UMTS as the one all encompassing mobile Internet standard for Japan, Europe, the US, and the rest of the world.

Our answer is that if NTT DoCoMo is a great competitor and its price strategy drives product development, and promotion and place marketing, iMode could become the universal wireless standard rather than be isolated only in Japan and few other areas of the world.[1] No reason exists for iMode to be a cultural artifact only for the *nihonjin* culture of Japan. Today, mobile phones, m-commerce, and the wireless Internet are a global telecom technology, and tomorrow iMode could become a global wireless brand, especially if iMode captures the early adapters in the airport lounges, hotels, coffee shops, and other "high loiter" areas.

INTRODUCTION

Here's our segmentation strategy:

- Make forecasts for 2001, 2003 and 2005 for similar market segments across national frontiers. Adjust these forecasts as UMTS technology becomes universal for most national cultures worldwide. Make new forecasts each year as more precise data becomes available for 2002 and 2004. Assume the telecom providers will get behind one universal standard and its capabilities will be accepted by customers across the globe. Determine the new revenue stream from the wireless Internet as telecom providers and their customers give up wired landlines in favor of mobile phones.

- Use soft information on values and lifestyles. Minimize the possibility that outliers or non-representative examples might color the decisions of telecom providers about the appropriate groups of people who make up the national segments that offer the best opportunity for selling mobile phones, m-commerce, and the mobile Internet. Let early adapters of wireless Ethernet networks show the way towards what is the most appropriate mobile Internet technology for the future.

- Avoid dubious predictions about real growth rates in the mobile Internet by employing hard demographic data on disposable personal income, age, ethnic background, gender, and urban and rural living. Stay away from the temptation of overselling Web-enabled products before customers are willing to pay for the new wireless content. Follow how much money companies are willing to spend to cater to the needs of customers and employees on wireless services in airport lounges, hotels, business and university offices, and coffee shops.

- Develop promotion and advertising campaigns from focus group research about the willingness of people in actionable segments to pay for "free" content. Watch how early adapters among professional women, senior business executives, young netrepreneurs, and younger teenage women pay for content because their expenditures will set the rules for m-commerce payments in the future. Look for monthly accounts paid for by companies and how much over these amounts employees are willing to pay for themselves.

DUBIOUS PREDICTIONS

The years 2001–2005 frame a rapidly expanding wireless m-commerce world, one of dramatic innovation, rapid obsolescence and compatibility constraints. The mantra is "If you build it, they will come." As carriers build more broadband capacity and turn "dark" wire into "light" wire – that is, add electronics to the wire – more suppliers around the globe become a part of the community that supports m-commerce brands. European carriers demand the WAP brand. Japanese content providers insist on the iMode brand. American telecom firms observe the significant rise of the CDMA brand, but they don't know whether to choose CDMA or jump ship and go with what may turn out to be the universal standard, GSM, iMode, and UMTS. All m-commerce brands are pushing innovation and technological change, forcing analogue and primitive digital into swift obsolescence, and refusing compatibility with one another. Right now customers are confused because they have to make choices about technology and its diffusion when they would prefer to let experts decide on standards. Yes they will come, but to what standard, for what use, at what price? Let's not make predictions prematurely.

Brand community

Since European carriers have built a GSM infrastructure for Europe and other parts of the world, the GSM brand community now numbers 330 million customers. Moreover, they are probing the US market and have added another ten million members to the GSM community through the purchase of Voice-Stream Wireless and Powertel by Deutsche Telekom. The spokesperson for VoiceStream, Jamie Lee Curtis, does brand-building workshops for the firm's sales force, business customers, and consumers. These become true American believers in the wisdom of connecting with users in 70 other countries worldwide. GSM users are a community. These customers live in different nations. Their core values come from the ethnic, religious and cultural values inherent in their nation-state; their shared values come from the global community from which they learn about possible lifestyles among well connected people. Some lifestyle choices are similar across national frontiers, such as, the preference for wireless over wired telecommunications. Others are different because teenagers both in Europe and North America prefer short messaging services while business executives on both sides of the North Atlantic want quick and clear voice and data communications. Thus international marketers revere the WAP brand because it is the first wireless brand to be recognized as a global brand by the British, Germans, French, Italians, Spanish, Finnish and others in Europe, some Chinese in China, and a few Americans in the US.

CDMA is trying to build its brand community in the US. Its numbers of American users are growing, too. Nevertheless, CDMA is the second largest wireless community with American users totaling a bit over 33 million because so many American customers still use analogue and primitive digital mobile phones. As a consequence, Motorola builds CDMA phones for the US market while European firms, such as Nokia, build only GSM phones mostly for the European market. In 2001, CDMA users are not emotionally involved in the CDMA brand as GSM customers are with the GSM brand name. Right now CDMA is not a community. Rather, CDMA is just a local brand competing for market share among wired PCs, pagers and PDAs, and primitive digital wireless offerings in the US market.

On the other hand, iMode is a brand community only in Japan. Its numbers of Japanese users is growing exponentially. Within Japan, iMode is the dominant brand with Japanese users numbering 13 million customers. In 2001, iMode is a national brand among the Japanese. With the investments being made in Europe and the US by NTT DoCoMo, iMode may turn out to be a significant competitor for GSM and CDMA. By 2005 DoCoMo could turn out to be more of a global brand than it is today, or the global brand for almost all wireless users.

Brand-name predictions

Which brand will dominate the others throughout the world? Will some of them join the "dead brands society" as customers pick winners and reject losers among Vodafone AirTouch, NTT DoCoMo, ATT Wireless, and others? Which firms will provide m-commerce content of soccer scores, *manga* cartoons, and stock transactions first as luxuries, then as nice-to-have goods, and finally as necessities? Here are a few early predictions.

If we use the data we have available today, GSM has first-mover advantage and the dominant market share in Europe, and GSM is trying to capture share in the US. It's not clear whether GSM will do in North America what it has done in Europe, East Asia, and parts of Latin America. Since the pre-2001 wireless application protocol for GSM works with a bitmap format on a constrained bandwidth, 2G-based GSM has substantial technical problems with displaying graphics on the small screens of mobile phones, and GSM handsets without GPRS, 2.5G and Web 2.0 are obsolete. Thus GSM customers may buy the upgraded 2.5G mobile phones from Nokia (the GPRS Communicator) and Ericsson (R520), or they look for another user friendly wireless technology from iMode, CDMA, or something else not yet known to carriers, service providers and customers. If consumers want more and better content, the current crop of GSM phones cannot do what iMode (with W-CDMA infrastructure) phones can do now in Japan. Right now there is a small but growing risk that GSM phones may go the way of Betamax in the VCR wars with VHS as iMode gains users. By 2005 at the latest, this forthcoming epic battle will have been decided by users similar to you and me.

Data difficulties

The computation of comparative market segment data about these goods and services is not all straightforward, especially as marketers try to sort out the real cultural similarities and differences among nations in Europe, East Asia and the Americas. Also the combination of hard demographic data, and soft values and lifestyles information from which to select targeted market groups within nations is equally difficult. Moreover, positioning competitive products and services within local markets is highly subjective, one that faces marketers each day. Unfortunately, such decisions may lead to both pleasant and unpleasant consequences for firms because only a few of them can win the competitive race for market share and category dominance.

The impact of wrong decisions reaches deep into whether wireless will overtake wired telecom quickly. Also these decisions affect whether WAP has a chance in the US, CDMA has an opportunity in Europe, or whether iMode could dominate m-commerce both in Europe and the US. The task for market researchers is to put weights on the crucial factors affecting wireless decisions and to drop the unimportant ones from the equation. This is called chain-weighting in market research.

For example, when bandwidth expands rapidly and prices for such bandwidth drop sharply, the weights assigned to the rapid transmission of data, voice communications, transaction capabilities, streaming video, and other items go up or down in tandem with the drop in prices. Why? Quality improvement in wireless services makes good products and services cheaper. This is the practical paradox of the wireless revolution. As prices drop for better quality wireless content, more people join the wireless bandwagon and free themselves from wired landline connections.

Price elasticity of demand

The exponential growth in Internet usage and wireless m-commerce requires wider high-capacity fiber pipes as both services anticipate an 80 percent annual increase through 2004 in the amount of data fiber optic communications networks can carry. Some suggest capacity will outstrip demand, but this is a dubious prediction. Capacity estimates include "dark" fiber, which is laid but not activated by network operators. To "light' fiber with the necessary electronics costs twice as much as simply sticking the fiber in the ground. Here is the forecast: "Lit" or activated fiber will expand by 79 percent a year, and by 2004 will amount to 160 percent of peak demand, which is growing at 69 percent a year.[2] Hence, prices for bandwidth will drop sharply.

No "lit" fiber will remain dormant. Technologically simply marches on and marketing refuses to be quiet about telecom progress. The galloping force of wireless m-commerce will connect even the last mile into the home through cable modems and digital-subscriber lines, and all of this will eat up bandwidth. Wireless m-commerce products and services are price elastic; this means that any large increase in supply means a substantial drop in prices, or the price elasticity of demand. As prices drop, demand expands, perhaps exponentially.

Even if we don't know how quickly customers will adopt wireless phones and, even if we don't know which technology and type of content they will choose, we do know one fact. As prices drop for wireless services, users will adopt the new, wireless technology at an increasing rate. Between 2001 and 2005 let's predict a doubling forecast of users annually across Europe, within the US and throughout Japan. This prediction is a no-brainer.

Discontinuous marketing change

Moreover, these years of introducing m-commerce represent an era far distant from the wired Internet world of the previous decade. For example, the shift to users paying for content on wireless handheld devices from free information on the Internet is a discontinuous marketing change with profound implications for how customers react to and what users do with wireless m-commerce devices. These two worlds of paying for m-commerce content versus free Internet content cannot be described in terms of the same promotion and pricing characteristics. Also those characteristics with similar product and place terms don't really mean the same thing under wireless m-commerce as they did under the wired Internet. The choice of characteristics in which to measure success from one era to another is essentially a subjective one.

Unfortunately, dumb investors indiscriminately compare Internet apples with m-commerce oranges. Even some investors who are "crazy like a fox" use some form of hedonic indexing to reflect even small improvements in product quality and even larger changes downward in adjusted average prices for mobile phones, PDAs, wireless laptops, and peripheral equipment as they tout one wireless firm over another. Smart investors acknowledge the possibility that the shifts from the Internet to m-commerce and away from WAP to CDMA or iMode are less robust than the advertising pros might make them out to be. Therefore, let's be careful about m-commerce going from triumph to triumph without some setbacks, detours or difficulties. If we want to avoid dubious predictions during the years 2001–2005, marketers must apply chain weights to the marketing techniques of segmentation, targeting and positioning before we can make predictions with a 95 percent confidence level for this "new economy" industry.

CONTENT FOR CONSUMERS

Japan's iMode alerts the rest of the world to the possibilities from m-commerce. The enthusiasm of Japanese consumers for *manga* cartoons, karaoke, and on-line dating as well as ordering airline tickets, booking movie seats, and trading stocks tells us a great deal about the future potential of the wireless Internet. On-the-move people in Japan, China and elsewhere in Asia want these on-line activities and many more.

Actionable segmentation

In terms of hard demographic data, about 170 million people in Asia (out of total of 3.5 billion) have mobile phones, 60 million (or nearly 50 percent) in Japan, 60 million (or five percent) in China, and 30 million (or 60 percent) in Korea. Except for China and India penetration rates are high, even approaching the almost universal use of mobile phones in Finland, Sweden and the other Nordic countries.

However, soft value-based information portrays mobile phones as luxuries in China and India, nice-to-have goods in South East Asia, and necessities in Japan and Korea. These are qualitative numbers, and they help marketers refine concepts, obtain general reactions, and explore new areas of opportunity. Notwithstanding the high penetration rates in Korea and Japan, m-commerce is still in its infancy in China, India and South East Asia.

Therefore, for marketers to evaluate alternative marketing strategies under the rubric of actionable segmentation, they must review both predictive and descriptive data, select crucial analytical variables, and chain weight the m-commerce factors that are important to customers. Since wireless m-commerce appears to appeal to similar market segments across national frontiers (or teenagers and business executives), the likely responses from Japan, Korea and China about access speed, content, reliability, and variety of applications could be interpreted as answers from one cross-cultural focus group. Or the responses could be misinterpreted as dangerous misinformation of the highest order from many different groups of dissimilar respondents who were picked for the sample for convenience only. If the latter is the case, marketing research does the firm a disservice by generating and disseminating bogus data on the mistaken similarities of wireless users in Japan, Korea, China and elsewhere in Asia.

Notwithstanding the cartoons and other fun things, the financial data and other business information, and the high penetration rates in Korea and Japan, the mass ownership of mobile phones, Internet-enabled or not, does not in itself forecast a tidal wave of m-commerce. "When [mobile devices] are fast and always on [one of iMode's attractions in Japan], the potential will be huge," says Craig Ehrlich, group managing director of Sunday, a Hong Kong mobile telecoms operator.[3] However, m-commerce today "is not a very sophisticated shopping experience yet," says Masahiro Okabe, a manager at the Tokyo office of Andersen Consulting. "For the telecoms side, 3G will be epoch-making, it will be a very big jump ... but it will mean nothing to subscribers."[4] M-commerce customers will want exciting content so that buying on-line is quick, easy, and secure.

Here is why NTT DoCoMo is such a great success in Japan. iMode has links with 280 banks and stock brokers, and 540 product and market Web sites. Their tie to iMode underscores their reliability so users will get the merchandise they paid for on a timely basis. And the tie of debt-free users to iMode insures the firm's Web site partners get access to up-scale, higher income, pre-cleared customers. iMode guarantees fulfillment to users and payments to partners. Time will tell whether iMode can export this approach to relationship management elsewhere in East Asia, and to Europe and the US.

Enthusiasm from carriers

According to Ian Stone, the chief executive of Hong Kong's SmarTone Tele-communications, in which British Telecommunications owns 20 percent, "the challenge is to convert to customer solutions. It is about making people's lives a lot easier."[5] Stone's director of interactive applications, Christopher Lau, adds the following: "The customer is not a technophile ... Services need to be easy to use and localised."[6]

Others agree. "We have to understand the customer better, not just sell voice ... We see a huge revenue potential here ... So we need to educate and convince our customers ... [At the same time,] we are shifting our business focus from voice to data and m-commerce, and we are making services available across all technology platforms – including GSM, which is stronger in Europe but also present in Asia," says Eden Lau, general manager for market-ing mobile services at Cable & Wireless HKT, now owned by Pacific Century CyberWorks.[7]

However, iMode, which uses W-CDMA or non-GSM technology, is all the rage among industry insiders and users, consumers and customers alike. Each group brings its own imagination to the spread of m-commerce. Even so consumers will have to be weaned onto m-commerce with content, applica-tions and security. Today, only iMode in Japan does all three.

HOTELS AND BUSINESS TRAVELERS

"The new generation of business travelers rated technology support higher than any other hotel service ... Today's traveler needs real time access to pick up emails and [sic. to gain] access [to] the Internet. They want immediacy and do not want to waste time dealing with technical problems,"[8] says John Wallis, Hyatt's senior vice president. The hotel used a focus group to discover that it needs to help its customers through a user-friendly Web site that will resolve laptop problems, such as logging-on, having the wrong adapter or incompatible plugs, converting one m-commerce platform to another, such as iMode (W-CDMA) to GSM mobile phones and vice versa. Hyatt has introduced a "technology concierge" to help its business customers settle into the hotel with their wireless laptops and mobile phones.

Catching up with customer demands

Hyatt's broadband service is Worldroom Connect. Hong Kong-based I-Quest Corporation provides this service to Hyatt. The single most important advantage of this system for the hotel is that Worldroom Connect relies on existing telephone wires and does not require the hotel to put in new cabling within its properties.[9] This means older Hyatt hotel buildings and all new ones can be connected to a high-speed Internet access portal by May 2001. This is an impressive goal for the firm in its quest to dominate the soaring telephone revenues for connected laptops from one crucial market segment – business executives who travel extensively, about 50 percent of their time, around the world. If done properly, Worldroom Connect gives Hyatt Hotels a key competitive advantage.

Similar market segments

Who are these business travelers who prefer Hyatt's m-commerce and technology services? Are they Japanese, Europeans, Americans, Chinese, Australians, or any other nationality that can afford luxury hotels in which their telephone connection charges are high? They are all of these. Are they iMode, GSM, or CDMA users? They are all of these. Hyatt appeals to business travelers who are part of a global lifestyle. In terms of telecommunication services, these business executives have more cultural similarities than cultural differences. For marketers, these hotel guests form similar market segments across national frontiers, which is the essence of a global lifestyle, the basic data for a global marketing strategy, and crucial ingredient to build a global brand.

VIABLE SEGMENTS

Three Chinese market segments are crucial to the success of m-commerce in China. These segments are similar to those found in Hong Kong itself, Japan, and elsewhere in East Asia.

Lifestyles of professional business executives

The first includes professional women and men who are on their way up in the corporate hierarchy of foreign expatriate firms. These foreign direct investments are in southern China, in the coastal cities of China and in Manchuria. Although professional people are mobile phone users all around East Asia, the Chinese market segment differs in one respect in that these folks work for foreign investors rather than domestic firms. They want and demand on-line hotel and banking services. Otherwise, this market segment is not unique to China, but can be found in Japan and throughout East Asia.

Lifestyles of young dot-com netrepreneurs

The second includes younger professional women and men, the "netrepreneurs," who are building up their own dot-coms and issuing IPOs in the Shanghai and Hong Kong stock markets. All of them have relatively high disposable personal incomes, and spend it at lavish rates in the discos of the best world-class cities in China, such as Shanghai. They live mostly in southern China, within the coastal cities, and in the capital city, Beijing. This market segment is not unique to China, but can be found in Tokyo's Shibuya neighborhood (or "Bit Valley") and throughout pockets of East Asia, including the dot-com startups found in the Duxton Road area of Singapore and in Sydney, New South Wales, Australia.

However, the real soul of China's Silicon Valley can be found in the student activity room at Quinghua University Dormitory No. 20. Here graduate Chinese students are trying to do what Cisco and Sun Microsystems did in California, and make Zhongguancun, a chaotic neighborhood in the Haidian district in northwest Beijing and the site of some of the nation's best universities, the Chinese government's designated high-technology industrial zone. The Microsoft Laboratory is here along with many other domestic and foreign software, hardware, and Internet investors. These are managed by ethnic Chinese from the United States who have come back to China and by Taipei Chinese from Taiwan who have agreed to live in Beijing, China.

Will Zongguancun rival Silicon Valley? Kai-Fu Lee, Microsoft's director at the laboratory in Beijing is skeptical:

> *"I believe the 'real' differences between Silicon Valley and Zong-guancum are: culture, different types of talent, different definitions of innovation, different types of venture capital and different involvement of academic institutions … Silicon Valley has evolved a culture that is tuned to market-driven innovation, while in China innovation is still largely driven by technology."*[10]

One other difference needs to be noted. The Chinese government is a great deal more involved in encouraging new high-technology start-ups, especially those tied to fiber optics, wireless telecom services, and the Internet than the Japanese government. The Chinese government has laid out "dark" fiber cable lines north and south, east and west, so all the places without landline connections can be attached to mobile telecom services at the lowest tariff rate possible. This strategy of market economics with socialist characteristics means lower profits for foreign investors, and domestically-owned state and private firms. What is unknown is how this will affect Zongguancum's quest to be China's Silicon Valley.[11] The answer will come in the future.

Lifestyles of crucial decision makers

The third includes senior government executives who are already at the top of state-owned firms and the ruling Communist party. They live in Beijing and the key provincial cities of China, and they too want on-line hotel and banking services. These officials will benefit from the investments of government and foreign investors in wireless Internet services, and their lives will change for the better as they improve their work habits and family life. This market segment is unique to China.

Rural poverty

Most of China's people are not connected to the wireless Internet. About 900 million rural farmers in China's vast hinterland (for example, in Jiangxi, Anul, and Shandong provinces) and recent rural immigrants to the coastal cities of China do not have wired or wireless telephones. Given their deep poverty and their lack of disposable personal income, Chinese farmers are not potential customers of mobile phones as are farmers in Japan, Korea and Malaysia.

Mobile phone content is a moving target within China, Japan, the rest of East Asia, Europe, and the US. The marketing assignment is to be sure marketers use somewhat the same marketing strategies for similar market segments among those consumers whose cultural similarities are substantially greater than their cultural differences. More on this later.

RESPONSE MODELING

Segmentation is the art of defining groups in a way that is useful to marketers. The latter look for patterns in the data to see whether clusters of customers emerge to form viable market segments. This marketing research technique is called "response modeling."

For example, in Japan iMode mobile phone users represent a national market of customers. It is divided into two broad categories. The first puts together demographic market segments, such as age and income groups, urban and rural residents, and ethnic groups. The second groups values-based market segments, such as the lifestyles and consumption habits of unmarried men, those of unmarried women (or OLs, office ladies), and salarymen and their families, and many other groups of Japanese business executives. Put the two categories together to obtain actionable and viable market segments – i.e., those that have a minimal market size with sufficient purchasing power to buy goods and services on a long-term basis

Among all these groups a paradigm shift in the value of wireless over wired telecom services has occurred. This means wireless is now the preferred choice of Japanese consumers. NTT DoCoMo has been highly successful in connecting iMode to the goals and values of Japanese consumers for wired telecom services. Theirs is a brand community writ large for the wireless Internet whose infrastructure is built on W-CDMA technology and iMode mobile phone service.

Wireless m-commerce retail marketing campaigns now are used in Japan to sell all sorts of electronic gadgets, different types of *manga* cartoon books, smaller appliances for the home, and many other consumer goods. These campaigns also are used to reduce the number and cost of middlemen in the supply channel of distribution. Japan has come a long way with its B2C and B2B business, especially by putting both into m-commerce. In this way, response modeling has become an effective tool for Japanese marketers to do data mining, and to convert their suppliers and customers to the real-time benefits of the wireless Internet.

Effective data mining

Let's look at how response modeling or data mining works for wireless customers in Japan.

- Marketers must let the data speak for themselves, or what marketing researchers tell us about how the customer is the data.
- Marketers must mine m-commerce data for patterns, or what researchers tell us is pattern recognition. Sample questions: "How much is the monthly bill for wireless services?" "Is the monthly bill increasing from month-to-month?" "Which group of Internet services is growing faster than the others?" "Which group of services are expanding at a decreasing rate?" "Which group is in decline absolutely?"
- Marketers also look through m-commerce data for clusters of customers, or what marketing researchers tell us is the clustering of like users. Do all Japanese teenagers incur the minimum monthly bill, or $75 per month, or $155? Are some teenagers paying more per month? Can we pinpoint

and label them as the high-spending group? Are there economic reasons or changes in lifestyle values why the high-spending teenage group is spending more per month?

▦ Marketers must seek out a minimal market size with effective purchasing power, or what marketing researchers tell us about how firms make money from customers, the data about them, and the responses found by researchers. Does the high-spending teenage group meet the test of minimal market size? Of course, a group of one is not a viable market segment. A larger group could be a viable market segment if the persons within the group have sufficient purchasing power.

Therefore, the work of marketers is to recognize patterns, cluster customers, and find the minimal segment size. As always the customer is the data, and iMode means fast communications for Japanese consumers.

Criteria for effective segmentation

Ask yourself these questions about effective segmentation:

▦ Can marketers measure the size and purchasing power of the segment (*measurability*)?
▦ Is the segment the largest possible homogeneous group worth pursuing with a long-term sustained marketing program (*substantiality*)?
▦ Can marketers reach and service the segment effectively (*accessibility*)?
▦ Can marketers devise a tailored marketing program and an effective marketing strategy to serve the segment effectively (*actionability*)?

These four criteria are the bedrock of how marketers segment markets. Let's look at how these criteria play out in Japan.

DEMOGRAPHIC SEGMENTATION

NTT DoCoMo's enthusiasm for m-commerce captures the imagination of iMode's brand community. Here's how marketers segment markets from hard demographic data about users of iMode mobile phones in Japan. They are presented with the most helpful first and the least helpful last.

Disposable income spent on m-commerce

Most of the age groups listed above spend at least $75 per month for *haiku* poems, daily *manga* cartoons, waves on the coast of the Japan Sea, news about sumo wrestling, soccer and baseball, short messaging services, and minimum purchases from Internet providers. Stay-at-home moms spend more time per month on the Net searching for fresh fish and other food items in lieu of Tupperware-type parties that are now out-of-fashion for non-working women. Business executives, especially women who own their own firms and men who are in upper management of the larger Japanese corporations, spend $155 per month or more for all the above services plus minute-by-minute financial transactions, such as stock and bond purchases, investments in mutual funds, and the acquisition of US Treasuries. These hard demographic data tell marketers a great deal more about what are the preferences and possible expenditure patterns for users of mobile phones. If the high-spenders among women who own their own firms and senior business executives have only a minimum difficulty with wireless technology, then disposable personal income data by market groups are sufficient to give marketers viable market segments.

Ethnic groups

Although Japanese society is largely homogeneous, about 120 million total, the large Korean minority numbers about 500,000. Some of them own lucrative businesses that depend on the m-commerce wireless Internet, including Softbank. Those Korean-Japanese who are affluent do deals with Korea and other East Asian countries and the US. Also the much smaller expatriate community of Americans, Europeans, Russians and others who do white-collar work and run their own businesses, supply medical/dental services, and trade with the larger Japanese community, use mobile phones to communicate with others in their own ethnic communities and with customers throughout Japan. For the most part, Korean-Japanese, South East and South Asians, and Japanese-Brazilians who do more menial work in Japan, are not mobile phone users or they get by with very low monthly fees paid to NTT DoCoMo. The hard demographic data on ethnic groups are sufficient simply to point out those clusters of customers who may be users of iMode services. They do not give us a viable market size, but suggest a smaller niche or targeted group for special promotional campaigns by marketers.

Age

Teenagers, young male adults, OLs (office ladies), newly married men and women, recent parents, stay-at-home moms, full-time business executives, and retired grandparents all own mobile phones and use iMode. These demographic data tell marketers something about where groups are in their life cycle, and the data hint at what each may prefer from their mobile phones. Except for the younger groups who view the wireless Internet as a birthright and a necessity, especially for short messages to friends, the older groups may not be as willing to jump in with both feet and use cell phones for all their intended purposes. Also the older business executives and the retired persons may still have some technological phobia against wireless communications. The hard demographic data on age groups are not solely sufficient to give marketers measurable and viable market segments.

Urban locations

Tokyo, Osaka and most larger cities in central Japan have many mobile phone users. Smaller cities on the Japan Sea (Nigata), and to the north and south of central Japan, especially on the other islands, all have mobile phone services.

Rural locations

On most family-owned farms where the father or one son and daughter has a job in a nearby city, mobile phones are used, too. Nothing unique exists among these data to show patterns, cluster customers, and display minimum market size. The hard demographic data on the geography of potential customers are not solely sufficient to give marketers measurable and viable market segments.

Causal relationships

In summary, hard demographic data show the following causal relationships. Higher levels of disposable income for everyone determine the pattern of usage of mobile phones, and these are viable market segments. Although some age groups, such as teenagers and students, need mobile phones to connect themselves to their social friends; and although some ethnic groups, such as the affluent Korean-Japanese and the American expatriate community, need cell phones to run their businesses, these demographic data do not alone determine or cause the pattern of usage of mobile phones. Instead, both age and ethnic groups need high levels of disposable income, or joint causality, to provide marketers with viable market segments. Without high levels of disposable personal income, age and ethnic groups, especially the latter, are simply niche markets for marketers.

VALUES-BASED SEGMENTATION

Of course, niche markets can be transformed into viable market segments as marketers use soft values and lifestyle information about users of iMode mobile phones in Japan to build strong brand communities. Again the most helpful are presented first, and the least helpful last.

Lifestyles of professional women

More Japanese women are following the example of how the Crown Princess lived her life before she married the Crown Prince, the heir to the Japanese throne, in the mid-1990s. She had a key job in an important Japanese government ministry. Today, professional women hold these executive jobs in government and industry, and some own and manage their own businesses. As the Crown Princess did, most live with their parents and siblings, and together they do their own household chores. However, the lifestyle trend in the 21st century is for thirty-somethings women to live alone rather than with their parents.

Gen-X women use their designer cell phones to let their parents know when they have left the office, whether they have stopped off to have drinks with their male co-workers, to remind their parents this is the night for their ballroom-dancing lessons, and to let their family know which JNR train they are on for their journey home. These thirty-somethings are fashion-conscious, picky about the color of their mobile phones, and unpredictable about commitments to older and new Web sites. They are known to tire of new trends in a matter of weeks, a piece of qualitative data that puts fear in the hearts of marketers. Nevertheless, the marketing trend is for them to replace their *kaden* (home electronics) with *koden* (personal electronics), such as popular electronic pets and iMode phones.

7.7 million Japanese were born between 1971 and 1974; half of them are women; and today they represent one of the largest and most powerful market segments in Japan. Given their importance, several Japanese firms formed the WiLL alliance to target this specific market segment, and sell consumer electronics, beer, soap and personal care products, mobile phones, and other products.[12] All carry the WiLL logo. Gen-X (thirty-somethings), Gen-Y (twenty-somethings) and teenage women all have similar tastes in mobile phones; they tend to spend almost $200 on elaborate enamel designs for their cell phones; and they are very clear they don't want more functions than they now use in their wireless phones. In this, professional and teenage women are different than their parents in what they expect from mobile phones.

This market segment is growing in size, increasing its purchasing power, and shows every willingness to spend more money on wireless Internet usage than other groups. This is a viable market segment. The iMode phones must give these women the ability to download *Love manga* cartoon books, read the romance stories and look at the ads for expensive branded handbags, perfume, and jewelry, and buy full-price tours overseas. For them shopping is a social activity in Ginza, Tokyo's premier shopping district, for Tiffany jewelry, Prada handbags, Louis Vuitton luggage, and other luxury goods. Also for them on-line shopping by themselves is still limited to specific products, such as cosmetics for specific skin ailments, and cheap books. However, the future forecast is for this market segment to lead other Japanese consumers in a great change in Japanese shopping habits over the next five years. Knowledge of these product and service attributes are crucial to the success of iMode mobile phones in Japan.

Even though these women are in their late twenties or early thirties, age plays almost no part in the decision on mobile phone usage. Neither does geography, or urban or rural locations. Moreover, ethnic minorities do not hold high-level professional jobs in government in Japan and do not rise to senior executive positions in business firms. These are reserved for Japanese. Therefore, college-level training, the professional job, and disposable personal income are the defining characteristics of this market segment, and this combination of hard and soft more than anything else causes usage rates of mobile phones to go up. In summary, this market segment meets all four of the criteria for effective segmentation: measurability, substantiality, accessibility, and actionability.

Lifestyles of business executives.

These are graduates of the best law schools and universities in Japan. The very best go into government service at the Ministry of Finance, the Ministry of International Trade and Industry, and the Bank of Japan. Others work for the big business firms. A few are Silicon Valley-types who have set up their own dot-com start-ups in the Shibuya (incidentally, it means Bitter Valley in Japanese, and is referred to as "Bit Valley" by netrepreneurs) neighborhood of Tokyo. All of them have high levels of personal disposable income. They range in age from their late twenties to early forties. They live in and around Tokyo and Osaka. They are Japanese-Japanese, or simply *nihonjin* (or We Japanese).

Even though the hard demographic data are useful, they are meaningless in describing this market segment. Here the customer is really the data, and the customer is a combination of values, lifestyle and high disposable personal income. These business executives need instant voice and data communications, and the ability to do transactions without a moment's hesitation. Although some of them do fun things with their mobile phones, such as download the daily *manga* cartoon, their reason for using iMode phones is to connect to the wider wireless Internet for data, to their suppliers for shipments, to their customers for purchases, and to do a few fun things, too. Their business lifestyle is the primary reason why they will spend more than $155 per month using their mobile phones. This is a viable market segment. In summary, this market segment meets all four of the criteria for effective segmentation: measurability, substantiality, accessibility, and actionability.

Lifestyles of business commuters.

Japanese business executives commute by train rather than drive a car as do their counterparts in the US. The former use their wireless phones as miniature information devices. On the bullet train between Tokyo and Yokohama, for example, Japanese business people use their iMode phones to browse the Web through one or more portals, such as Yahoo and AOL, and find out about the nearest place for cold buckwheat noodles and green tea (*zaru soba* and *o-cha*), a great lightweight meal at the end of a hard business day. Of course, they get the latest financial, sports and local news over their mobile phones, too, and they can download information about their next set of business calls from the firm's secure Web site.

The iMode phones together with the portals are providing as much content as possible based on the location of their customers. This is putting wireless cell phones into non-PC space, or as marketers say, creating new market space. This too is a viable market segment, and it meets all four of the criteria for effective segmentation: measurability, substantiality, accessibility, and actionability. At the moment, only those European countries in which business executives commute substantial distances by train have similar market segments. Neither the US, Singapore, Hong Kong nor China shares this one important cultural similarity with Japan – long distance commuting by the train.

Lifestyles of "Bit Valley" teenage men

Until the start-up boom in B2B and B2C business-networking, dot-coms, and Internet venture capital deals came along in the late 1990s, marketers could not find an initial market segment among teenage boys and young men that might lead one-on-one to its own market segment replacement among professional business executives. Today, these young twenty-somethings netrepreneurs carry out their business in the hip Tokyo neighborhood of *Shibuya* (which means "Bitter Valley"). They are young innovators who want to sell their Web-enabled products on the handheld, Net-ready communication devices now in wide use by their information-savvy high school and university friends.

Some 17 million Japanese, or about 14 percent of the population, now log on to the Web. However, by 2003 more than 52 percent of the Japanese population will log on to the Net. According to Joichi Ito, chairman of Infoseek Corporation's Japanese subsidiary, "We're seeing a shift from early adoption of the Internet to mass penetration."[13] If these start-ups are successful, their IPOs and stock will trade on either the Mothers or Nasdaq Japan exchanges in Tokyo.

On thing is certain with the "Bit Valley" market segment. These young netrepreneurs will not become business executives similar to their fathers. Instead, the ranks of these Net innovators will be filled with drop-outs from the large corporations and the major universities. They are a blue-jean generation that prefers a high-risk, informal, non-hierarchical work setting. This market segment meets all four of the criteria for effective segmentation: measurability, substantiality, accessibility, and actionability. Unlike the "Supli" teenage market segment that grows up and becomes the professional women's market segment, the "Bit Valley" market segment will grow up, stay very different, and over several decades recreate the business executives' market segment in the image of information-savvy netrepreneurs.

Lifestyles of "Supli" teenage women

These are high-school girls (aged 16–18) and college women (19–22) who seek to keep their thin figures and be part of their peer community by drinking fizzy water, lightly flavored with fruit juice, and enhanced with vitamins and minerals (*niah-wotah*), such as the brand name "Supli." Sales for established drinks, such as Coca Cola, beer and bottled tea, are flat. "The way to start a trend in Japan is to get high-school girls to buy your product," say marketing executives at Kirin Beverage, the firm that launched Supli, the first near-water drink in 1997.[14] High schoolers like Supli; they are the important trend setters in Japan; and they are big spenders because they live with their parents who foot the bill for housing.

Teenage women are a part of the always connected generation who seek out personal relationships, acquire fun things, and do transactions through their iMode mobile phones. Their disposable income is from an allowance given by their parents and from whatever part-time jobs these young women may hold in retail shops or as clerical employees. Young women who go to college want a career and marriage, if the latter is possible, but they do not want to become OLs (or office ladies) who do dead-end jobs in larger Japanese corporations. As the "Supli" women mature, graduate from college, and take lower-level managerial jobs, they enter the ranks of unmarried professional women.

This is a viable market segment. The iMode phones also give these young women the ability to download *Love manga*, read the romance stories, and buy inexpensive tours overseas. These product and service attributes are crucial to the success of iMode mobile phones in Japan among teenage girls and young college women. This market segment meets all four of the criteria for effective segmentation: measurability, substantiality, accessibility, and actionability; and it creates its own market segment replacement among the values and lifestyles of unmarried professional women.

Lifestyles of unmarried young male adults and office ladies

Both use short messaging services to arrange for their Saturday afternoon parties in which young men wear the hard blue jeans with cuffs and motorcycle boots, and young women dress in poodle skirts and saddle shoes, and both dance to the rock-'n'-roll music of the late 1950s on blocked-off streets in the local neighborhoods of Tokyo and other large cities. The recession in Japan is in its tenth year and hence people are marrying later in life. Although this market segment is growing in size, its purchasing power is in decline. Therefore, this market segment is no longer as viable as it once was and cannot compete effectively for the attention of marketers who look for long-term growth in revenues. Since no one knows when and how the government will pull the Japanese economy out of recession, this market segment lacks actionability – that is, the ability of marketers to devise a sound marketing campaign to grow segment size and purchasing power.

Lifestyles of married salarymen

They are salesmen who wear the traditional shining blue suits go out after work, eat and drink together, use the personal form of speech to clear the air at the office, and call their wives when they have caught the last JNR train home. Their rate of mobile phone usage is limited by the lack of high levels of disposable personal income and the unwillingness of their wives to give them more spending money or allowances. Salarymen are lucky to get one week's vacation a year and supremely lucky not to have been fired during this long recession; most will be retired early as Japanese firms seek to rid themselves of excessive middle-level employees. This market segment has measurability, but lacks the other three criteria of effective segmentation: substantiality, accessibility, and actionability.

SIMILAR MARKET SEGMENTS

Japan's NTT DoCoMo has alerted the world to the possibilities of iMode mobile phones both at home and abroad. After its great success in Japan, the firm has taken minority positions in telecom companies in Europe and in the US. The intent of NTT DoCoMo is to transfer W-CDMA technology, provide fun and functional content, offer buy and sell applications, and to disperse marketing expertise to its local partners and affiliate firms. These are the firm's most important business goals for 2002–2003.

Will marketers who work for NTT DoCoMo find similar market segments overseas? The answer is yes for some, such as professional women, senior business executives, and younger netrepreneurs who are part of the global lifestyle for m-commerce. Concerning wireless telecommunications, these three Japanese market segments have more cultural similarities than differences with similar persons around the world. The answer is no for others, such as "Supli" teenager women, unmarried young males, office ladies, married salarymen, and women in the water trade, who are not part of the global lifestyle for the wireless Internet. With regard to telecom services, these several market segments have more cultural differences than similarities with other mobile phone users in foreign lands.

Surely, high levels of disposable personal income go hand in hand with the purchase of mobile phones and higher usage rates for the wireless Internet in virtually all national markets. Also the younger ages of teenagers and students play a key part in who buys wireless service in Europe, the US and elsewhere in East Asia. Geography is important in those national markets in which landlines are insufficient and the wired telecom firm will not add to capacity, e.g., Ireland. Ethnic background is key in the poorer areas of the American cities where landline telecom firms refuse to provide service; for example, African-American mothers buy cell phones for themselves and their children who are in local, neighborhood schools. Age groups, geography and ethnic background reflect real cultural differences while high levels of disposable personal income show real cultural similarities in most national telecom markets around the world.

Therefore, NTT DoCoMo's international marketing strategy must focus on three crucial market segments: professional women, business executives, and young netrepreneurs. NTT DoCoMo provides them with the same promotional message whether they are in Japan, Europe, the US, East Asia and elsewhere in the world. "Buy the mobile phone. Use iMode. Get connected worldwide. If we build it, you will come. You will like our content, our applications, and our availability worldwide."

VALUE-BASED MARKETING DECISIONS

Here are the value-based decisions made by mania-driven stock pickers in Korea. These show real cultural differences between young South Koreans and their equivalent demographic age groups in Japan and China.

What is the context of a decision?

Young twenty-something (Gen-Y) and thirty-something (Gen-X) Koreans prefer stock picking to their old way of life in which they went to *noribang* (or singing rooms) to perform karaoke, and to computer rooms to play cybergames, such as Star Craft. For young Korean men stock picking is an addiction for winning and losing money. In fact, 70 percent of e-commerce business in Korea is on-line share trading, says the Boston Consulting Group.[15]

South Korea is tailor-made for the boom in Internet share trading. The population is computer-literate, and the stock market is dominated by retail investors, who account for 70 percent of the turnover on the Korea Stock Exchange. Also more than half of all shares trade in South Korea comes from Internet transactions.

Although the age of Koreans in m-commerce stock trading is the same as the "Bit Valley' Japanese and Zongguancun Chinese, these young South Koreans are more similar to other Koreans who prefer short-term trades, deals, and fast turnover. As they see it, since the government has banned gambling, stock picking is the best substitute for Packinco parlors, horse tracks, and casinos. In this case, young Koreans make up a market segment whose cultural differences with young Japanese and young Chinese are exceptionally wide. Therefore, mobile phones must have content that permits young South Koreans to trade stock quickly and often.

What is the object of a decision?

What do parents really know about what their children do once they move from rural Korea to Seoul? Lucky children who graduate from the university find jobs with the bigger Korean firms who send them to Internet-gaming events in Europe, Asia and the US. Kim in Kyung is one of those lucky ones. She works for Samsung, is an internationally ranked player of a popular intergalactic-conquest Web game called Star Craft, and she is part of a company team that competes all over the world. And what of her parents: "they don't know I'm living in the Internet world. They just know I have a good job,"[16] says Kim.

This is a young professional woman who works for a big Korean-owned firm. Here too young Korean women make up a market segment whose cultural differences with young Japanese and young Chinese women are wider than one would have thought at first glance. Therefore, wireless phones must come with the job so these young South Koreans can keep in contact with team members, parents, and friends.

What is the impact of a decision?

Notwithstanding these real cultural differences, talented business executives are defecting from the large conglomerates, or *chaebol*, to form start-ups in mobile telecom services. In this respect, they are culturally similar to executives in Japan, and others in Ireland and Finland. In this case of business executives transforming themselves into netrepreneurs we have similar market segments across national frontiers.

Here are two other examples of cultural similarities. Korean teenagers have been going to cybercafés to use the PCs for games, do stock trading, watch movies, check email, surf the Net, and maintain a temporary office away from their parents. At these same places are Korean housewives who surf the Net to buy fish and other food for their families, purchase furniture, and acquire cosmetics and personal care products. However, since 60 percent of all South Koreans now use mobile phones and some 50 percent will be on-line by the start of 2001, m-commerce is fast replacing fixed cybercafés for m-commerce. In both cases, these South Koreans are ahead of their counterparts in both Japan and China in using mobile phones for m-commerce, but Japanese teenagers and housewives are catching up to the Koreans. Nevertheless, both segments show the dominance of similar market segments across national frontiers at least in East Asia.

Decision opportunities

The problem in South Korea's success story is that the old ways of secret arrangements among *chaebol* and with them and the government still dominate the business environment. Korea does have key players in place among its

younger professional people and those business executives who have transformed themselves into successful Net enterprises. However, they are too few.
It is possible that Korea will fall behind Japan and even China rather than
becoming another digital champion in East Asia.

M-COMMERCE TRANSACTIONS

In contrast, Singapore's transparency in m-commerce means young Singaporeans have the opportunity to take risk with the blessing of the Island's government. It has a US $1 billion fund to support technology start-ups, build incuba-
tors, and create netrepreneurs. The government subsidizes up to 80 percent
of costs to equip everyone in the firm from the receptionist to the chief executive for globalizing these emerging techno-entrepreneurs. According to Liam
Brown of the British Council, which is doing some of the training within local
firms, "Singapore compares favorably with Europe."[17]

Also in Australia, which uses technology to overcome the enormous distances that divide the country from the rest of the world, Telstra, Australia's
largest company, gets 53 percent of its revenue from mobile phones, data
communications, and the Internet. However, growth in mobile telephony has
slipped from 17 percent in the first half of 2000 to 7 percent in the second
half of 2000;[18] this confirms the results for another country in which growth is
increasing at a decreasing rate for mobile phones, m-commerce, and wireless
Internet. Telstra, which has been government owned, is going through privati-
zation, and faces competition from three new mobile networks in 2001.

However, m-commerce can succeed in Australia as it has in South Korea
because Australians are the heaviest gamblers in the world. About 82 percent of Australians bet, wagering twice as much per capita as Europeans or
Americans, some of it on poker machines in betting shops and the rest through
Telstra's mobile service.[19]

Throughout the region of East Asia and Australia, young netrepreneurs
are working very hard to become masters of a new digital mobile world. Each
country has twenty-somethings, thirty-somethings and a few older folks who
are investors in start-ups, dot-coms, Internet firms, mobile telephone firms. All

of them have the technical knowledge to come up with m-commerce solutions to B2B and B2C problems. Let's summarize what we know today:

- Japan has whacked GSM with its iMode service at home, but it has failed to push its unique W-CDMA service into other regional and global markets.
- Korea, Singapore and Australia are fully mobile, with their governments taking different roles in the process to train and equip local citizens to be netrepreneurs.
- China is just at the beginning of a fast climb towards widespread use of mobile phones, m-commerce, and the wireless Internet.
- The competition among iMode, GSM, CDMA and other wireless technologies is heating up across the region as all countries seek to make the best decisions possible for the years 2001, 2003 and 2005.

Clearly, more m-commerce transactions are in the future for everyone in East Asia. Who will succeed? Who will fail? The answers are still covered by the veil over news from the future.

MONEY-MAKING DEALS

Let's answer the segmentation questions.

Observing brand community

- *Is our current knowledge on similar market segments across national frontiers and the cultural differences among nationals of different countries about m-commerce sufficient to make accurate forecasts for the years 2003 and 2005?*

No. We don't know enough because we don't have a sufficient number of years from which to make good forecasts. However, we do know that if all telecom firms had gotten behind one standard platform, the telephone companies could have gained new revenue by giving up fixing landlines and simply issuing mobile phones to all customers. A great opportunity was missed, one that would have found favor with virtually all nationalities throughout the world.

Currently, technologists have given us competing, incompatible technologies in mobile wireless service. They have done everything to impede the swift deployment of mobile phones, wireless services, and m-commerce. These professionals tell us that everything will get better once 3G is deployed and that the newest mobile phones will have the capability to switch from one platform to another with little initiative from users.

Think where we would be today if wideband code division multiple access (W-CDMA) and its packet switching capability had been adopted by the US, Europe, China and others and not just by Japan. Think where we would be today if GSM and its circuit switching capability had been adopted by the US, Japan, China and others, and not just by Europe and a few others around the world. Think where we would be today if CDMA had been adopted by Japan and Europe, and not just by the US and a few others. Of course, a single standard is wishful thinking today, but one platform would have eliminated customer confusion about what choices to make, how many different phones to carry, and whether the decisions about phones and service were worth the effort.

The brand community of believers in m-commerce would be substantially larger, perhaps double or triple its current size. The wireless folks would have overwhelmed the wired ones so that traditional telephone companies could cease spending money on repair service. Instead of coming to the home or office to check the wired connection, the telephone firms could have issued mobile phones and ended the pretense that they were really interested in the expense of keeping up their installed base of wired connections. These cost savings in service might even have been passed on to customers, or invested in more "lit" fiber, or both, especially in countries in which m-commerce still has not achieved mass penetration.

Predicting customer choices

Do we gain more detail for our forecasts by using soft information on values and lifestyles?

Yes. We are able to minimize the possibility that outliers or non-representative examples may color our decisions about the appropriate groups of people who make up the segments that offer us the best opportunity for selling mobile phones and wireless telecom services.

Today, early adapters among groups of people with higher levels of disposable personal income and a professional stake in fast communications have adopted the new technology without looking back. Professional women, senior business executives and netrepreneurs have made the initial global market for m-commerce what it is in 2001 for Japan, China, Korea, Singapore and elsewhere in East Asia.

Yet we don't know enough about these national segments, how they interrelate across nation-states, and whether real cultural differences will get in the way of creating a truly uniform market for m-commerce from Korea in the north to Australia in the south. Even though iMode has done well in Japan, it does not have first-mover advantage, market share, or even presence in most parts of the world. Turn this around for GSM. It has done the impossible and imposed one platform standard across the corporate cultural differences between state- and privately-owned firms within 70 European, Asian, and other countries of the world. Lastly, CDMA needs to show it can dominate the US before others will pin their hopes on it for future deals outside North America. Early adapters who have both the money and status as decision makers will compare technologies, after-market services, marketing campaigns and returns on investments, and then decide which one or two of the three will offer the rest of the market the best opportunity for mass penetration in an already crowded world telecom market.

Planning for falling prices

■ *Do the hard demographic data from the government census and private sources on disposable personal income, age, ethnic background, gender, and urban and rural living help us avoid dubious predictions about real growth rates in mobile services when national economies prosper and go into recession?*

Yes. We are able to withstand the temptation of overselling Web-enabled products before customers are willing to pay for the new wireless services.

In 2001, m-commerce is in the never-never land between not yet being a mass-market product in all countries and on its way to mass-market penetration in a few countries. Prices for Web-enabled products from iMode in Japan continue to rise even as more and more people adopt wireless technology, but the increases are going up at a decreasing rate, a sign that pricing is indeed a crucial part of the NTT DoCoMo's 4 Ps marketing strategy. On the other hand, prices for Web-enabled products from GSM in Europe will be going up substantially to pay back the high costs of new licenses in the UK, Germany and elsewhere on the Continent. This pricing strategy will slow down the use of m-commerce transaction capability from 2G to 3G, and from GSM to UMTS by non-early adapters. Without these other market segments, the promise of m-commerce to connect everyone at anytime, anywhere will remain just that – a promise rather than a reality.

Hard data about disposable personal income limit prices on the upside because some folks from the middle and lower income brackets will not have sufficient disposable income to spend more money on m-commerce. Soft information on values and lifestyles offer a range of offers on price-quality-service for the upper and middle income brackets, especially as GSM providers reconfigure their value chains by investing in the US. Segment knowledge about early adapters shows what they are buying today in wireless functions and hints at what they will buy tomorrow in enhancements for m-commerce; although these choices do not translate one for one into decisions by non-early adapters, the choices made professional women, business executives, and young netrepreneurs foretell the future direction for m-commerce.

Forecasting the impact of discontinuous change

▓ *Will those people in the actionable segments be willing to pay for content through m-commerce that is currently free for the asking on the Internet?*
We don't know. Marketers have not carried out focus group research to determine whether wireless access is sufficient to change expenditure patterns for Web-based content. If professional women, senior business executives, young netrepreneurs, and younger teenage women choose to pay for content, these early adapters will set the m-commerce payment boundaries for other market segments, targeted groups, and market niches.

The willingness to pay for what was once free is the great unknown for m-commerce. If Japan is the example, then young netrepreneurs and "Supli" teenage women will lead the way in paying for content. However, there is a caveat. These picky young Japanese will pay only for what they want, and will not pay for everything that is offered in the wireless market. Also the folks in these two segments will go from Web site to Web site with no loyalty to one or the other.

In Europe and especially in the US, similar market segments may not want to pay for content unless GSM and CDMA providers create new market space, recreate the value chain, and retool their 4 Ps marketing strategies. Customers must get something new for their money, or they won't give up the known for the unknown.

REAL OPTIONS

The value of real options to m-commerce is to give marketers the ability to time the selection of appropriate market segments for the wireless Internet, and to cost out the crucial elements of a 4 Ps marketing strategy for shifting customers from free Internet content to paid m-commerce content. Real options formalizes what is noted above (i.e., mobile commerce) faces discontinuous change in how it is delivered to customers. The segmentation options discussed in this chapter include the following:

- Join a brand community, then disband it, and later form a new one; or a set of platform and investment options.

- Go from a miniature information device business, then face price elasticity of demand, and later become a commodity business; or a set of options to switch or terminate, or both.

- Segment national groups by demographic data, then by values and lifestyle information, and later determine that actionable segmentation depends on cross-cultural similarities across national frontiers; or a set of options to chose effective segments with high levels of disposable personal income, and a customer base with the knowledge and desire to become believers in m-commerce in one or more countries.

- Create new market space, face competitive pressures over price-value-service, recreate this new market space without the expectation of ever crossing the finish line; or a set of options to chose a set of different 4 Ps marketing strategy as wireless products and m-commerce services go through a discontinuous change in their product life cycle.

Smart investors want to make investments in promising similar market segments across national frontiers and in successful cross-cultural marketing strategies among m-commerce customers. They bet on the long shot that wireless will replace wired telecommunications between 2001 and 2005. The optimum set of options for smart investors permits wireless firms to make just enough investments in appropriate market segments to raise their returns on invested capital to the level of NTT DoCoMo without suffering the slow earnings growth of AT&T Wireless.

CONCLUSIONS

How to conquer the wireless world? Apply segmentation strategies to m-commerce, especially to show how young entrepreneurs and professional business executives view their investment opportunities in wireless telecom, in-house hotel services, and on-line financial services. Here is a checklist of things to do:

■ Put all types of services on the Web for anytime, anywhere connections through 3G-enhanced mobile or cell phones.

■ Build market share with marketing segmentation strategy that is carefully adapted to making money from the young and restless netrepreneurs.

■ Offer an unbeatable value proposition to early adapters among Gen-Y and Gen-X who establish dot-coms, and who are stock pickers, gamblers, and all who form the new Net Generation.

■ Create value by reconfiguring the value chain for m-commerce for all market segments, young and old, throughout East Asia.

Next let's look at how marketers use targeting strategies to find the most appropriate group for Web-enabled products in which content is based on location, utilization is based on the creation of new market space for mobile phones, and higher price points are based on promoting mobile phones as miniature information devices.

CHAPTER 5

Targeting National Markets

EXECUTIVE SUMMARY

M ARKETING MANAGERS ASSEMBLE smaller like groups of people who are bound together by their professions, such as entertainers, or by their skills, such as athletes, and by their personal tastes, habits, and values, such as info-tech geeks.

Marketing managers must also find like people who share the following cultural characteristics:

- similar preferences about appropriate food to eat and clothes to wear;
- similar personal habits about the use of the TV or the PC or both for viewing sports and entertainment;
- similar family values about saving or spending money;
- similar group lifestyles about work versus recreation; and
- similar preferences for brand names.

If marketers do their jobs well, they come up with target groups to whom they can sell products and services. Here's what marketers must do to keep their m-commerce customers, dominate the product category, and grow market share.

- Select sports marketing as the niche. Start with twenty-something professional athletes or the Gen-Y age group. If possible, include all their thirty-something agents and investment advisors to sports stars or the Gen-X age group. Although unlikely, add some forty-something coaches and team owners or the boomers age group. Throw in male fans, especially those who are between 25 and 35 years old who follow two to six sports, and are currently interested in extreme sports. The sports may vary between American football and FIFA soccer, and the play on the field may differ between in-your-face injuries and face-saving fluidity towards the goal posts. Nevertheless, sports personalities are among the first target group to use mobile phones, m-commerce, and the wireless Internet on and off the field.

- Do the same for entertainment marketing. Start with Ben Affleck and Matt Damon, and other younger Gen-Y movie stars. Include their agents and investment advisors who tend to be the same for sports personalities, such as Tiger Woods, Michael Jordan, and Steve Young. Add some studio heads, network executives, and Ted Turner. Throw in movie fans, especially teenage boys and young adults. The movies and sitcoms may vary between more or less violence, nudity, and crude language. Nevertheless, entertainers are also among the first target groups to use the mobile Internet on the movie sets, in their cars, and at home.

- Look at Information Technology marketing. Start with info-tech geeks, applications providers, software developers, and hardware manufacturers. Add in wireless marketers who understand changes in telecom technology. Throw in all those venture capitalists who are providing cash for start-ups. The wireless system may vary among iMode, WAP, and CDMA. Nevertheless, wireless providers won't let a little thing like no universal standard get in the way of building new wireless networks for other target groups.

- Give actionable target groups among airline passengers, hotel executives, stock traders, on-line bankers, and coffee shop managers help in choosing an appropriate wireless standard for their service businesses, one that best suits their customers.

- Don't forget that target groups in such diverse countries as Japan, China, Singapore, Australia, the US, Finland, Germany, Italy, Israel, and India all have different attitudes towards sports, entertainment, IT, stock trading, and on-line banking.

- Do deeper data mining to understand all the nuances about substitutes, structure, and scalability – or the "3 Ss" of targeting – that make some target groups more attractive and others less attractive for long-term, sustainable sales prospects.

- Carry out the *new* 4 Ps marketing strategy that offers marketers the option to recharge WAP with more SMS and W-CDMA with more broadband content, to reconfigure the value chains of digital versus vocal portals for m-commerce, and re-conceive the accompanying 4 Ps marketing strategies for m-stock traders and m-bankers.

Invest in like people as target groups

Since targeting is more culturally tied to fundamental psychographic and socio-cultural personal habits than is segmentation, marketers find the lack of similar target groups across national frontiers a major stumbling block in developing a single coherent global marketing strategy for selling mobile phones, m-commerce, and the wireless Internet to all the world's potential customers. Hence, the wide use of cell phones in Japan and Europe has not become a fact in the US. If marketers do their m-commerce initiatives well, they will encourage potential on-line customers from the target groups mentioned above to jump into all forms of m-commerce and the mobile Internet. Here's how marketers create actionable target groups.

▦ Add personal data about habits, tastes, values, and lifestyles. American entertainers, agents, info-tech geeks, and venture capitalists tend to be bi-coastal people with many living in California. American, Japanese, and European athletes tend to live in the major urban markets large enough to draw big crowds of fans to the sports stadiums. Both target groups need instantaneous access to their agents, stock brokers, bankers, and other on-line support people as well as to their family and friends.

▦ Offer m-brokers, m-bankers, m-insurance agents, and many others personal data about the high-income earners among twenty-something athletes and entertainers. Find them and thirty-something netrepreneurs in their expensive homes and apartments in LA's Beverly Hills, New York's Upper East Side, London's Notting Hill, Paris's 17me arrondisement, Shanghai's former International Zone, and Tokyo's far western and southern suburbs.

▦ Establish virtual work and play places for all target groups who want to get away from their offices in Burbank, Kings stadium in LA, and homes in the Hollywood Hills. They want to take in skiing at Vail, Colorado and in Klosters, Switzerland; deep-sea fishing off Cabos, Mexico and off Cape

Town, South Africa; scuba diving in the Celebes, Indonesia, and Cancun, Mexico; and ranching in the Big Sky country of Montana and near Bariloche, Argentina. Although these entertainers, athletes, and others want to get away from their everyday life, they still want to be in contact with agents, investment advisors, tax consultants, accountants, stock brokers, bankers, and all other support personnel.

▓ Increase the awareness of teenage movie fanatics, male fans of extreme sports, their friends and spouses, and many others who live in the reflected glory of the entertainers and star athletes about the possibilities of m-commerce to change the lives of those who are not well known today. Help these others make their own luck by concentrating their work on those areas of m-commerce in which they will receive a high return for greater effort and higher risk. Sell the fan club phenomenon as the way to boost m-commerce.

Recommendation

The trick for marketers is to turn rabid fans into followers of athletes, entertainers, and info-tech geeks in the new world of m-commerce. The stars are the early adapters. They can pay the higher prices as new technology is introduced. Then come business executives who have the funds of their firms behind them to pay for some of the new technology as it begins to be adopted in manufacturing, banking, and other industries. The last group to come to the table will be the middle-class fans who finally decide the new technology is affordable and that they cannot live without it.

This roll-out happened to analogue cell phones and then to primitive 2G mobile phones. It will happen to 2.5G and a bit later to 3G miniature information appliances. Get ready for the rapid increase in the number of income-producing m-commerce target groups as hotels, banks, sports, dot-coms, venture capitalists, and many other businesses target all the groups listed above and their fans to carry out their business transactions through m-commerce.

Here is the marketing assignment for wireless marketers:

- Segment digital customers into those segments that have the most probable like groups of people for the purpose of selling products and services to targeted groups.
- Target digital customers among those professional athletes, movie stars, music artists, and IT geeks who are early adapters and who can persuade their fans to become followers in the new world of m-commerce.
- Position iMode mobile phones, dual-band iMode and WAP phones, UMTS phones, and wireless Ethernet networks as the choice of early adapters who want m-banking right now.

Thus get ready for wireless marketers to use all their powers of targeting as they roll out 2.5G and 3G mobile phones to early adapters in 2001–2002, and to followers in 2003–2005. Once the latter occurs, marketers will have one or more global brands upon which to build a long-term 4 Ps expansion strategy. If m-commerce is to come about quickly, marketers must be flexible and self-confident, instill corporate culture on-line, build m-commerce networks, make their customers feel special, and be knowledge managers.[1]

INTRODUCTION

Here is our targeting strategy:

- Acknowledge that we do not have sufficient information to make accurate forecasts for 2001. We probably will not have sufficient data to do these forecasts for 2003. By 2005 we may have sufficient information to make more accurate forecasts, especially if the early adapters are joined by their followers into the world of m-commerce.
- Do deeper data mining on the habits, customs, attitudes, and values of specific target groups, such as professional athletes, entertainers, and info-tech geeks. Scale up by adding agents, investment advisors, business executives, and, most importantly, the fans. Structure targeting by offering on-line stock trading and on-line banking to all of these target groups. The Nordic and Baltic countries in Europe provide good examples.

- Collect primary data through questionnaires to help make better choices about substitute mobile phones, platforms, and telecom providers. Use secondary data to support efforts to roll out m-commerce to all appropriate target groups.

- Find actionable target groups among like people who are willing to pay for content through m-commerce in Japan and Europe. Decide how to sell content to those actionable target groups in the US who are used to getting content free of charge. However, marketers should realize that athletes, entertainers, and info-tech geeks may say no to this discontinuous change in their m-commerce surfing habits. Thus the long-term sustainability of the primary target group's interest in wireless versus wired links is still open to question about how long, how much, for what purpose, and whether money can be made in this new world of m-commerce.

BETTER CHOICES

At what point does the increasing use of mobile phones for m-commerce, require us to redefine what we mean by telecommunication services? The answer is now. Or how do twenty-somethings stay out in front as gurus of bandwidth, start-ups, venture capital, Internet banking, and mobile telecom services? The answer is by doing everything right now through the wireless Internet. However, reconceptualizations do not come easily. For all the daily evidence of a wireless culture – and for all the popular excitement about iMode and WAP – the work of recrafting the language of instantaneous on-line communications, is just beginning to find its way. Let's start making more precise choices for this "new economy' industry.

If you ask a group of twenty-somethings (or Gen-Y), they tell you wireless Internet is a necessity whether they are in Hong Kong or Tokyo, or Helsinki or Stockholm. Gen-Y customers of wireless Internet products and services form a brand community.

In Hong Kong, virtually all customers (that is, Gen-Y, Gen-X and boomers) consider cell phones a necessity to maintain a good lifestyle. This is also the case in South Korea, Japan, Singapore, Finland, Sweden, and Italy. However, most German and British customers from the Gen-X and the boomers age groups still use their landline phones and consider mobile phones something nice-to-have, but not absolutely necessary to maintain a good lifestyle.

Twenty-somethings who aspire to be professional athletes, entertainers, and info-tech geeks are the primary target group in most countries for the wireless Internet service, sports marketing via m-commerce, and virtual m-banking. They come to the market for cell phones from professional sports, dot-com start-ups, venture capital, corporate and traditional banking businesses, hotel travelers, and other Internet players. Each of them is a member of at least one target group whose members form a collection of like-minded people. Some of them are members of two or more target groups; because professional athletes are travelers, dot-com start-ups are venture capitalists and m-bankers, and so on. Twenty-somethings all share one thing in common. They just became adults. Their teenage years were spent with laptops, mobile phones, and the Internet. They have no hang ups that hinder the diffusion of technology among the general population. In this they are different from the thirty-somethings (Gen-X) who grew up with PCs, or the forty-somethings (boomers) who must rewire themselves to stay competitive in the market.

THE "3 Ss" MODEL OF TARGETING

Substitutes, scale, and structure are the "3 Ss" of targeting groups within market segments. If all the target groups got rid of their landline connections tomorrow and went solely to wireless service, would anything radically change in their day-to-day lives? They would still call their families (Italian men would still call their mothers) on their new wireless phones. Would these voice phone calls have any measurable effect on growth in sales revenue per head for telecom providers, or is this simply substituting one service for another? If the price of wireless drops substantially or if telecom service becomes free via the Internet, then wireless communications would have an enormous impact on the bottom line of telecom firms. Since voice communications would become a commodity, then marketers must make money through mass penetration and a high volume of sales. However, once mobile products become commodities, the value of targeting specific groups ends and firms lose the ability to raise margins.

If professional athletes combine their public persona with the dot-coms ideas of twenty-something netrepreneurs and both of them together reconceive, recreate and reorganize sports-related Web sites for ESPN, would the delivery of sports information become more efficient? If one or more m-bankers combine their financial talents with the venture capital ideas of the new "rain makers," would the delivery of financial services become more productive? This is scaling up sports services to fans and fanatics alike, to long-term bank customers and new clients as well, and it means finding the right target group for each set of information available for the market as a whole. Is this process of scaling up sustainable? Is there a "long wave" in the future of sports via m-commerce and banking via virtual m-Internet banking? Or will target groups tire of sports as entertainment and shift to movies, music, and other Internet venues? Or will target groups go with non-traditional financial institutions and away from old-fashioned banks who are dressing themselves up with minimum technology to become e-banks?

Lastly, if Japan gets substitution and scale correct for m-commerce via iMode mobile phone connections, can this structure be transferred to Europe or the US? Or does the structure need serious modifications? WAP phones are common in Europe, smart cards in France, and electronic wallets are common in the Nordic and Baltic countries. Laptops and credit cards are common in the US. However, none of those things are the common thread that makes the mobile Internet work in Japan. Instead, personal iMode phones or kiosk connections at 7-Eleven shops are the way in which m-commerce is carried out there.

This is targeting in a nutshell. No easy answers exist to represent mobile service in all countries, among all age groups, within all market segments, and for all target groups. Each has its own self-reference criteria. If more investment goes into m-commerce and the telecom providers make massive organizational changes, all to reflect the demand of customers for one compatible platform, then each target group will get improved product quality, time savings, and convenience. But these are big ifs, and we are just at the beginning of a great adventure in which globalization, information technology and m-commerce come together and are recreated as one joint activity in the minds of customers. Could something yet unknown from government, business or some place else slow down the change or stop it in its tracks? Yes, because competitive life among telecom providers is about training users how to gain as much as possible from mobile phones, wireless Internet and m-commerce, and getting them to spend more of their disposable personal income on these value-added services.

ACTIONABLE TARGETING

Here are the crucial questions:

- Where does the important marketing opportunity lie within the market segment?
- Are there groups within the market segment that share demographic characteristics, and present to the world the same core values and lifestyles?
- Do these groups have unique mind sets about their expectations of the goods and services they use?
- Can marketers collect data about the purchasing habits of groups, array them into easily recognizable product categories, give the groups an easy-to-remember moniker or call sign, and label them according to well-established norms of consumer behavior?

Twenty-somethings are the important marketing opportunity within the market segment of young adults, some of whom are still college students, others who are professional athletes, agents to the stars, start-up gurus, and investment advisors. Twenty-somethings share positive attitudes towards technology. Their mind set includes cell phones, m-commerce, and the wireless Internet. The call sign of twenty-somethings is Gen-Y or the generation that grew up with the Internet.

REAL OPTIONS

Targeting is the science of finding marketing opportunities among groups of like-minded people. Collectively, they share similar self-reference criteria. Targeting turns these unique mind sets about product choice into sales. What do these groups share in common? Can marketers use this information to grow sales, seek dominance in the category, and become number one or two in market share? The targeting options are as follows:

Option 1: pursue and invest

Pursue some target groups within a market segment because members of the groups already have formed brand communities and are ready for an aggressive set of marketing strategies, or a set of platform and investment options. Examples are:

- technology personnel at the Grand Hyatt hotels within the market segment called five star hotels;
- m-bankers at the Overseas-Chinese bank of Singapore, Merita-Nordbanken of Finland and Sweden, and Citigroup of the US within the market segment of an alternative channel of distribution for financial services;
- dot-com start-ups whose cash burn rate is below industry averages, especially those in Sweden, Finland and Germany; and
- professional basketball players as brands, especially Michael Jordan of the Chicago Bulls, within the market segment labeled NBA, or other athletes from the NFL and MLB.

Option 2: postpone and switch

Postpone the pursuit of other target groups for some future date because members of the groups can switch from one brand community to another even with an aggressive set of marketing strategies, or a set of options to switch. Examples are:

- long-term residents at three-star hotels who need more technology support and can afford five star accommodation;
- back-office personnel at private banks and their m-banks, especially in Germany, the UK, and France, who could move to the Nordic and East Asian countries;

- dot-com start-up investors whose cash burn rate is higher than industry averages, especially those in the UK, France, Italy and Spain; and
- professional hockey players as brands, especially Wayne Gretzky of the Edmonton Oilers, Los Angeles Kings, and other teams, within the market segment labeled NHL; champions from the Olympic movement; and semi-professional, amateur and college athletes.

Option 3: terminate

Terminate the pursuit of still other target groups because members of the groups do not have the ability to form brand communities, offer actionable targeting, and create new market space even with the aid of marketers who could invest in the *new* marketing concept, or a set of options to terminate. Examples are:

- hotel customers who lack competence in technology, cannot use computers, and are unfamiliar with the Internet;
- bank customers who prefer personal relationships with bank tellers rather than links to computer software;
- traditional investors who shun start-ups, dot-coms, and venture capital deals;
- professional soccer players, especially the two greats from Brazil and France, or Pele and Zidane respectively, who never found brand community in the US within the market segment labeled FIFA Soccer.

Brand management

Currently, Michael Jordan, the world-famous former NBA basketball player, promotes long-distance voice communications for MCI. As a celebrity similar to Paul Newman (actor), Oprah (TV personality), and Martha Stewart (household goods), Michael Jordan is doing product development, product positioning, advertising and brand management for his own line of products. He hopes his brand name on sports merchandise and, perhaps, telecom products, will outlive his playing days as consumer brands watch their chief executive officers come and go at business firms.

In Japan, Hinano Yoshikawa, a popular model, is the "Supli" face in the TV advertising campaigns by Kirin Beverages, and Namie Amuro, another model and actress, promotes Nice One drink. Both famous Japanese women appeal to teenage women and office ladies (OLs) because the models have beautiful faces, great figures, and suggest what is possible if only women drink *niah-watah*, or near water. Also Satoshi Koike comes to Japan from Netyear Group, Inc. in Redwood, California to find and show twenty-something Japanese how to organize a business-networking group and later launch an e-business. He meets with them in Shibuya's Bunkamura theater and art center, dressed in blue jeans, and promising them a great Web-based mobile Internet future.

Moreover, in Sweden Jonas Birgersson is the proponent of fixed broadband while in France Loic Le Meur and Marc Reeb show how dot-com start-ups gain first round venture capital, term sheets, and IPOs in the stock market. All these Gen-Y global marketers, some more famous than others, are doing brand management as a prelude to great marketing success both in their home countries and overseas. Only Michael Jordan and Jamie Lee Curtis are older thirty-somethings, but their famous faces and names push the telecom products and services they endorse into strong competitive positions worldwide.

Product development

M-banking tied to the mobile Internet has taken off in Finland, Sweden and Estonia with their commitment to electronic wallets, and m-commerce has done the same in France with its universal use of smart cards for debit and credit cards. Unique product development languishes at Deutsche Telekom in Germany and at Vodafone AirTouch in the UK. The European wireless telecom providers do not have spokespersons to capture the hearts and minds of twenty-somethings. Instead, most of these firms use the WAP as the key selling point for product development throughout Europe.

In the US, Michael Jordan, Wayne Gretzky and other former professional athletes do product development as a second career. Their professional sports segments are ranked according to their paid attendance at games, and their revenue from TV broadcasts and the sale of merchandise: National Football League (NFL), National Basketball Association (NBA), Major League Baseball (MLB), and National Hockey League (NHL). Each has championship games (Super Bowl or World Series) in which the winner is labeled the world's best team. Of course, this really means the US for the NFL and NBA, and the US and Canada for MLB and the NHL, and Europe for Formula 1, the Tour and Giro. Only FIFA Soccer has a championship game (World Cup) in which the winner is really the world's best team, but this professional sport has only a small following in the US.

At the moment, the product manufacturers of Nokia, Ericsson, Siemens, Motorola, and Samsung (of Korea) believe the product will sell itself. They have not found celebrities to endorse and push their mobile phones. Rather, they use clever well-placed advertisements in print and TV media to show the features of their cell phones. The marketing problem is as follows: as cell phones become commodities and prices drop, the costs of marketing remain too high relative to the sales generated from the ads themselves. In the longer run, this is an unsustainable strategy and violates one of the 3 Ss of targeting.

Product positioning

The Grand Hyatt hotel has used its technology savvy personnel to convince travelers their Internet needs will be attended to while they stay at the hotel. The On Command wireless system tied into the television is a bit awkward to use from the select button on the remote control device; other hotels attach a DSL converter to their phone lines and this makes all the difference in the world in terms of speed and ease of use to gain access to email and the Internet. Twenty-something guests want speed and ease of use whereas thirty-somethings want ease of use over everything else, and boomers will put up with old-fashioned landline telephones and faxes.

European m-banks outside of the Nordic and Baltic countries are still trying to work out what they will offer customers in terms of virtual products, back office support, and non-bank financial services. Forty-something Germans have begun to use non-bank e-financial institutions as a way to enhance their pension portfolio. Only the Overseas-Chinese bank in Singapore has done everything possible to position its financial products successfully into an m-bank structure. Its target group are the thirty-somethings who are married with one child with each partner having a good, high-paying job and the need to pay for the care of their aging parents and put some money away for retirement.

Of course, primitive digital cell phones are common among American players, coaches and owners. Players use them to talk with their agents and investment advisors, wives or girl friends, and their teammates; coaches make calls to check up on players and find out what their spotters have found among college athletes who could become pro ball players; and owners bark out orders to be sure coaches and players are following instructions about how to play the game to fill seats. Given the state of wireless technology in the US all the current crop of mobile phones are good for in early 2001 is voice communications.

And this is not all bad. Virtually everyone in Italy has a primitive cell phone. Unmarried Gen-Y and Gen-X men who still live at home call their mothers three times a day to chat and their unmarried sisters who also live at home to let their mothers know where they are and that they are safe during the day. Of course, their mothers call them to be sure they are working rather than playing with the opposite sex. Cell phones are the unbreakable umbilical cord that keeps Italian families closely tied to one another.

Marketing to the primary target group

As location awareness takes hold among US telecom providers between 2003 and 2005 and they carry out option 1, (pursue and invest), twenty-something pro ball players (who are among the highest paid employees in the US) and their sports agents and investment advisors will be one of the first groups to buy the new phones and promote themselves as early adapters of the new 3G technology. They will be ripe for content from Web-masters in Silicon Valley, the new alliance between AOL Japan and NTT DoCoMo, Network of the World from Pacific Century Cyberworks, and whatever comes out of the Microsoft Laboratories in China, Malaysia and elsewhere in the world. Also these high net worth customers only will stay at Web-equipped hotels and carry out their financial transactions at m-banks.

One thing needs to be noted. Although similar market segments exist across national frontiers, target groups tend to be local and carry with them many of the national cultural characteristics of their home countries. Their habits, attitudes, values and lifestyles rarely offer marketers a global target group. In the next few pages, let's explore in detail two industries, sports marketing in the US and mobile Internet on-line banking in Europe, and show the unique differences among target groups.

SPORTS MARKETING

Within the market segment of sports professionals, several target groups leap out and suggest some broadly focused self-reference criteria (SRC).

- Players provide insight into the preferences of high-paid, mid-twenty-somethings and thirty-somethings for more advanced mobile phone products. As teenagers just a few years go, they grew up with cell phones and the Internet. Today, as one element of Gen-Y or the Net Generation, they adopt most new technology as quickly as possible so long as it is priced right and does the job better than older technologies.
- Coaches are older. They may be from the last gasp of the baby boomer generation. Thus they will help us understand how quickly forty-somethings adapt new wireless technology. If mobile phones with 3G technology can transmit the statistics on potential new collegiate players, coaches will make every effort to learn from marketers how to maximize their use of m-commerce. Some may have problems with the diffusion of new technology.
- Owners will help us understand whether older persons will slow down the move to the new economy because of the problems inherent in diffusion. These are self-indulgent people who made their money the old fashioned way – they inherited it from their parents – and they have let others take care of the more mundane parts of life. If older people make the transition to the new technology, then m-commerce, the wireless Internet, and mobile phones free all of us from technical dependence on staff. Owners may not

want to give this "perk" up and could slow the transition to m-commerce within professional sports.

Leagues, teams and fans

Within each league (or segment), teams represent target groups whose fans display loyalty by wearing baseball caps and T-shirts with the team's name on them. For MLB baseball, intra-city rivalry within Chicago is legendary between the Cubs and the Sox. The Cubs mean white-collar, wine-drinking, upper-middle-income people on Chicago's North Side, and the White Sox mean blue-collar, beer-drinking, lower-upper and middle-middle income people on Chicago's South Side. These are two distinct target groups, the first with more disposable personal income and the latter with less. White Sox fans tend to be ethnic-Americans, the Irish, Slavs, Mexicans and others who live on the South Side and who essentially live among their past glories when Chicago was the factory to the world. On the other hand, Cubs fans tend to be as diverse as the American landscape and are the city's future in banking, insurance, dot-com start-ups and venture capital. These are all good targeting data. Can you guess which group of fans, those who favor the Cubs or those who support the Sox, use cell phones?

Of course, cell phones are owned and used at higher rates by Cubs fans because of business needs and nice-to-have family connections. They have studied the various offers by wireless carriers and made their choices about service without too much thought on costs. In many cases, the employers of Cubs fans pick up the costs of the cell phones, the bulk minutes of service purchased, and the roaming charges outside the home territory of the wireless provider. In fact at Cubs games, mobile phone users may even be getting a quote from the office to pass on to the client sitting next to them.

If Sox fans have mobile phones, these are used for voice communications with the family. The cell phones are usually in the car and the conversation is about how long it will take to get out of the parking lot, drive down the Dan Ryan expressway, and make it home before the children go to sleep. These phones are not in their pockets, carried on their belts, or in their briefcases.

Therefore, a new car that comes with a cell phone as a small extra will be purchased, and the family will become a wireless user without the effort of searching for the best mobile phone deal. However, the wireless firm won't make a great deal of money from Sox fans. They will use their cell phones sparingly to avoid paying more money for extra minutes.

DEEPER DATA MINING

However, let's do a bit more data mining so that we have the exact categories of information in front of us to develop appropriate marketing strategies for the sale of sports-related products. We are drilling down layer by layer until we have unearthed our target group of customers.

Within Wrigley Field, the baseball park of the Chicago Cubs, two target groups are present at the same game. They are there to take in the game, sing along with the announcer, and do the "Seventh Inning Stretch." One target group sits in the sun in the outfield bleachers, is unmarried and at the game with his buddies, drinks a great deal of beer and eats copious amounts of junk food, and takes the day off from work as a vacation day. Fun is the shared experience. Sports mania for the team and bad behavior in public are core values.

Another target group sits in the covered seats, is married and at the game with business clients, drinks a little white wine and eats healthy snacks, and counts the day as a work day. Getting to know clients in an informal setting is the shared experience. Sports interest in the game and quiet behavior in public are core values.

As men go through their life cycle, and marry and have children, the first target group (the so-called sports brutes) who are college graduates and work in professional fields become part of the second group (the sedate sports fans). Both root for the same team, the Cubs, but their demand for food and drink, T-shirts, pennants, and other memorabilia is different. Hence, the need for two separate marketing strategies by the Cubs organization within Wrigley Field.

SIMILAR TARGET GROUPS

Fans are loyal to the sport, the team, the player and their buddies at the park.

Some fans are loyal to more than one sport, teams in different leagues, and players who stand out from the crowd. For example, in the US, over 90 percent of American males are self-styled sports fans; 50 percent of them follow six sports; and 30 percent use their PCs to follow the game and the players. American men have a tribal devotion to sports teams. Today, their sports heroes turn themselves into brands (Michael Jordan, Tiger Woods, and Wayne Gretzky). If they were sports heroes before sports became entertainment in the 1960s and 1970s, sports marketers have turned them into myths (Lou Gehrig, Babe Ruth, Jackie Robinson, Joe DiMaggio, Mohammed Ali, and Pele).

Under specific promotion and advertising circumstances for world championship events, devotion to local teams gives way to spectator interest in the game. MLB's World Series draws millions of fans in the US, Canada, Venezuela, Cuba and Central America to their TV sets to watch the games and check out the ads. NFL's Super Bowl also draws over a billion fans throughout the world to watch two American football teams battle it out for a world championship. Both sports provide statistics on the game and sell merchandise via their Web sites.

However, these cross border attempts to reach fans and sell merchandise do not represent what marketers think in terms of similar target groups across national frontiers. The SRCs of American fans is vastly different than the SRCs of most fans overseas because most championship sports in North America sprang from US soil, culture and history. In the case of US-based sports, similar target groups across national frontiers (except for Canada) is more of a fiction than reality.

Realities of FIFA soccer

One professional sport crosses virtually all national boundaries and is the dominant, most important sport in all countries save the US and Canada. This is FIFA Soccer. Loyal fans follow Zidan from his Algerian-French home in Marseilles, France to professional teams throughout Europe, and to the 1998 World Cup in Paris where he scored the first two of three goals for France against Brazil and brought the world cup back to France. His sports fans bought his memorabilia and that of his national team so they could stroll down the streets of Paris with him, the team and the French president singing the French national anthem. For this short time, the target group was national. Then it reverted to the local teams once again as it does in the US after the World Series and Super Bowl.

Manchester United is a local English team that earns 99 percent of its income in the United Kingdom. The average fan with his family can drop $1000 per visit when the travel, hotel, food and merchandise costs are added up. Manchester United's target group must buy the merchandise with its logo on it, such as boxer shorts, T-shirts, posters, and replica red-and-white uniforms for the kids, and stay at the team's hotel where they just might see a player from the team doing a walk-about among the fans.

This local target group is different than the one in China called the Shanghai Supporters Club. From satellite TV they see the games in England, or use the team's Web site to purchase the VCR tape or see it through video streaming, buy merchandise from the team, and subscribe to the team's magazine. Although the revenue from overseas venues amounts to about $150 million per year, it is small potatoes compared with what Manchester United gets at home from its loyal British target group.

The reality is that marketing target groups in sports don't travel well outside their home country. Some teams do better in gaining attention abroad. A few players do the same. But rarely is cash put on the table to buy seats. If the Web site is interactive and easy to use, then local teams sell merchandise worldwide. Here then is a real marketing opportunity for m-commerce to do a bang-up job and get an additional revenue stream from the wireless Internet. Let's see how sports marketing and m-commerce interact with the target groups we can distill from the business segments we presented in Chapter 4.

MARKETING STRATEGY

Firms engaged in selling mobile phones, wireless Internet content, and m-commerce service should concentrate on selling to influential twenty-somethings who can carry the day for change with other, more senior business executives.

- *Product.* The wireless mobile phone must do its job without substantial drops in service.
- *Price.* The upper limit on monthly charges for wireless Internet service is about $150.00.
- *Promotion.* The ads must show younger, hip people, such as Jamie Lee Curtis, talking to Helsinki, roaming to Rome, and finding a Seoul mate.
- *Place.* Location awareness means mobile phones and m-commerce service must be everywhere in all countries around the world.

These same firms must offer a different 4 Ps marketing strategy for forty-some-things. In this case, the job of marketers is to teach older business executives how to use and be more productive with the new wireless technology. This is the application of the *new* marketing concept. How do potential older customers learn about a new technology and how do they use this new technology to improve their performance? Once learning takes hold, marketers begin to merge their marketing strategies for twenty-, thirty-, and forty-somethings as this whole segment becomes more similar across age groups and across national frontiers.

One goal for marketers is *product standardization* for all age groups within the segment of business executives. Another goal is *promotion and pricing adaptation* so that appeals reflect the real interests of different age groups and their ability to pay for technologically superior products, faster interconnect services, and secure transaction capability. The task for marketers is to craft a marketing strategy that sells product to all age groups irrespective of their technological savvy. To do this they must know the SRC of very specific target groups within the larger segment of business executives.

ON-LINE BANKING SERVICES

We asked this question in Chapter 4. Do you want your m-bank to operate like a technology firm that works in banking, or do you want your m-bank to operate like an established bank that works with technology? Let's get answers from the target groups. Which ones have formed brand communities and are targets of marketing opportunities?

Netrepreneurs and athletes

Twenty-somethings netrepreneurs suggest their m-banks operate like a technology firm that works in banking. Although professional athletes tend not to be netrepreneurs themselves, they may want to invest in dot-com start-ups because of hype from agents who also represent successful fans. Also players want to save more during their high-income years, and they need financial help from agents, investment advisors, and m-bankers to turn savings into long-term investments.

Pursue this target group because its members already have formed brand communities. They are aware of different brands and the relevance of each to their financial lifestyles. The members of this group know retail banking costs go down and expect prices for various financial products to decrease, too; if the m-banks do operate similar to a technology firm that works in banking, prices are found on the Internet and are transparent for all users of the various financial products from m-banks. This target group demands 24/7 anytime, anywhere service through the call centers of m-banks. A good m-banking marketing strategy is based on deep data mining for the narrowly focused self-reference criteria of the target group, or actionable targeting.

Venture capitalists and coaches

Thirty-something venture capitalists demand their m-banks provide a bit more personal service through both the m-bank and its companion bricks-and-mortar bank, or provide a wider range of financial services through both the alternative and traditional channels of distribution. Although coaches tend not to be venture capitalists themselves, they may need to learn to trade their fame for a piece of the action in other businesses; some put their names on restaurants, discos and other retail venues. Also coaches are old enough to start worrying about retirement planning because their playing days are over and their coaching days could end too with one or more bad seasons of play by their teams.

Postpone the pursuit of this target group because its members are giving m-banks mixed messages about brand awareness and brand relevance. The members of this group understand intuitively that prices and costs of retail banking will go down, but they look at their financial needs and wonder whether m-banks can do the job with the various financial products venture capitalists may need to secure their future. This target group demands the private placement of funds as part of the financial package from their m-banks. Here too we learn more by doing deep data mining and asking questions about self-reference criteria of the target group, or again actionable targeting.

High-net worth executives and owners

Forty-somethings high-net worth business executives insist their m-banks don't interfere with their traditional banking relationships. Owners of professional sports teams want old-fashioned personal service from their bankers; the former consider the latter family retainers rather than professionals of equal merit. These wealthy individuals don't want to learn about new technologies and new ways to get information because they expect others to carry the cash, pay the bills, and do all the other mundane things of life.

Terminate the pursuit of this target group because members of the group will not form brand communities, offer actionable targeting, and create new market space even with the aid of marketers who could teach them how to use the new technology under the rubric of the *new* marketing concept. It's not worth the effort to spend time or money on folks whose self-reference criteria are against the new economy of m-commerce and the wireless Internet.

THE TARGET GROUP

After substantial marketing research, the important marketing opportunity for m-commerce is the brand community formed by the twenty-somethings, ne-trepreneurs, professional athletes, agents to the stars, and investment advisors. They share demographic characteristics, such as high levels of disposable personal income, and they present to the world the same core values and lifestyles about sports as entertainment.

When Wayne Gretzky was traded from the quiet vastness of northern Alberta and the Edmonton Oilers to the Hollywood buzz of the Los Angeles Kings, the deal was done to drive the NHL into the consciousness of American customers throughout the US. Planet Hollywood owners, such as Bruce Willis, and other Hollywood royalty (Mel Gibson, Sylvester Stalone, and Charlie Sheen) made the scene at the arena and watched the game for a short time. Gretzky was raised to mythic heights as the "Great One" by media spin artists. The word went out to all NHL players that Gretzky was the NHL's meal ticket for future TV revenue, and he should be spared the dangerous shoves into the boards and high sticking attacks made on other players that caused them to lose teeth, suffer face damage, and worse. He and his southern California blonde wife with their squeaky-clean children were media darlings for all to worship and adore. When the "Great One" put his name on a product its sales soared. When his playing days were over and he retired from NHL play in his mid-thirties, Gretzky had become a brand name for sports memorabilia, Web-based sports news, and many other products.

This target group has a unique mind-set about their expectations of the m-commerce goods and services they use. They want to move beyond primitive mobile phones and get what is already available in Europe and Japan. If 3G were available in the US, this target group would be big spenders because the Hollywood buzz and master spin doctors would be behind the roll-out of promotions and advertising by athletes, netrepreneurs and others. Other consumers would join the bandwagon of this new and exciting brand community. This is elementary consumer behavior in marketing.

Marketers collect data about the purchasing habits of groups, array them into easily recognizable product categories, give the groups an easy to remember moniker or call sign, and label them according to well-established norms of consumer behavior. Their marketing strategy for rolling out 3G m-commerce must be focused on one important target group above all others. This is their route to success.

In the Nordic countries of Finland and Sweden this target group is the twenty-somethings. They not only know about technology, its uses, applications and possibilities. They also want the services they know they can get from this technology – for example, a complete array of financial services through Internet banking. Twenty-somethings have taken command of the venture capital, Internet banking, and mobile Internet investment markets. The question is no longer when and by how much, but how long it will take to acquire m-banking services in other Nordic, Baltic and northern European countries, and convert all their twenty-somethings to Web-based banking as well.

VENTURE CAPITAL

There's good news and bad news from Europe's Internet companies. As of October 2000, they have on average 20 months to go at current cash burn rates before they run out of cash – up from 13 months at the start of 2000, according to PcW, the consulting firm. That's the good news. The bad news is they are spending three times gross profit on sales and marketing.[2] It is bad because the cash burn rate is unsustainable. All Internet firms together (including dot-coms start-ups, mobile telecom providers, and m-banks) will either reduce the costs of marketing and raise prices because no one firm individually can take these business actions alone and survive – a classic tale of the prisoner's dilemma. No doubt some of them will fail and be taken over by those European dot-coms with heaps of cash: T-Online, Terra Lycos, Wanadoo and Tiscali.

At the beginning of 2001, Germany has 56 of Europe's top 150 Internet companies, and half of Germany's dot-coms are profitable. The UK has 35 of Europe's Internet firms, and 26 percent of UK's start-ups make money. B2C companies are the most vulnerable with burn rates of 15 months while burn rates of 23 months exist for B2B firms. Also m-commerce firms are the strongest, while content and software sectors are the weakest.

Of course, m-banks are burning cash along with the weaker dot-coms. Not enough traditional bank customers from the forty-something group have shifted over to the alternative channel of distribution and none of the folks from the twenty-something group want to keep their funds with the banks or their retail m-banking units or both. The latter target group together with teenagers prefer to buy their financial service products from non-bank institutions, e.g., discount brokers and mutual funds, and through the floats of venture capitalists. Therefore, marketing campaigns in Europe for m-banking have to be targeted at those who will actually do m-banking at traditional private banks.

In terms of real options, European m-bankers should pursue thirty- and forty-somethings with a more traditional promotion and advertising campaign, and they should postpone an integrated marketing communications campaign targeted to the twenty-something group. Let's look at the facts country-by-country.

Forty-somethings in Sweden

According to the Swedish Venture Capital Association, 140 early stage venture firms exist today in Sweden, up from 25 in 1994. The investments of the twenty-somethings' group were "unfocused and opportunistic," says Per-Ola Karlsson, a principal at McKinsey. This was because "there was too much money, too many business ideas, and too few experienced people," from the thirty-somethings group, says James Mannerfelt at Alumni, a headhunting firm.[3] Even though the forty-somethings group from the banks and pension funds put their firm's money into these start-ups because they thought that the twenty-somethings knew what they were doing, the failures were spectacular ones, including Boo.com, Dressmart, and others.

These failures taught the forty-somethings a great lesson: be a technology firm first; understand the technology inside and out; and teach it to customers. Only after this is done be a venture capitalist or a bank. Of course, this is the same rule for bankers who make alliances with twenty-something dot-com "experts" for m-banking, and expect it all to work out in the end. Nothing could be further from the truth.

Twenty-somethings in France

French business school graduates even from the best b-school in France, Ecole des Hautes Etudes Commerciales (HEC) start Web businesses fast. For example, Loic Le Meur's B2L built Web sites for Chanel and Twentieth Century Fox. He then established Business Pace, a company that starts companies, such as Marketo.com (a Web site that puts small businesses in touch with suppliers) and Actibox (a messaging system).[4] Also Marc Reeb set up Netcrawler, a way to track advertising campaigns over the Internet. Many more are housed in the incubator LeDefi in the Pompidou area of Paris.

Such start-ups get their first round financing from the likes of Leonardo Finance. Although a bit late to the game, the French are trying to create an equity culture and then trade the new IPOs on the Nouveau Marche, France's version of Nasdaq. The problem is the lack of liquidity on this market and the preference for similar markets with greater liquidity in Frankfurt and London.

Unfortunately, these new start-ups face higher taxes, a short work week, and more cumbersome inspection procedures in France versus the UK. This is why one of France's twenty-somethings, Oliver Cadic, set up Info-Elec, a computer electronics business in Ashford, England, the first UK stop for the Eurostar train. Also this is why some 50,000 French twenty-somethings are working in Silicon Valley, California rather than in France.

Thirty-somethings in France

In smart cards, France is ahead of its European neighbors and the US because of decisions made by mid- and top-level business executives. All credit and debit cards issued in France have an embedded chip with a dedicated identification code, which makes on-line payments more secure. Also telecom service providers offer bundled services such as a subsidized handset price, a subscription fee, and talking time for a flat monthly rate. In this case, Wanadoo, France Telecom's ISP, has copied what is already in place in Japan through NTT DoCoMo.

INTERNET BANKING

Forty-somethings who manage the big nationally-owned European banks must choose between forming alliances with Internet companies and setting up their own m-banking Web sites. If they chose the former, they would have to share revenues with twenty-somethings, the upstarts who own the dot-coms, and, perhaps the thirty-somethings, the folks who provide the venture capital. If they chose the latter, these older executives would have to move ahead quickly to learn about how business is done and who makes money on the Internet. This they seem incapable of doing within any time frame that would be helpful to their traditional banks.

One big exception of the failure of forty-somethings in the dot-coms of Sweden to see the future is Merita-Nordbanken, the Finnish-Swedish bank, that leads in terms of Internet users. These banks are moving into cross-border deals because they face low growth at home, cannot find even more cost savings, and need to raise new money for investments in technology. Also Merita-Nordbanken now have one million Internet banking customers; and 35 percent of the bills of SEB's Swedish customers are paid over the Net.

Thus Finnish banks are in a major drive to persuade customers to adopt electronic and phone banking. Today, some banks in the Nordic region are already getting more Web visits than branch visits. Twenty-something Finns and Swedes never visit the branches; they can pay their bills, check account balances and trade shares more easily, and more cheaply, on the Web. Customers also receive their bills on their WAP phones, and pay them at the touch of a button.

Since almost 100 percent of twenty-somethings are actively engaged in Internet banking and the percentage of thirty-somethings doing banking on the Web will climb to over 50 percent next year in Sweden and Finland, growth will have to come from acquiring banks in other Nordic and Baltic countries. The branches are becoming centers of advice rather than the place for transactions; many branches have no tellers and no windows; instead, the whole floor is dominated by cash dispensing machines for deposits and withdrawals. The Web is definitely altering the face of banking in two of the Nordic countries.

Target groups In Germany

Standing still is not an option in a world characterized by global consolidation, Web-based technological change, and Internet banking, say Germany's larger banks, Deutsche Bank, Commerzank, and HypoVereinsbank. Germany continues to be a country with too many banks, each placing too much emphasis on branch networks as opposed to new distribution channels, such as the Internet. Nevertheless, the bigger German banks have formed separate subsidiaries to do m-brokerage transactions. These m-German brokerages have become big players in the direct stock investment field. More importantly, a few of these m-bank subsidiaries have become as innovative, flexible and fast-thinking as most m-commerce start-ups in the Nordic, Baltic and northern European countries. In fact, these German m-bank SBUs have rejected the slow and ponderous habits of their venerable parent German banks. These m-direct brokerages are better at marketing today than ever before, but this is not saying much. They haven't been able to build up brand awareness, brand relevancy, or the brand name itself as has happened in Sweden and Finland across the Baltic Sea to the north.

Contrary to the sports lifestyles information from the US and Europe that high-paid athletes and their retinue of followers, and contrary to the age group data from the Nordic countries that IT geeks and their start-up partners – all of whom are twenty-somethings and will be the first to use m-brokerage services, this is not the case in Germany. Instead, German forty-somethings are middle income employees and housewives who want to manage their pension assets a bit more aggressively than the staid German banks. These forty-somethings are in the first wave to convert to the advantages of on-line stock brokerage business, but thirty-somethings, especially men, dominate trades through direct brokers. Over the years, the forty-somethings have complained to their banks and asked for a discount when trading shares, and they got rebuffed. Through Comdirect, Germany's leading on-line brokerage, they get a huge discount, and since they are always on-line, they can check their stocks as often as they wish. Discount brokers expect to service over 3.3 million German customers by 2002 because of the huge surge in Internet use by Germans.

Target groups in the UK and Ireland

Some are offering the highest saving rates possible (or loss-leading interest rates) as a way to attract customers to their Internet sites (e.g., Egg, the UK Internet and telephone banking arm of the Prudential, and Dublin-based First-e or now Unofirst).[5] Instead of viewing e-banking as a future profitable business unit, senior executives see it as an extra layer of costs for a completely new channel of distribution in which the wireless application protocol on mobile phones, interactive television, integrated statements and accounts, and other technologies all exist under one e-banking roof. Forty-something bankers fail to see m-banking and the Internet as a great new marketing opportunity for cross-selling financial products and for the future of their brand-named bank.

VALUE-BASED MARKETING DECISIONS

Here are the value-based decisions that made young soldiers turn into high-tech netrepreneurs in Israel. These show real differences in attitudes towards mobile phones, m-commerce, and the wireless Internet between twenty-somethings from Israel, and their equivalent Gen-Y age groups in East Asia, Europe and the US.

What is the context of a decision?

Young twenty-somethings are drafted into the Israeli Defense Forces (IDF) army at 18 for a military tour of six years. This is their coming of age. Many of them serve in one or more of the high-tech units of the Israeli military. For young Israeli men and women military service is the training ground to initiate wireless start-ups, put together m-commerce dot-coms, and go to market in New York with software IPOs. Usually, they base all research, development, and product planning in Israel, and move the strategic operations – including marketing, sales, and business development – to the US.

Some success stories include Compugen, Check Point Software, Nice Systems, Floware Wireless Systems, SoftLink, Whale Communications, Repli-Web, Back Web Technologies, Jerusalem Global Innovation Centers, and Concord Ventures.[6] Most Israeli firms don't want to spend money on public relations and marketing, and they have been remiss in getting their message out to the larger global population in both Europe and the US.

What is the object of a decision?

Why New York? Israel's home market is too tiny for an Israeli company to become a significant player either at home or overseas if it tries to sell just to buyers at home. Many young Israeli men and women have family and friends in the United States, and a broad network of well-placed individuals who have deep pockets, Wall Street experience, and links to venture capitalists in Silicon Valley. Since money-making mobile Internet deals are always possible within Israeli society, even young *haredim* (Hebrew for "quakers") men from the Orthodox Jewish yeshivas are doing deals along with their Talmudic stud-ies. The few native *haredim* women and men are far outnumbered by the *hare-dim* who have migrated from English-speaking countries and who have the better high-tech skills, or the Anglo *haredim*. Most Orthodox rabbis prefer cell phone communications with their followers and mobile phone negotiations within the Israeli government to maintain strong religious rules for an increas-ingly more secular society.

What is the impact of a decision?

All Israeli society thrives on very loud voice communications either personally or over mobile phones. Israeli women and men use to argue face-to-face; now they also argue over mobile phones about their high-tech start-ups and when and how to make the big money in New York.

Decision opportunities

The problem in Israel's success story is that their new high-tech ideas must compete for financial market space in New York with those from Silicon Valley, California, Bangalore, India, and several countries in East Asia and Europe. Although twenty-somethings from Israel have good ideas about technology, so do other ethnic groups within the US who also have the backing of their com-patriots, such as Jewish-Americans, Chinese-Americans, Indian-Americans, Greek-Americans and others. Unfortunately for Israel and the other countries involved, they lose their best and brightest permanently to the US.

According to Rami Beracha of Polaris Venture Capital, "The number of Israeli companies that don't succeed because of technology is less than one percent ... But the number that fail because of business reasons like poor po-sitioning or internal strife is much larger."[7] Polaris has 60 Israeli start-ups in its portfolio, and it has hired a professional therapist to help the firms operate effectively in both Israel and the US.

M-COMMERCE TRANSACTIONS

Silicon Valley competition for Israeli, French, Finnish, Swedish and other start-ups is real. American companies, such as HeyAnita, Inc., offer customers the ability to gain access to the content of the Internet not through computers, but with the telephone. Since 50 percent of all American homes do not have PCs, nor do many more people around the world, the ability to use a common landline phone for information has great potential for linking them to the wider Internet world. They dial into a toll-free number and orally ask for stock quotes, restaurant locations, airline schedules, or news stories. The answers are delivered almost immediately through voice synthesis, and the caller then can be connected to the specific phone number of the broker, food establishment, or airline. The bulk of the phone calls come from landline telephones rather than from cell phones, a surprising turn of events and a warning signal to wireless telecom providers.

Charles Schwab, the brokerage firm, has offered its customers a voice portal since 1996. America Online and Sprint both started voice portals in early 2001. AT&T uses the service of Tellme Networks, Inc. for its corporate customers who have employees that travel without their computers and need information from the home office. HeyAnita offers voice portals in Korean, Mandarin Chinese, and Spanish as well as in English.[8]

The danger that telecom providers may have spent too much money on wireless licenses and setting up the m-commerce Internet infrastructure has crossed over to the banks that lent them $171 billion in new loans. Over 40 percent of the total was syndicated out to European telecom providers. Thus European banking regulators are questioning these loans and their impact on bank solvency; the former think the banks have taken on too much risk in one sector; the banks may be overexposed and unable to weather a downturn in the ability of wireless telecom providers to gather in new users, sell more minutes, and encourage them to do m-commerce Internet transactions over cell phones. Already, landline phones that are connected to voice portals are eating into potential wireless business. Of course, the banks involved may have sold or refinanced the loans to wireless telecom providers, but the collective action of

European bank regulators is a shot across the bow of the high-flying telecom sector.

Telecom firms are now highly leveraged. As a consequence, British Tele-communications, Deutsche Telekom, France Telecom, and Dutch-owned KPN have seen their credit ratings drop from double "A" to single "A." The latter is still above investment grade, but lower ratings raise the cost of borrowing funds. If the stock market's sentiment about their equity performance drops too, these telecom providers will find it hard to reduce their debt and float the shares of their wireless subsidiaries. In 2001, the wireless providers are not forecasting the robust profits they did a year earlier, and no targeting strategy seems to be on the horizon to change this picture any time soon.

MONEY-MAKING DEALS

Let's answer the targeting questions.

Structure: targeting twenty-somethings

■ *Is our current knowledge on target groups within national markets and their specific, local choices for mobile Internet banking and other wireless services sufficient to make accurate forecasts for the years 2003 and 2005?*
No. We don't know enough because we don't have a sufficient number of years from which to make good forecasts. However, if all telecom providers start providing structure to their targeting efforts and go after the twenty-somethings or Gen-Y – the primary target group – then those who best understand their needs will be ahead in the race for dominance of e-business.

Within the Internet banking community, the word is out that a decent idea executed quickly is far better than a perfect idea executed late. Twenty-some-things like new ideas proposed early in the life of products or services. They want to catch these ideas during the beginning of the expansion phase of the product life cycle so they can be investors and make money too.

Alex Au, who is the chief executive of the Oversea-Chinese Banking Corporation in Singapore, launched Asia's first Internet-only bank, finatiQ, 100 days before actually building it at all. The launch is promoting the brand name with a quirky campaign that is charming younger Singaporeans. Promoting brand name awareness is the top priority of this Internet-only bank and OCBC.

FinatiQ started out in July 2000 by offering unit trusts and holding deposits; then in September it began offering fixed deposit products; and it will have a full array of financial products and services sometime in 2001. Is this a good marketing strategy? Or does it create bad publicity? None of this seems to worry twenty-something Singaporeans because they do have the beginnings of the first Internet bank for the island nation.

Moreover, the parent OCBC bank formed an alliance with the Australian and New Zealand Banking Group (ANZ) to offer a regional Internet bank for the region as a whole. ANZ bank brings high-tech skills to the regional Internet deal, and its technology could spill over to finatiQ in Singapore.

Alex Au came to Singapore from Hong Kong as the island nation seeks to infuse foreign talent and ideas into the local banking business. He brought with him his highly competitive background from years of work at the local Hong Kong offices of HSBC bank. There the local banking scene has big banks with many outlets in all parts of the Special Administrative Region, and smaller banks with fewer outlets that must compete on personal service through the traditional and alternative channels of distribution for banks. Both big and smaller banks in Hong Kong view Internet banking as a way to inject a new wave of competition for the twenty-something target group. Au's new task is to do the same in Singapore.

FinatiQ provides structure to Internet banking in Singapore, and the alliance between its parent and ANZ bank enhances that structure throughout East Asia. Other banks are watching finatiQ's roll-out of Internet financial services and whether Alex Au can deliver substantial revenues and steady profits starting in the year 2003. Most traditional bankers are unwilling to subsidize Internet banking for more than a few years, and they want Internet bankers to carry their own weight within a relatively short period of time.

Therefore, Internet bankers must build structure, and spend their money on information technology and brand development rather than on new variations of existing financial products. The latter will sell if the other two are done well.

Scale: doing deeper data mining

■ *Do we gain more detail for our forecasts and the ability to scale up quickly our m-commerce initiatives by doing deeper data mining on habits and attitudes of target groups?*

Yes. We are able to focus on twenty-somethings who are sports professionals, their agents to the stars, their investment advisors, and their fans; and on younger business executives who want to convert traditional banks to on-line banking, and their customers who want easy-to-use financial services.

Also within the Internet banking community, the word is out that building m-banking portals and scaling up in-house information technology means setting up domain knowledge teams within the bank and with their foreign partners. IT people must say to their colleagues "I understand your trusts, smart cards, and your financial products." In building scale into Internet banking, ethnic communal ties go a long way to creating wireless bankers. Indians in Bangalore and the US design semiconductors that lower the cost of Internet access, and provide software packages that help small businesses handle customer requests received by fax, phone and the Internet.

Today, "the greatest value is in something scalable, and that means products"[9] for domains such as Internet banking, says Hans Tapaaria, a director of ASG-Omni, a Bangalore- and Connecticut-based investor and corporate adviser. Selling financial products through e-banking requires deep pockets, world-class talent, and marketing muscle, and this means tapping into the highly successful Indian-American target group of Silicon Valley. These thirty-somethings have turned their domestic successes (in either India or America) into products for the global market. They are the muscle behind building up scale in Internet banking.

Their taste in sports is cricket, soccer, and Australian-rules rugby. However, the taste of their American children in sports is boys' high-school football and girls' basketball. In Internet banking, information technology and sports mania, Indians must compete against the Chinese, Israeli and other talented ethnic groups in America's East and West Coast Silicon Valleys and their overseas laboratories in Singapore, Hong Kong, Taiwan, and Tel Aviv.

Substitutes: collecting primary data

■ *Do the primary data collected through questionnaires and from the media help us make better choices about substitute mobile phones, platforms, and telecom providers?*

Yes. We are able to decide whether GSM, iMode, or other Web-enabled phones will migrate from their home markets to overseas host markets.

Here's the background of the wireless application protocol and GSM. In the early 1990s, WAP was designed originally to run over limited bandwidth that worked on a compact binary code rather than with HTML language. Then in the mid-1990s short messaging services (SMS) or short text messages were put on GSM phones. SMS has the luxury of not interfering with GSM's use of bandwidth; instead, SMS and WAP co-exist on one GSM phone. Nevertheless, the introduction of SMS added value in the build up of the margin for marketing GSM phones.

In the later part of the 1990s, GSM phones went completely digital with text screens on the handsets and the now famous (or infamous to users) three-letter keys on the keyboard. By the start of 2000, WAP became a development platform for GSM. Telecom providers, such as Sweden's Tellia, began offering the following GSM services: voice communications with roaming capabilities, SMS text messages, data transfers, and Web gateways to the Internet. All of these GSM services appear on Tellia's monthly bill, so-called microbilling in the language of DoCoMo.

Here's what respondents tell us. They expect WAP to deliver the Net on handheld mobile phones – but are disappointed when it cannot do so. The problem is bandwidth limitation not with the protocol. WAP is "G." However,

WAP needs infrastructure investments by telecom providers to go digital with 2G, give it GPRS and EDGE speed with 2.5G, and provide "always on" speed with 3G. Today, WAP is evolving into WAP 2.0 as the protocol seeks to protect GSM security. At the same time, WAP 2.0 may be merging with iMode's cHTML.

Both GSM and iMode will in future deliver a dual-protocol mobile device for the 3G infrastructure that comes to Europe by 2003. The antennas are going up, the equipment is being deployed, and the licenses are being issued by governments. At the moment, marketers are working on the name for this new mobile phone. Respondents want to know what they can call this new miniature information device that works virtually everywhere in the world.

GSM phones do best when they act as enhancements of successful mobile phone practices, such as SMS (or short messaging services). These include OAG, the publisher of flight schedules in electronic and print format for more than 800 airlines, and its ability to deliver SMS about delays and the status of current flights. Amadeus, Galileo, Sabre and Worldspan are booking agents for on-line travel sites, and with GSM phones, they show travelers how to redo their travel schedules and tell the folks waiting for them what will be the new likely arrival time.

With SMS enhancements GSM phones and GSM-enabled personal digital assistants (or PDAs) can become power tools for travelers. If the mobile phone manufacturers don't provide these enhancements, iMode through W-CDMA or the convergence of TDMA with UMTS, or lightweight wireless laptops, or voice portals may do the job better and cleaner. The years 2001–2003 will determine whether European-owned GSM technology extends itself into other areas of the world, or whether GSM gets overwhelmed by other technologies in its home market.

Sustainability: paying or not paying for content

■ *Will those people who make up the actionable target groups be willing to pay for content through m-commerce that is currently free for the asking on the Internet?*

We don't know. Marketers should anticipate that the Gen-Y Japanese and other East Asians, and some Europeans may be willing to pay for content. However, marketers should realize that the twenty-somethings in the US may say no to this discontinuous change in their m-commerce surfing habits. Thus the long-term sustainability of the primary target group's interest in GSM, W-CDMA and UMTS, and in wireless versus wired links is still open to questions about how long, how much, for what purpose, and whether money can be made in this new world of m-commerce.

The broadband content market is up for grabs. NTT DoCoMo does a deal with AOL Japan to get the latter's content up on wireless phones. In the process, wired laptop-based AOL learns how to transmit content over wireless phones, and gets itself ready for what can be major breakthroughs in mobile Internet connectivity in the US and Europe. Pacific Century Cyberworks does deals with Cable & Wireless (UK), Telstra (Australia), CMGI (US) and others with technology, hard cash, and worldwide contacts; the former's goal is to develop non-TV interactive content. And many more alliances, partnerships and investments.

Skulking about with interactive broadband content is a race to be won by only the swiftest runners. All of them need to get a good idea out quickly rather than wait for possible perfections in the future. There's money to be made by making the right choices.

CONCLUSIONS

How to conquer the wireless world? Apply targeting strategies to m-commerce, especially to show how young professional athletes and younger e-bankers view their investment opportunities in wireless telecom, sports marketing, and on-line financial services. Here is a checklist of things to do:

- Put all target groups in play for anytime, anywhere telecom services.
- Build market share with a marketing targeting strategy that is carefully adapted to making money from athletes, m-bankers and other twenty-somethings.

▨ Offer unbeatable value propositions to early adapters among twenty-some-things who establish start-ups and dot-coms, and obtain venture capital.

▨ Create value by reconfiguring the value chain for wireless sports marketing and m-financial services in which content is based on location awareness and the creation of new market space for all forms of m-commerce.

Now let's look at how marketers use positioning strategies to match the most appropriate Web-enabled products with key target groups among Gen-Y, Gen-X and the boomers, and what marketers can do to raise price points, promote expanded services, and deliver these goods everywhere in East Asia, Europe, and the US.

CHAPTER 6

Positioning Local Goods and Services

EXECUTIVE SUMMARY

MARKETERS MATCH POSSIBLE ON-LINE Internet products with probable customers; the former offer the latter enhanced customer relationships to try out m-commerce and the mobile Internet. Also marketing managers match goods and services with the cultural needs, habits, and values of target customers by improving customer relationships through call centers, on-line ordering, virtual supplier networks, and timely delivery to factories, offices or homes.

Moreover, marketers perfect fulfillment or accurate delivery for their customers. In the process, marketers learn to be m-managers. Here's what they must do to position goods and services successfully:

▨ Pursue the option to invest in on-line stock-trading because the mass affluent, business customers of airlines and five-star hotels, and many professional athletes and entertainers, agents, coaches and directors, and team owners and studio heads are all familiar with and want to trade stocks with their PCs or mobile phones. Money can be made quickly on trade with on-line buying and selling of stock.

▨ Postpone the option to invest in interactive TV. Lease or buy rather than create content. Leave the creation of content to Hollywood firms, their entertainers, agents, and studio bosses, such as LivePlanet. Money is harder to make in Hollywood. All types of expenses are charged against gross receipts before residual owners of content – venture capitalists who provide angel and start-up capital, and vendors who provide financing for operations – see any money. Unless the movie, TV sitcom, or cable production is a big blockbuster hit, expenses *always* are greater than the "grosses."

- Terminate the option to invest in Internet banking. The commodity pricing of on-line financial services is inadequate to pay back the investment and operational costs. Also many smaller and mid-size traditional banks seem incapable of turning themselves into on-line Internet banks that capture the hearts and minds of their customers. Moreover, these traditional banks with an on-line Internet operation have the following problems: decisions about which of the many legacy computer systems to abandon; decisions about which of the many off-the-shelf back office middleware systems to install; and decisions about how to get customers to love impersonal, on-line financial services and pay the new fees. Traditional banks need a price-lining strategy for their on-line Internet operations – that is, commodity prices for many financial services and higher value-added prices for those more limited services that need in-depth customer relationship management (CRM).

- Prepare for the impact of the NTT DoCoMo-AOL Japan alliance on all three types of on-line personal services in Japan, Europe and the US, as this alliance of a telecom provider with a content provider upsets most traditional ways in which services are positioned through both the wired and the mobile Internet.

- Thrive in the world of the wireless Internet by employing the *new* marketing concept, preparing a *new* 4 Ps marketing strategy, putting in place a *new* marketing organization, and creating a framework for real options analysis.

Invest in customer relationship management

Positioning requires marketers to improve their techniques of CRM. Customers are our data and our business. Make them feel special by creating a "wow" experience. Let customer service, not the price, sell the product. Deliver help on-line to twenty-somethings; deliver help both on-line and via the telephone to thirty-somethings; and deliver help over the telephone to forty-somethings. Perfect on-line customer-support systems. Put together many legacy data bases into one coherent whole middleware system to gain more accurate information about how to retain. "Simply knowing more about your customers makes it easier to keep them,"[1] says Avid Modjtabai of Wells Fargo's Internet services group.

As airlines have done for many years to fill seats, firms now can quote different prices for different quality and services to different customers. To reinforce something spelled out in Chapter 3, marketers now know that price marketing is the most important element of a 4 Ps marketing strategy because the name of the marketing game today without effective CRM is profitability, nothing more. Marketers are turning those goods and services without CRM, such as last-minute availability of airline seats and hotel rooms, into commodities. Here's where firms do a good job in selling their products through on-line Internet services.

Banks don't have the same time pressure. Their financial services are always needed, and customers expect to receive interest and pay fees. Banks are not airlines trying to fill seats before the plane takes off or hotels trying to fill rooms before the day is over. This misunderstanding about the timeliness of bank transactions causes bank marketers to think all customers want to carry out financial transactions on-line. This is far from the truth. Only some bank customers from Gen-Y and a few customers from Gen-X truly want all their financial services on-line. Most persons in older age groups prefer some social interaction with bank personnel who solve financial problems for customers.

These banks turn financial services into "experiences" for customers. The banks get higher margins, greater customer loyalty, and more fee income. By watching how customers select among and pay for many different financial services, bank marketers get an early insight into which services are in favor and which are out of favor among bank customers. The Internet provides the detailed information about customers. However, bank marketers use follow up personal contacts through CRM to raise prices, and complete both the first sale and all additional, repeat sales. Effective CRM means a continuing relationship with customers either through the Internet and personally, or only with personal contacts between bank marketers and customers. Knowing which to use and when is how marketers make money from their positioning strategy.

- Add CRM to the kit of successful marketing strategies for banks and non-bank financial situations.

- Offer commodity prices for on-line stock-trading and some on-line financial services, and a range of prices for higher quality information and better, more personal financial services.
- Establish interactive content for on-line cable, TV, PC and mobile phones to watch sports and entertainment, do stock trades, and engage in financial services for those target groups that prefer on-line service.
- Increase the use of mobile phones, m-commerce, and the wireless Internet through both the virtual and real worlds.

Recommendation

The trick for marketers is to convince more and more customers to try out on-line services and turn one-time users into permanent on-line customers. Also the trick for marketers is to offer personal services to those customers who are familiar with the traditional ways in which they do business. CRM means doing both and making money from on-line and traditional services. Here is the marketing assignment for wireless marketers:

- Segment digital customers into those that are willing to carry out on-line financial services and those who reject the use of on-line services.
- Target digital customers who prefer on-line services with low cost, commodity prices, and others who prefer both on-line and personal services. Give both target groups the quality of service they prefer, and charge higher prices for the highest levels of CRM.
- Position CRM as the tool for discriminating among customers, different levels of services, and multiple price levels.

Thus get ready for multiple positioning strategies as on-line service providers, especially bank marketers, use mobile phones, m-commerce, and the wireless Internet for all sorts of financial transactions among preferred on-line customers, such as twenty-somethings or Gen-Y info-tech geeks, entertainers, and professional athletes. Add more positioning strategies for older age groups and give them additional follow up personal services via the telephone. Effective positioning flows from effective targeting and both flow from effective segmentation. More on this below.

INTRODUCTION

Here's our positioning strategy:

- Deepen brand equity of on-line stock brokers by making these brands relevant to values and lifestyles of customers. Insist brand names meet the expectations of younger, upwardly mobile professionals (or the Gen-Y age group) users of on-line stock-trading for risk, income and wealth creation. Reinforce the creation and delivery of value for both wired and wireless users of on-line stock-trading.

- Make brand names for interactive PCs and TVs relevant to the values and lifestyles of Gen-Y entertainers and professional athletes. Offer them short messaging and email services. Insist interactive content take a page from on-line stock-trading before investments are made in the alliances of Hollywood and Silicon Valley firms.

- Build up brand name recognition for Internet banking. Make these Internet bank brand names relevant to the values and lifestyles of target groups. Employ the *new* marketing concept to train potential customers about the benefits of m-Internet banking, especially those age groups who are familiar with on-line stock-trading. Don't rush the move to on-line Internet banking because most customers with money are uneasy with the concept and will not make the move in their lifetimes.

- Ensure that the brands for on-line stock-trading, interactive content for PCs and TVs, and m-Internet banking have careful definition, clear and meaningful differentiation, insightful deepening of the brand's connection to users and their lifestyles, and a disciplined defense of the brand name. Test all of these brands with a real options analysis. Then decide which investments to pursue, which to postpone, and which to terminate.

CUSTOMIZE CONTENT

So, what happens when m-commerce providers move from dubious predictions to better choices and then to customizing content? The reality is that brand expectations (in the form of awareness, relevance and equity), product opportunities (in the form of handheld devices, databases on the Web, and PC software), and media-rich content (in the form of chat, interactive TV and outsourced broadband information) don't last long. This fast-paced growth in the expansion phase of the product life cycle, which is usually diagrammed as a concave curve rather than the traditional S curve, affects all users, business firms, and government decision-makers. Many substitutes exist, come and go quickly, and are never heard from again. This is especially true in m-commerce and the wireless Internet business.

Today, m-commerce has created a business environment in which firms face open boundaries, greater flexibility, and more-focused market decisions. They sub-contract more even up to the point in which some never touch products because their inward and outward supply chains are totally outsourced. The value chains of some companies look like a piece of Swiss cheese in which the holes are filled by suppliers, partners and dealmakers.

Therefore, no m-commerce businesses are planned to last forever. Their executives have an option to pursue target markets and invest in content that lives on-line only for a short time. To keep content too long on-line means to be out of date and opens the firm's market space to newer, more aggressive competitors. In haste, these firms create value, exploit its opportunities, and make it obsolete with new products and services. If their first round investments don't run out of cash, the "burn rate," and instead keep revenues ahead of expenses, then the option to postpone some target markets and switch investments should be reconsidered and joined together with the current set of pursue and invest options. These options require further rounds of investments from venture capitalists who look for newer and better opportunities wherever they may be. All they require is speed. Do the deal fast. If it is better and cheaper, fine, but speed is essential. Successful m-commerce firms must be able to accelerate quickly and capture opportunities as soon as they become a reality. Their organizational structure must serve marketing strategy and m-commerce opportunities. That is the reality of the wireless Internet.

ACTIONABLE POSITIONING

Here are the crucial questions. How do marketers customize expectations, opportunities, and content? Providers that buy or lease content do a better job customizing content for users than those providers trying to create new content on their own. Teenagers and upwardly mobile twenty-something professionals prefer to buy their Internet services from the former. They obtain a wide variety of content choices from this first group of providers. Once 3G is widely available, both target groups will want to interact with the content and change it to suit their own needs. They perceive that they have the best chance of being interactive with content by subscribing to the services of providers who buy or lease content. The aim of the younger target groups is to be as interactive as possible. Therefore, marketers must customize content based on the expectations of users.

How fast is the expansion phase of the product life cycle for content? If providers do customize content based on the expectations of users, then the curve will have a fast-past concave shape rather than the slower S curve. How do marketers deal with open boundaries and greater flexibility? They employ the *new* marketing concept, create a *new* marketing organization, and prepare a *new* marketing strategy. Let's look a some guidelines for carrying out positioning effectively.

THE 4 Ds MODEL OF POSITIONING

Successful positioning involves affiliating a brand with some category that customers can readily grasp, and differentiating the brand from other products that belong to the same category. For example, AOL, Yahoo! and Pacific Century Cyberworks are three brand names in the fixed wired category. Both AOL and Yahoo! buy or lease content whereas Pacific Century Cyberworks is investing in new studios to create its own content. These are two different marketing strategies and users must decide which they prefer. Also NTT DoCoMo's iMode and Vodafone's GSM are two brand names in the fixed wireless category. They too buy or lease content rather than create it for users. The AOL-DoCoMo fixed-wireless alliance differentiates these brands from others in the wired and wireless categories.

Then marketers should draft a positioning statement that is product-focused, sets the product within an attribute-defined category, and shows executives how to measure the success of the product within the category. Here are the four positioning tasks that should be included in a positioning statement.

Definition

Positioning means the careful definition of what is the brand. America Online (AOL) is the world's largest Internet service provider (ISP). NTT DoCoMo is one of the world's leading mobile phone operators. Together, they have joined in a strategic alliance which gives AOL a way to expand its reach through wireless terminals other than PCs, and offers NTT DoCoMo iMode mobile Internet service a higher profile outside Japan. This partnership takes the Internet beyond the dial-up PC connection into other Internet appliances, such as mobile wireless phones and, sometime soon, interactive TV. The launch of AOL's instant messenger service on iMode will be the killer application for 13 million iMode subscribers who want to chat similar to AOL's 24 million US subscribers and AOL Japan's almost 500,000 Japanese subscribers. The outcome is for AOL Japan to become a really powerful brand, and for AOL in the US to gain a foothold in the wireless Internet. AOL will use the funds from its alliance with NTT DoCoMo to buy more content.

Both brands are well defined in the minds of their users. The alliance gives additional definition to the brand names AOL and NTT DoCoMo. Content users have expectations about the two brands, are aware of their importance to shifting how connections are made to the Internet, and users can now see their relevance to a substantial change in the *new* interactive lifestyle coming down the road in 2001.

Differentiation

Also positioning means a clear and meaningful differentiation from similar products. The AOL-NTT DoCoMo partnership differentiates itself by offering Internet services through both PCs and cellular phones. This is called "fixed-wireless convergence." The partners will take their alliance into another joint venture between DoCoMo and the Dutch-controlled cellular provider, KPN Mobile NV, so AOL's fixed wire service and DoCoMo's wireless service are both in Europe together, and then they will take their partnership into the US, too.

Through the deal with DoCoMo AOL gets ahead of its rival, Yahoo!, in seeking a crucial foothold in the Japanese, European and US wireless markets. Also AOL moves more quickly into the unknown in seeking ways to predict consumer habits in a world of changing technologies. Moreover, the marriage between AOL and DoCoMo combines content with two types of telecom services, wired and wireless carriage. With AOL's instant messaging service, users now have an open line of immediate communication among target groups of AOL users and with DoCoMo users, too. Tie this to the future interactive capability of the alliance versus those from competitors, such as Disney and Vivendi Universal. Thus AOL-DoCoMo may eventually gain collective dominance over other providers, especially Pacific Century Cyberworks, which creates English-language content in London for a largely Mandarin- and Cantonese-language audience.

Deepening

Moreover, positioning means an insightful deepening of the brand's connection to goods and services over time. With about 500,000 subscribers in Japan, AOL is far behind Fujitsu's Nifty service which boasts 2.3 million subscribers. DoCoMo gives AOL Japan deep pockets and 13 million subscribers from which to buy language content in the main East Asian languages as well as English. Of course, DoCoMo gets AOL's email and instant messaging service. For both brands, the frame of reference is more than the product category, because it includes the goals and values of national target groups, and similar market segments across national frontiers.

Clearly more chat means less phone use. Chat or instant messaging service allows real-time conversations between on-line parties by typing out messages on keyboards, and these appear instantaneously on the computer screens of recipients, or AOL's list of buddies. Instant messaging means no more phone tag, the bane of most fast-paced, upwardly mobile professionals. It has become so popular that most observers think that chat by instant messages will be the killer application for the fixed-wireless alliance between AOL and DoCoMo.

Disciplined defense

Finally, positioning means the disciplined defense of the position as competitors react and consumer tastes change. Are there contenders for AOL's market share besides Yahoo!? Yes. Richard Li, Hong Kong's media mogul, is building studios for his Network of the World in a former shoe polish factory on the outskirts of West London in the UK. Here he hopes to create English-language content for a market that speaks Mandarin, Japanese, Cantonese, Korean, Bahasa, Hindi, Tamil and other languages prevalent in East Asia. Li's Cyberworks wants to become a one-stop provider of connections and content from software to IP backbones. This puts Li's firm in competition with the global media giants (such as, Disney, Vivendi Universal, and AOL/Time Warner) as well as local producers, an almost impossible situation for Cyberworks.

To overcome this problem, Li tried to make deals with others (CMGI, Telstra and Giga), but they pulled out, sought better terms, or dragged their feet in going forward. His mastery of news flow in late 1999 and early 2000 was unparalleled – that is, until investors took a second look at the debt Pacific Century Cyberworks took on to buy Hong Kong Telecom from the UK's Cable & Wireless, and the latter decided to sell the first tranche of its newly acquired stock in Cyberworks.

So in September 2000 stock pickers decided they wanted tangible progress, not promises about the unique content Cyberworks could create in the future. Some of them saw Li's firm as a tried and true telephone utility. A few of them lamented their trading losses by thinking of Cyberworks as a beatified shell company, one in which Richard Li used the earlier heady valuations of Internet stocks to raise money to buy real assets.[2]

This is where AOL comes in. It offers a better alternative. AOL provides the wired platform, email, and instant messaging services. Then AOL goes into an alliance with NTT DoCoMo in which AOL gets access to a wireless platform, too. For both platforms AOL buys or leases multi-language content from others. It does not make investments in studios nor does it seek to create wholly new content. AOL's marketing strategy is different than the strategy of Cyberworks. This is how AOL defends itself against Cyberworks.

In summary, AOL already has 24 million subscribers worldwide and another 13 million DoCoMo users in Japan who are ready to join AOL's commanding lead in market share among teenagers and upwardly mobile twenty-something professionals. Cyberworks has no such commitments from these two important target groups. Also AOL does not need to make large-scale investments in studios as is the case with Cyberworks. Moreover, AOL will not create content as is the plan of Cyberworks for its London studios. Instead, AOL buys or leases content from anywhere in the world. This *new* marketing strategy of AOL is the only one that commands respect from investors and users alike for the future of interactive PC and TV connections.

REAL OPTIONS

Positioning is the discipline of matching up the expectations of target groups with the product offerings of business firms. Together, they depend upon the awareness of brand names and the relevance of these products to the habits, attitudes and lifestyles of customers. Positioning forms brand communities among like users. Can marketers take this information to make their product or service the dominant one in the product-attribute category? The positioning options for content providers are as follows.

Option 1: pursue younger upwardly mobile professionals and invest in providers that buy or lease content or both.

First, pursue those target groups (e.g., teenagers and young upwardly mobile twenty-something professionals) that are the best set of potential customers for new fixed-wireless service.

Second, recognize these users as a brand community. Let's call them AOL buddies and their new DoCoMo and KPN friends.

Third, use the *new* 4 Ps marketing strategy to gain sales from members of the AOL–DoCoMo–KPN brand community.

First round investments

Fourth, invest in those content providers who can accomplish the following marketing tasks:

- Create competitive transparency. Recognize that goods and services from content providers tend to be the same in the minds of buyers. This is the *new* approach of marketers towards product marketing.
- Establish financial nakedness. Deliver the lowest possible prices and minimum transaction costs for goods and services from content providers, because users demand this competitive pricing structure in return for maximum purchases. This is the *new* approach of marketers towards price marketing.
- Put in place distribution exposure. Provide the maximum number of suppliers and minimum inventory levels, because customers insist on success in fulfillment or the delivery of accurate orders. This is the *new* approach of marketers towards place marketing.
- Raise up marketing openness as the norm for customers who want promotion and advertising to provide information rather than new entry barriers. This is the *new* approach of marketers to promotion marketing.

These are the ingredients of a *new* marketing strategy for those providers who buy or lease content for users, and they form the backbone of all alliances or acquisitions among wired and wireless providers for the new 3G fixed wireless service. Build this base first before moving on to other target groups.

Option 2: postpone the pursuit of other, slightly older thirty-something professionals until it is clear they will switch to the new 3G technology and go interactive, too

Fifth, postpone the pursuit of other target groups (slightly older thirty-something mid-career professionals and forty-something senior executives) until it is clear they will switch to the new 3G technology and go interactive, too. Some of them may be less willing to switch to the new 3G technology because they have established their routine social patterns with existing wired or wireless services or both. Until their careers are threatened by their failure to adapt to technological change and to accept wholeheartedly the diffusion of fixed-wireless service, these target groups will remain the second best set of potential customers for new interactive telecom services.

Future rounds of investments

Sixth, if and when most other target groups are willing to accept fixed-wireless interactive 3G technology as part of their lifestyle (i.e., mass market penetration), seek additional funds for new rounds of investments in those content providers who have done the best job in rolling out the *new* marketing strategy for users at home and abroad.

What are investors willing to pay for?

Today, AOL Japan in alliance with Japan's NTT DoCoMo has the best chance for first-round success in fixed-wireless service. The reasons are obvious. AOL has 24 million American and worldwide subscribers for dial-up wired service, a very long list of buddies for instant messages, email, and access to whatever content its subscribers want AOL to buy or lease; of course, AOL Japan has only about 500,000 subscribers, but the opportunity to gain many more. DoCoMo has 13 million Japanese subscribers for iMode wireless service, a very long list of local Japanese content providers, instant messages, and email. Together, AOL and DoCoMo will be the largest fixed-wireless service in Japan, and expand their competitive service to both Europe and the US.

AOL and DoCoMo are good first-round investments. Investors should take an option in their future success. If Yahoo! gets a good wireless partner and if Vodafone's recent deal with China Mobile works out well, these will be good second or future rounds of investment. Investors should consider taking an option in their future successes, too. Why? No one knows how well all the competitors will do. Some will do very well. Others will do OK. Still others will fall by the wayside. Cyberworks seems to be out of the running for a competitive position in fixed-wireless service.

What do I get?

Let's look at the possible forecasts. Which ones will have doubling success, a rapid rise in the expansion phase of the product life cycle, present investors with a concave curve in sales revenue, and double-digit growth in long-term profits? Which ones will have amplifying success, a slower rise in the expansion phase of the product life cycle, present investors with an S curve in sales revenue, and single-digit growth in medium-term profits? Which ones will have continuing success, a very slow rise in the expansion phase of the product life cycle with the possibility that first-move advantage will be lost, and almost low real growth in short-term profits?

Obviously, investors want to put their money into investments in which marketers can guarantee a doubling success. Tom Perkins, the legendary co-founder of Kleiner, Perkins, Caulfield & Byers, once explained that his venture capitalist partners invest only in companies that create products or services that are ten times faster, cheaper or more convenient than the competition. "Unless a product or service is several orders of magnitude more valuable for users, it will be difficult to get them to switch over to something new."[3] Doubling success comes about when marketers use the *new* marketing strategy to gain sales among the most probable customers within the brand community for fixed-wireless services. Let's see how this will work out in several different industries.

INTERACTIVE TV

The number of interactive TV viewers in early 2001 is low, a mere 3.5 million subscribers to Microsoft's WebTV service and Excite@Home. Yet the number of subscribers will increase fast. Forrester Research predicts that by 2003, 71 percent of all business enterprises and 33 percent of all households will have broadband access; the firm also predicts that by 2004, program guides, enhanced broadcasts, and TV-based browsing will generate US $11 billion in ads and $7 million in commerce.[4] This is the beginning of the creation of new market space in Web TV and its speedy re-creation several times over as Internet TV during the expansion phase of the product life cycle.

The first target groups to buy Internet TV service will be some of AOL's 24 million on-line subscribers and some of its 62-million-strong instant messaging audience. Also add some of NTT DoCoMo's 13 million on-line Japanese subscribers. Moreover, throw in whoever in Europe and the US buys into their alliance, and you find the riches discovered by the venture capital firms. The numbers for set-top boxes (from Phillips Consumer Electronics) that connect to cable boxes, video recorders and phone lines, and for AOL's monthly fee will be significant within one year or two.

Both Yahoo!, which already offers daily interactive broadcast content on financial markets through PC connections, and Rupert Murdoch's News Corporation, whose satellite system reaches about 65 percent of the world's viewing public and will be converted into an Internet service provider, will compete directly with AOL. Nevertheless, AOL and News Corporation have an inherent advantage over Yahoo!, because they both can produce and deliver content. The others cannot do both things for interactive TV.

Real options

AOL has the commanding lead in the US as a deliverer of content and a producer of content (through its acquisition of Time Warner) over fixed wired lines. Through its alliance with DoCoMo, AOL gains the same commanding lead in Japan over wireless. Together, they will take their fixed-wireless convergence into Europe and the US. Right now a small set of similar market segments across national frontiers has AOL-DoCoMo customers ready to interact with their television sets and PCs. Here's where the first round of investments should go by venture capitalists and stock pickers alike. However, these investments are being postponed; because of the problems discussed below, and the wait-and-see attitude over the future of LivePlanet.

News Corporation has the same type of lead outside the US in satellite-based wired service. Its subsidiary, Sky Digital, offers interactive betting on horse races in Europe. Along with Canal Plus, a Vivendi Universal subsidiary, Sky Digital's interactive TV horse race betting is popular with young twenty-something men. About seven million European homes currently have set-top boxes for interactive TV, and one-half of them tune in and bet on the horse races while the rest get customized weather reports, consult electronic program guides, send email, change camera angles, replay sports segments, access text formation, order pay-per-view films and sports events.[5] Yet most Europeans prefer passive TV watching to active interactive TV participation; they do not want to work at making the technology perform properly at home.

In the US, direct broadcast satellite (DBS) operators, such as EchoStar and Direct TV, now have 13 percent share of the cable TV market. The forecast is for them to double their market share by 2003. News Corporation wants to buy DirectTV from GM's subsidiary, Hughes Electronics; however, Disney, NBC and Viacom are also potential buyers. According to Jimmy Schaeffler, the founder of the Carmel Group, he forecasts DirectTV to control 61 percent of the direct-to-home market and EchoStar to take 39 percent of the market.[6]

Even though News Corporation has a deal with Taiwan-based Giga for additional wired-based content, it does not have a deal in place with anyone to deliver content over the wireless Internet. This is unfortunate. If it had a wireless connection, News Corporation would be a competitor on par with AOL-DoCoMo. Without such a link, News Corporation is a second best option. To put it another way, News Corporation joins the ranks of postpone options in which a second round of investments could be made once News Corporation puts a few additional pieces of fixed-wireless service together for its subscribers.

Yahoo!, Microsoft's Web TV, and Excite@Home all exist in the realm of options to postpone or eventually terminate – that is, until some information comes along that shows these firms can give investors a concave expansion curve and a doubling of yearly earnings. The same is true for many content only firms, such as Atom Films and TheFeedRoom; they should be watched when and if the Internet market space takes another turn at re-creating itself. Moreover, if Bertelsmann AG, the German media giant, or Pacific Century Cyberworks is able to buy EMI, the world's third largest music company, then they may be put in play once again as firms to look at in terms of future rounds of investments by venture capitalists.

Without an m-commerce and wireless Internet strategy, most of these firms will end up as also-rans in the race to deliver interactive content in the homes of Web subscribers. Today, the AOL-DoCoMo alliance has the best chance to make interactive TV happen for them and their investors. News Corporation and Vivendi Universal are next in line for success. The rest have fallen behind and may never catch up.

INTERNET BANKING

Can investors get a better return by investing in m-banks? Are the products and services from Internet banks ten times faster, substantially cheaper or more convenient than those from interactive TV or other Internet industries? Are e-financial services several orders of magnitude more valuable for users? Will national target groups be willing to switch over from traditional teller-driven banking or PC-based home banking to m-banking for their mortgages, stock-trading, their small and medium enterprise corporate accounts, and their personal high-interest account balances? Are m-bankers creating new market space?

Actionable positioning

Is it possible for m-bank marketers to create a doubling success from a *new* marketing strategy that positions financial products and services for one or more target groups? Let's list the possible m-banking scenarios and determine the target groups the most likely to use all or some m-banking financial products and services, or none at all:

- Those who use all possible Internet banking services. Young upwardly mobile professional twenty-somethings (or Gen-Y) who already use mobile phones, wireless laptops, and PDAs for stock-trading, B2B industrial purchases, B2C personal shopping, data and voice communications, and for interactive sports programming via the TV and PC, are highly likely to use Internet banking. They have no technological difficulties with other forms of Internet business activity, and accept the diffusion of new technology as part of how their business and personal lifestyles will be improved with the coming of the Internet era. Gen-Y people need no inducement to switch their financial products and services to e-banking.

- Those who use some Internet banking services especially those they are familiar with through home banking via their PC. Middle-level professional thirty-somethings (or Gen-X) who use older wireless devices for some business communications, shopping transactions, and unidirectional sports and entertainment programming via the TV and PC are somewhat likely to use Internet banking. They have some difficulties with the most advanced technologies, but would be willing to learn how to gain access to many e-banking services if the training were simple, easy and convenient, and the bank gave them a cash payment for their willingness to switch from their routine banking habits to m-banking.

- Those who use just a few Internet banking services to check account balances. Younger forty-something boomers who may use mobile phones only in an emergency are not likely to use most Internet banking services. They have experience with automatic monthly deposits of pay checks and automatic monthly withdrawals for mortgage payments and utility bills, but they are reluctant to use ATM machines for cash deposits and withdrawals. Many boomers still do their basic financial transactions through teller stations at the branch bank, and know when the lines at the teller stations will be the shortest.

- Those who will not use Internet banking services. Older boomers who prefer the social interaction with tellers at the bank and who come from a generation that pays bills by cash or check, and who use a credit card for big ticket items, are unlikely to use e-banking services. They might change their minds if they were forced to pay substantial charges for maintaining

their traditional accounts at the bank, or they might switch banks altogether.

Clearly, Gen-Y twenty-somethings will put their financial accounts into m-
banking without thinking too much about the change in their routine social
practices. They will form a brand community for m-banking financial services
and, if the *new* marketing strategy is crafted carefully, some Gen-X persons
will join up as members of the brand community, too.

Actionable targeting

Gen-Y will not form a sufficient market size for the investments needed by
banks in new computer systems, middleware, and software, and the training of
personnel to double revenues each year. Also Gen-Y will not give m-Internet
banking a rapid rise in the expansion phase of the product life cycle. Moreover,
banks will have to dip into their cash reserves because venture capitalists will
not put up the additional funds required to move a traditional bank into becoming an Internet bank.

    Thus Internet banking must pick up target groups apart from Gen-Y pro-
fessionals. In many East Asian countries, women control the family's finances.
They pay bills, deposit cash, and give their husbands allowances. If these
wives are from the Gen-X thirty-something group, then bank marketers need
to prepare a *new* marketing strategy for Gen-X women with an emphasis on
safety, ease of use, and convenience. If Gen-X women join the Internet banking market, then its size will become sufficient for investors to take a new look
at making investments in Internet banking.

Actionable segmentation

In Europe, the cross-border merger of Merita-Nordbanken, a Swedish and
Finnish bank combination, is an unqualified leader in Internet banking with
1.1 million customers on-line. This means the most technologically sophisticated Gen-Y and Gen-X men and women from these two countries, plus
other Swedes and Finns who are willing to learn how to use the technology

for Internet banking are making price comparisons by a click of the mouse – shaving margins and driving down bank shares in the stock market.

Close behind is Barclays with 600,000 net users in the UK. They too hope to shift their customers out of branches and onto the Internet. As soon as possible, they will offer mobile phone Internet access and seek customers from less technologically advanced banks. Also they may expand outside the UK and undercut local brands. For example, Lloyds TSB seeks one million customers throughout Europe by 2003. Also SEB, the Swedish bank, uses small Danish and German banks that it owns to advance Internet banking across the national frontiers of the European Union. Moreover, Spain's Banco Bilbao Vizcaya Argentaria has joined with Telefonica, the Spanish telecoms company, to launch Uno-e.com with the aim of getting one million French, Italian and Portuguese customers by 2003. Many more cross-border EU deals are in the works as Europeans seek ways to join forces across the continent in building up Internet banking.

What do I get?

European banks need to cut costs through Internet banking. Their bank marketers point to actionable segmentation as the way to accomplish this important cost-cutting goal. Yet segmentation, targeting and positioning are not enough to make people use m-banking financial services. Most bank customers need something more, something exciting such as betting on horse races in Europe or using on-line banking services for initial public offerings in Hong Kong. The most recent IPO to be offered on-line was the Mass Transit Railway Corporation (MTRC) of Hong Kong in October 2000. Both HSBC (Shanghai Bank) and Hang Seng Bank saw their on-line transactions double after the MTRC's IPO, and their transaction costs drop from US $1.07 to US $0.01.[7]

Booz.Allen & Hamilton report that a typical US banking transaction by phone costs $0.54, at the ATM machine $0.27, and through the Internet $0.01. Nevertheless, American consumers seem to have a general lack of interest in switching from traditional banks to Internet-only banks. They do not see they will get very much in economic benefits from m-banking and perhaps lose a great deal in social relationships when they give up traditional banking.

Here's what banks must do in terms of the 4 Ps:

- Create competitive transparency. Recognize that financial goods and services from banks tend to be the same in the minds of buyers. Thus delivering a bill and presenting it for payment on-line must be error free; traditional banks should enter into alliances with financial service providers such as Checkfree, Intuit and the insurance companies that offer a broad array of financial services. This is the *new* approach of marketers towards bank product marketing.
- Establish financial nakedness. Deliver the lowest possible prices and minimum transaction costs for financial goods and services from banks; because users demand this competitive pricing structure in return for maximum transactions. In fact, some on-line banks, such as NetBank, pay their customers to try out the new bill payment on-line services. Others offer no-fee, interest bearing checking accounts and high money market yields for savings accounts. This is the *new* approach of marketers towards bank price marketing.
- Put in place distribution exposure. Provide the maximum number of ATM locations and types of service through mobile phones, wireless laptops, PDAs and Web TV; because customers insist on success in completing their financial transactions anytime and anywhere, or 24/7 service. This is the *new* approach of marketers towards bank place marketing.
- Raise up marketing openness as the norm for customers who want promotion and advertising to provide information rather than new entry barriers. FleetKids is one, significant example of how to teach target groups about the future of Internet banking. This is the *new* approach of marketers to bank promotion marketing.

Within North America, the Bank of Montreal, the Harris Bank, and NetBank are just a few examples on how both traditional and on-line banks are linking up with mobile phones, m-commerce and the wireless Internet. Their customers want to do their banking on the road and not just at home, and those who are most sophisticated have watched as their counterparts in Estonia, Finland, and Sweden point their electronic wallets or mobile devices at parking meters, soda machines, or at each other to pay bills. The ability to transfer money between two mobile devices or the use of smart cards will make e-banking a success story in many parts of the world whenever the 3G mobile telecom infrastructure is up and running, and the banks themselves solve their back-office information technology and software problems.

ON-LINE STOCK BROKERING

When Hong Kong banks and overseas brokerage firms, such as Charles Schwab & Co., set up Internet stock-trading accounts for local Hong Kong and mainland Chinese, and Chinese-Americans, they always try to put a lucky "8" in the account numbers. To many Chinese, the number 8 is supposed to bring good fortune. Some brokers give gold Chinese New Year pendants to customers who deposit large amounts of cash, such as US $1,888, $10,888, or $ 20,888. During the Moon Festival in September, many give out traditional moon cake pastries, too. The very smart account managers usually keep a big goldfish bowl on their desks with, as you might guess, eight goldfish in the bowl.

These Chinese play the stock market similarly to playing mah-jongg or gambling on horse racing. They trade one-and-a-half to two times as much as other investors, generating a lot of commissions for the banks and stock broker-age firms. Long-term for them is six months, or less.

Charles Schwab estimates the Chinese community in the US holds as much as US $150 billion in assets ready to be invested in the stock market. About 69 percent of Chinese-American households are hooked to the Internet. Schwab has 14 Chinese-language offices in New York, San Francisco and else-where in the country. Its Chinese-language Web site gets more than five million hits by customers either making trades, looking up quotes, and checking financial news.[8] This is another example of how Charles Schwab creates new market space.

Marketing on-line trading

Schwab uses the *new* marketing concept to promote on-line trading. It educates investors through Web-based seminars and face-to-face, and calls them "smart investors." According to Money.com, Gomez.com, and SmartMoney.com, the three ranking services of Internet brokerage firms, Schwab is always among the top five and sometimes the number one firm in terms of ease of use, customer service, system responsiveness, products and tools, and cost. Gomez.com praises Schwab for the availability of on-line information and customer service, but notes its commission schedule is a bit more expensive than other Internet brokerage firms.

Structure, strategy and performance

Schwab built up its strength by giving its IT managers an amount of power equal to that of its brokers, so together they created its advanced Web site and made the back office do its work effectively. Once these were operational, Schwab built up customer loyalty through a superior value proposition and value delivery system.

- *Product.* Schwab provides Web tools to assist investors in finding investment specialists, guides them through the fundamentals of equity research, and sends email alerts to customers.
- *Place.* Even though 70 percent of all new accounts are opened at one of the many branch offices of Schwab, about 90 percent of all trades are conducted on-line. Schwab also provides trading information and the ability to trade stock via cell phones and other wireless devices.
- *Price.* Schwab commissions are more expensive than those from other Internet firms.
- *Promotion.* Print and media ads are targeted at ethnic groups who have money to spend on stock transactions; also several sports personalities are used in the ads to capture the interest of Gen-Y and Gen-X men.

The result is nothing but success for Schwab as an on-line trading firm. Even Merrill Lynch had to take notice and go into on-line stock transactions.

Internet brokering in Japan

In October 1999, the Japanese government deregulated the Japanese stock market. Within the last 18 months Nomura, the leading Japanese broker, has set up about 400,000 on-line accounts, Daiwa 300,000, Nikko 50,000, and Nikko Beans (a joint venture with Fujitsu) 60,000. Monex, the broker backed by Sony, has almost 100,000. Charles Schwab, DLJdirect, and E*Trade Japan, which is part of Softbank, are also setting up a client base for on-line accounts.[9]

At the moment, no one is making money in Japan. The self-reference criteria of the Japanese is for safety of their money at the post office or at traditional banks. Unlike the Chinese, the Japanese do not like to gamble. As post office accounts mature, and Japanese wives look for ways to invest their family's funds, they turn to funds of US government T-bills and other highly secure government bonds. Only about ten percent of these maturing postal accounts have found their way into the Japanese stock market.[10] Also the Japanese and foreign brokers do not offer additional services, such as credit cards, insurance products, and medical services. Moreover, the on-line brokers in Japan must teach potential Japanese investors computer and financial skills. Once Web-enabled phones take over, the Japanese, who spend long hours commuting, will do more stock-trading via the Web sites of on-line brokers. NTT DoCoMo has packed its popular iMode service with many stock-brokering services.

On-line trading in Germany

Commerzbank, one of Germany's big banks, set up Comdirect to take care of its on-line stock-brokering accounts. Comdirect has been separately listed on the Neuer Markt, Germany's stock market segment for young, high-tech companies. Besides Germany, Comdirect is going into Italy because the Italians will use their mobile phones to do both direct banking and direct brokering with the bank parent and its stock broker subsidiary. Other German firms in the on-line stock-trading business include ConSors, Direkt Anlage Bank (DAB), and Deutsche Bank. In Germany, 60–70 percent of the direct brokerage customers are male, whereas the banks divide their customers at 50 percent for men and 50 percent for woman.[11] Most of Comdirect's customers have been lured away from small public-sector banks that do not offer on-line stock-trading services. They want the security of a big-named bank for on-line services.

In this regard, Germans and Japanese are more similar because they both prefer security and trust over anything else. On the other hand, the Chinese prefer to take high levels of risk and gamble several times a month on whether a stock will go up or down. Americans and British are in between these two extremes. Nevertheless, on-line stock-trading is a product that crosses national frontiers with ease because national segments exist in many countries that want to buy and sell stock on-line.

VALUE-BASED MARKETING DECISIONS

Here are the value-based decisions made by Internet banks and on-line brokerage firms that seek to improve customer relationship management. CRM means an integrated sales and marketing effort in which leads are identified, customers are kept track of in a single data base, and all executives work together as a team. Their goals are value creation, value delivery, and the creation of new market space.

What is the context of a decision?

Try to keep existing customers happy. It costs six times more to sell to new customers than to sell to existing customers. Identify the most-valuable target groups in the existing set of customers. If you increase the retention rate by 5 percent, you can boost profits by 85 percent. Also if you sell new products and services to existing customers, the chances for growing sales are better than 50 percent. Moreover, if you make a mistake and correct it quickly, 70 percent of those who complained will stay with you as existing customers.

In theory, you should keep the existing customers happy. In practice, they may not be the right kind of customers for the future. If the customers belong to the older age groups, they may have little experience in using PCs for home banking, and almost no interest in learning about Web-based Internet banking. You may want to get rid of existing customers and shift to younger, more technically qualified age groups. Then you can sell these new customers on-line stock-picking, which tends to be an easier sell, and later to on-line banking, which tends to be a harder sell.

Therefore, CRM means an integrated approach towards those customers who will deliver a rapid increase in sales and growth in profits. This is the context of decisions taken by entertainment firms to introduce interactive TV, banks to introduce Internet banking and by stock brokerages to introduce Internet stock-trading. Only Charles Schwab and other on-line stock firms have used CRM to create and deliver value.

What is the object of a decision?

Why CRM? Five core processes must be reviewed.

- Cross-selling and telemarketing must be done well.
- Both in-house and after-market service must be top notch.
- Maximum loyalty efforts must be made to retain customers.
- Customer support must be given high priority.
- Fulfillment must be done without mistakes.

Together these form a set of integrated CRM applications to acquire, enhance and retain customers.

What is the impact of a decision?

If CRM is done well, then entertainment firms, traditional banks and stock brokerages are able to match business functions with products and services used by customers. For example, banks stop thinking of themselves as banks and financial institutions, and begin looking at their work as serving customers through both traditional and on-line channels of distribution. Thus banks need kiosks at subway stations, ATMs everywhere, referral programs from all customers, call centers, merchant data, person-to-person selling, and fast Internet connections.

Decision opportunities

Interactive TV firms, Internet banks, and on-line brokerages need data warehouses to take in, assemble, and provide data on a real-time basis for all decisions. The use of data mining as the basis for decision-making is a paradigm shift for banks because they have not thought of themselves in this way. Their task is to manage financial services for consumers, trading firms, card issuers, and correspondent banks in ways not thought of before including new bill-payment systems, smart cards, back-office support, and new central databases.

In many cases, the outsourcing of IT and the use of ERP from either PeopleSoft or SAP are required for e-banks and on-line stock brokerages to be effective. These will streamline document distribution, facilitate market intelligence, and enhance team cooperation. The task is for firms, banks and brokerages to make decisions to go forward with new mobile-based IT, and then train their staff quickly in CRM and how to use the new tracking technology for ERP.

Value creation and value delivery

AOL, NTT DoCoMo, Yahoo!, Vodafone, Deutsche Telecom's On-Line, and other fixed wired and wireless services have all fully invested in the newest information technology. Some are developing partnerships in fixed-wireless services to get ready for the boom in mobile communications. For example, the AOL-DoCoMo alliance is doing a better job in value creation than other interactive firms.

Small Hong Kong banks need to invest in the latest IT. Otherwise, they will get further behind middle-sized and big Hong Kong banks. The small banks will find themselves taken over by other Hong Kong, mainland Chinese, or foreign-owned banks. Most banks seem to be unable to do a great job in value creation and value delivery. Traditional bank practices and legacy computer systems seem to get in the way of good marketing-management decisions by bankers.

Finally, Charles Schwab and other on-line stock brokerages have fully invested in the newest IT. Some are worldwide firms that have created new market space in East Asia, Europe, and the US. These on-line stock-trading firms are doing a great job in both value creation and value delivery because they have mastered IT and CRM, and put them to use in creating their new alternative channel of distribution through m-commerce and the wireless Internet.

If firms want to be stars in on-line value creation for insurance, supply management, retail services, and music, or in value delivery through new travel Web sites and new DSL, cable, and satellite portals, they too must follow the *new* marketing concept and the *new* 4 Ps marketing strategy discussed in detail in this chapter. Apply these ideas to international segmentation, national targeting and local positioning through the use of mobile phones, with m-commerce, and in the new world of the wireless Internet.

Interactive TV, Internet banks, and on-line brokerages are three good examples of both successes and failures in the new world of business that begins in 2001, takes us without too many changes to 2003, and then pushes us with many changes to 2005. After that, the world of m-commerce will be substantially different, and its distance from the present makes good forecasts suspect in the eyes of venture capital investors.

M-COMMERCE TRANSACTIONS

One of the wireless devices that takes us solidly into 2001 and should still be a great success story in 2003 is the smart card. It is a secure, portable, and tamper-resistant data-storage device. A smart card contains as much power as a minicomputer, but it is the exact size of credit card. The market for smart cards is 1.1 billion units in 2001, and the forecast for 2003 is 2.7 billion units.

What do consumers get?

Here are the benefits available to consumers from smart cards:

- convenience in transportation and rechargeable at Add Value machines, and convenience in telecommunications through GSM mobile phones;
- access to buildings;
- student and faculty identification cards, especially for borrowing library books, securing parking spaces, and paying for meals at the cafeteria;
- secure credit and debit transactions, and the ability to transfer funds from bank accounts to service providers. Multiple applications, such as medical records, frequent-flyer points, travel reservations, and personal financial information.

A smart card is compatible with PCs, mobile phones, and PDAs, and it connects any machine to the Internet.

Within closed environments, such as universities and military bases, smart cards work well. In open environments, such as the upper East Side of Manhattan, smart cards have not done well because of a lack of interest among the American public. Elsewhere in the world, such as in Paris and Hong Kong, smart cards are much more successful. Smart cards need a reader attached to a computer, a set-top box, cell phones, etc., and retail merchants and consumers alike seem to be unwilling to pay for readers.

The blue card from American Express has not been an unqualified success even though 1.5 million blue cards have been issued to American Express customers. As a consequence, American Express has started a new, alternative program: each time a customer performs an on-line shopping transaction, he or she gets a new credit card number for one-time use only. This is another way to give customers and firms the security they want in today's market. It's another example of how firms create new market space.

SWOT analysis

- *Strengths.* Most customers of firms, banks, and brokerages have credit cards. These can be converted easily into smart cards.
- *Weaknesses.* Many smart cards are already available. Many customers with credit and smart cards remain unconnected to the Internet. Some smart-card technologies are not compatible.
- *Opportunities.* Many features can be built into smart cards as customers demand more from their cards.
- *Threats.* Smart cards may be a transition technology until electronic wallets become common worldwide, as they currently are in Estonia, Finland and Sweden.

According to some analysts, smart-card usage will be driven by the proliferation of electronic technology and mobile telecom systems. They view smart cards as uniquely qualified to provide network security, offer m-commerce contracts, and provide for electronic signatures. Smart-card providers make these promises. What they don't know is whether customers accept the long-term importance of smart cards over electronic wallets or other mobile devices not yet introduced in the market. By 2005, these important decisions will have been made by customers and companies alike.

MONEY-MAKING DEALS

Let's answer the positioning questions.

Success stories

- *Are consumers aware of existing brand names in the on-line stock-trading category?*
  Yes.
- *Do customers consider these brands relevant to their values and lifestyles?*
  Yes.

- *Do these brand names meet the expectations of younger, upwardly mobile professionals (or the Gen-Y age group) users of on-line stock-trading for risk, income and wealth creation?*
Yes.
- *Do brand names, such as Charles Schwab, create and deliver value for both wired and wireless users?*
Yes.
- *Does the on-line stock-trading category offer other m-commerce categories a successful approach to employing the new marketing concept and the new 4 Ps marketing strategy in the wireless Internet world?*
Yes.

The success of stock-trading firms in creating and delivering customized content for on-line users is well known. How did these on-line brokerages jump ahead of on-line banks in the quest to create and deliver financial services? The former took to heart the *new* marketing concept, employed the *new* 4 Ps marketing strategy, and put in place a *new* marketing organization. These on-line stock-trading firms took advantage of the opportunities presented during the boom in the stock market, and made both Gen-Y and Gen-X age groups their customers for financial services. In fact, these age groups and some of the boomers now choose on-line brokerages and their money market opportunities as the only way to handle cash, savings and investments. Charles Schwab has positioned its brand name successfully in all major regions of the world. It is a good example of how effective real options analysis can be in making rounds of investment decisions.

Partial success

- *Are consumers aware of existing brand names in the unidirectional and interactive PC and TV category?*
Yes.
- *Do customers consider these brands relevant to their values and lifestyles?*
Yes.

- *Do these brand names meet the expectations of younger, upwardly mobile professionals (or the Gen-Y age group) users for on-line sports and entertainment events, and short messaging and email services?*
  Yes for some; no for others.
- *Do brand names, such as AOL, NTT DoCoMo, Yahoo! AirTouch Vodafone, and others, create value for both wired and wireless customers?*
  Some do, especially, the fixed-wireless alliance between AOL and DoCoMo.
- *Will this alliance put these two firms ahead of their competitors in the quest to deliver value to users through fixed-wireless services?*
  Yes!
- *Does the unidirectional and interactive PC and TV category need to take a page from the success of the on-line stock-trading category in how to build up another m-commerce category?*
  Yes.
- *Should the latter's successful approach to employing the new marketing concept and the new 4 Ps marketing strategy in the wireless Internet world be employed by the former category?*
  Probably yes.

Both Charles Schwab and AOL are well known brand names. However, the success of the former in creating and delivering customized content for on-line users is not as apparent in the latter's business. Why did these on-line PC and TV firms not jump as far ahead as on-line stock-trading firms in the quest to create and deliver services? Both did take to heart the *new* marketing concept, employed the *new* 4 Ps marketing strategy, and put in place a *new* marketing organization. Also the on-line stock-trading firms did take advantage of the opportunities presented during the boom in the stock market, and made both Gen-Y and Gen-X age groups their customers for financial services. Moreover, the on-line PC and TV firms are still waiting for the new 3G technology to be put in place rather than using what they have to get commitments from customers. If the two partners in the AOL-DoCoMo deal do their positioning job well, then their brand names will take their collective success from Japan to Europe and the US. Real options analysis can help in making new rounds of invest-ment decisions in the unidirectional and interactive PC and TV category.

Failures

- *Are consumers generally aware of existing brand names in the Internet bank-ing category?*
  No.
- *Do customers consider the on-line banking services these brands represent relevant to their values and lifestyles?*
  Yes.
- *Do these brand names meet the expectations of younger, upwardly mobile professionals (or the Gen-Y age group) users for on-line financial services?*
  No.
- *Do the brand names of traditional banks create value for the customers of Net banking?*
  Some do, especially, the very big banks such as HSBC, Citibank, and Deutsche Bank.
- *Will their on-line banking initiatives put any of these traditional banks ahead of their competitors in the quest to deliver value to users through fixed-wireless services?*
  No. None of them have put their mark on the on-line financial banking business.
- *Does the Internet banking category need to take a page from the success of the on-line stock-trading category in how to build up another m-commerce category?*
  Yes.
- *Should the latter's successful approach to employing the new marketing con-cept and the new 4 Ps marketing strategy in the wireless Internet world be employed by the former category?*
  Probably, yes.
- *Should traditional banks go into an alliance with on-line brokerage firms for the purpose of creating and delivering value to customers?*
  Yes.

Traditional banks must employ new approaches towards product, price, place and promotion marketing. These are respectively labeled: competitive transparency, financial nakedness, distribution exposure, and marketing openness. Back-office support, IT and CRM are crucial to the success of the *new* 4 Ps marketing strategy for all on-line businesses, especially the traditional banks that want to deliver Internet banking to their customers.

Newest on-line opportunities

HSBC (known as the Shanghai bank in Hong Kong) claims it has made it to the global top five "favorites list" with its on-line banking service. This traditional bank targets the mass affluent group of investors who have between US $100,000 and $400,000 in assets available for stock investments. HSBC divides them into two specific target groups:[12]

- One group is self-directed and comfortable with doing things on a PC, its members tending to make their own investment decisions. They are upwardly mobile, professionals who range in age from Gen-Y, through Gen-X, to young boomers, and who have made a great deal of money in computers, software and the Internet. HSBC thinks this target group will make up about 25 percent of the total mass affluent group of investors in the UK, more in East Asia, and lots more in the US. Of course, HSBC's footprint is strongest in Hong Kong, the UK and Europe, and weakest in the US.

- Members of the other group are not used to doing things on a PC nor to making their own money management decisions. HSBC believes this target group will make up the rest of the total mass affluent group of investors. HSBC uses its branches and call centers to help this target group make decisions about which funds to buy rather than to trade stocks frequently. Obviously, HSBC will not get as much transaction revenue from this target group as it does from the self-directed group.

The number of these mass affluent customers in Europe is about 40 million people. In the past, they have held their assets on deposit in low-return savings accounts. Recently, these Europeans have become more affluent through stock options, a booming stock market (especially, in the new markets for the high-tech sector), and through growth of their new economy businesses. These newly affluent Europeans are following what Americans did previously and are moving some of their financial assets to on-line brokers and mutual fund managers.[13]

HSBC together with Merrill Lynch are targeting these club class Europeans for their new joint venture, an on-line stock brokerage and Internet bank business. Credit Suisse is doing the same and calling their mass affluent customers "advice-seekers" (or self-directed customers) and "comfort-seekers" (or those who need their hands held). The Royal Bank of Scotland is pushing its National Westminster Bank subsidiary to offer similar services via the telephone and the Internet. And there is more to come as private banks in Europe take everyone into account.

The future

■ *Do some of these brands, especially in the on-line stock-trading and interactive PC and TV categories, have careful definition, clear and meaningful differentiation, insightful deepening of the brand's connection to users and their lifestyles, and a disciplined defense of the brand name?*
Yes.
■ *Are these and other m-commerce categories ready for a real options analysis?*
Yes.
■ *Can we decide which investments to pursue, which to postpone, and which to terminate?*
Yes.

SWOT analysis gives us a static, present-day view of what we have and what we can do in interactive PC and TV, Internet banking, and on-line stock-trading. SWOT is a useful tool in our analysis of AOL-DoCoMo, Deutsche-Comdirect, and Charles Schwab. However, real-options analysis is a critical tool in our analysis of how these firms and their competitors will pursue, postpone, or terminate their investment options. We need to answer two questions: What do customers get? What are investors willing to pay for in 2001, 2003 and 2005?

CONCLUSIONS

How to conquer the wireless world? Apply positioning strategies to m-commerce, especially to show how on-line stock-trading and interactive content providers can assist traditional banks in their quest to become Internet banks. Here is a checklist of things to do:

- Put all on-line business in play at one time, and compare their current and future performance through both SWOT and real options analysis.
- Build market share with a marketing positioning strategy that is carefully adapted to the ins and outs of each line of business.
- Offer new ways to create and deliver value, create new market space, and find support among venture capitalists.
- Create *new* marketing organizations for all on-line businesses worldwide, and train their executives into a transparent and open set of *new* 4 Ps marketing strategy.

Conclusions

EXECUTIVE SUMMARY

MARKETERS TRAIN M-COMMERCE CUSTOMERS to use mobile phones and to interact with unique content from the wireless Internet. The former turn the latter into true believers. This is the application of the *new* marketing concept to m-commerce. If traditional financial rules from the venture capital market are followed, marketers make money from m-commerce. These include:

- The "burn rate" of cash is no more than eight months.
- Positive cash flow starts within two years.
- Sales produce earnings in the third and following years after the initial investment.
- These financial guidelines help marketers determine whether they have implemented a successful *new* 4 Ps marketing strategy for the mobile Internet.

All together these marketing and financial rules apply equally to Japan, Europe, and the US, and also to China, India, and elsewhere in the world.

Let's review how marketers make money from m-commerce:

- They design new and different interactive content (such as, 2-D graphics, 3-D graphics, MP3, data, video, and voice) for the wireless Internet.
- They form fixed-wireless distribution alliances among telecom and content providers (e.g., NTT DoCoMo-AOL Japan). The marketers then force them to compete with other place marketing strategies, such as PC-based fixed-wired Internet, TV broadcasts and narrowcasts, satellites, cable and DSL, and DVD discs, and especially with the wireless Ethernet network.

- They turn iMode and GSM phones into miniature 3G-ready information appliances, and force them too to compete against other interactive platforms, such as wireless datapads (or PDAs), PCs, TVs, and game machines.
- They sell cell phones that cross national frontiers to the following age segments: Gen-Y (twenty-somethings), Gen-X (thirty-somethings), and boomers (forty-somethings).
- They market anytime, anywhere voice and data communications, and transaction capabilities within nation-states to the following values and lifestyles target groups: "Supli' teenage Japanese young women, unmarried American info-geeks, married European business executives, Chinese bureaucrats, and others.
- They build brand communities as product-based experiences for users by carrying out segmentation, targeting, and positioning strategies in Japan, Europe, the US, China, and elsewhere in the world.
- They put in place wireless Ethernet networks for airport lounges, hotel lobbies, and other places where high-income target groups congregate.

Best money-making deals

Let's pursue the best initial round of investments that we proposed in the Introduction and discussed in Chapters 1–6. They are listed in ranked order based on our review of their marketing and financial strengths and weaknesses. The first is definitely the best deal; the second one is second best; and the rest are in order further down the list:

1   The distribution alliance for wireless telecom connections and new interactive content between Japan's NTT DoCoMo and AOL Japan. This place marketing strategy is the best of the four deals. It has millions of subscribers, thousands of dot-com content providers, microbilling, and a walled garden to keep both DoCoMo and AOL customers coming back for more transactions, chats with 'Buddies," and daily access to favorite *manga* cartoon and Pokémon characters.

2   The use of wireless Ethernet technology for electronic wallets from the Finnish and Swedish jointly owned bank, Merita-Nordbanken. This

price marketing strategy is second best of the four deals. It has taken off only in the Nordic and Baltic countries where 50 to 75 percent of the people are tied to virtual networks through their Nokia and Ericsson Web-enabled phones. They keep using these electronic wallets for the purchase of everyday low-priced goods, medium-priced household goods, and even high-priced luxury goods.

3   The introduction of W-CDMA or CDMA 2000 from America's Qualcomm as the UMTS standard in Europe as it is for NTT DoCoMo in Japan. This product marketing strategy is third best of the four deals. Although W-CDMA or CDMA 2000 3G standard is backed by many firms, GSM has a commanding lead in the European market. It's only a matter of time before GSM converts itself into the UMTS standard and this will be strong competition for W-CDMA in Europe.

4   Web-enabled phones, whose screen or "home deck" shows books, CDs, airplane tickets, and other items to purchase, from Finland's Nokia, Sweden's Ericsson, Germany's Siemens, and America's Motorola are still several years away from perfecting their presentations on the screen. This product-marketing strategy is fourth best of the four deals. Wireless laptops, PDAs, and other new inventions may take away the wireless Internet transactions market from Web-enabled phones.

Second-best money-making deals

Let's postpone the second-best future rounds of investments. They too are listed in ranked order based on our review of their marketing and financial strengths, weaknesses, opportunities, and threats:

5   The dual-mode WAP and iMode phones from Japan's NTT DoCoMo and its Dutch partner, KPN, seems like a good second-best solution to multiple, incompatible standards. The costs of producing the dual-mode phone are higher. Customers say they want dual-mode phones. However, they are unavailable. Hence, marketers have no record of sales from which to make a forecast. The revenue stream from Europe is unknown.

6   3G wireless investments in the US wireless market are still "blue sky" proposals for which no spectrum has been allocated by the US federal government and no agreement has been reached among telecom providers over a universal standard. Also American customers for mobile phones do not think they want cell phones, and up to 70 percent of the US population gets along with landline connections.

7   Wireless portals generally and those in Europe, such as Vizzavi, go head-to-head with one another. A shakeout is bound to occur in these portals, and it is not clear that this one will become the dominant portal in Europe, or whether portals as surfing devices survive the rush to mobile devices.

8   Traditional banks are trying to set up m-Internet banks, but they are facing strong customer resistance among most target groups.

Prediction about wireless investments

Do remember the investments now being made in an innovative and highly disruptive technology called the wireless Ethernet network. Aerzone and Wayport are putting this type of wireless network in place for the Red Carpet Clubs of United Airlines, the lobbies of five-star hotels, and intranets for business offices, university campuses, and Starbucks coffee shops.

If Aerzone, Wayport, and others who sell wireless Ethernet networks produce burn rates of eight months or less, positive cash flow within two years, and earnings from sales in the third and following years, then existing fixed-wireless and other wireless technologies will become second-best options for investors. The wireless Ethernet network is the most important, new, disruptive technology to come along that it may be the deal breaker for all other m-commerce investments by telecom and content providers in the world of the mobile Internet. If this prediction comes true, the US may jump ahead of Japan's iMode and Europe's GSM by the year 2003. The wireless Ethernet network is so significant as an innovative technology that all bets are off for the years between 2003 and 2005. Let's watch together as the future unfolds.

Recommendations

Marketers spend a great deal of time creating and delivering value about mobile phones, m-commerce, and the wireless Internet. However, the devil is in the details. Throughout the book, we examine how and when interactive content, distribution, and platforms morph into interactive m-sports, m-entertainment, on-line stock-trading, m-banking, and other possible money-making mobile Internet deals. Sometimes, events get in the way and turn good predictions into less than stellar results. Nevertheless, when all is said and done – that is, in about ten years – the mobile wireless Internet will replace the fixed-wired Internet, because telecom providers want users to start paying for the content they now are getting free of charge from today's PC-based Internet system. This is one prediction marketers will place their money on as they create and deliver value for the mobile Internet.

Marketing assignment

First, marketers apply the *new* marketing concept to teach customers how to use mobile phones, m-commerce, and the mobile Internet as telecom and content providers introduce 3G wireless technology in Japan, Europe, the US, and elsewhere in the world. Second, marketers adjust their *new* 4 Ps marketing strategy as they watch how customers actually use miniature information appliances to enhance their lifestyles. Finally, marketers put together a *new* marketing organization in which providers become members of an open-ended wireless alliance.

Here is a summary of the recommendations in the book for how marketers *create and deliver value* for m-commerce. The companies discussed throughout the book are examples of how business firms are changing the rules of the telecommunications game.

CHAPTER #1: PRODUCT MARKETING

Get ready for a big expansion in the demand for m-commerce in 2001 in Japan, 2003 in Europe, and 2005 in the US. Marketers target the rich mass affluents and the upwardly mobile, relatively affluent customers with 3G-based smart wireless devices that incorporate location awareness, voice and data communications, and transaction capabilities.

- *Key phrase.* Roll out international wireless products, such as cell or mobile phones, or miniature information appliances, or both.
- *Crucial marketing strategy.* During the expansion phase of the product life cycle, the rapid introduction of new digital 3G-based mobile phone products permits customers to transmit voice and data communications, and complete secure m-commerce transactions quickly.
- *Recommendations.* Introduce new mobile phones ahead of competitors. Upgrade them as miniature information appliances on a continuous basis. Grow by offering customer-centered product designs, such as multi-colored phones, and support services, such as microbilling, to capture the network economies of the wireless or mobile Internet.

International wireless products

So many products, so many choices, and too little clarity as to which platforms, methods of distribution, and content will become the strongest competitor in the race to dominate the mobile Internet. Within a short time, cell phones went from being expensive toys to commodities; Motorola guessed wrong and its earnings took a dive, whereas Nokia made a good guess and its recent earnings are strong. Dot-coms went from being investment darlings to facing hard economic facts that they too had to show positive cash flow within two years of their start-up. Qualcomm's CDMA technology lost the mainland Chinese market, and then found it again with the help of China's entry into the World Trade Organization. Also the firm's W-CDMA technology, which is used in Japan, could become the UMTS standard in Europe. GSM, which is used throughout Europe, also could morph into the UMTS standard. Confusion reigns among telecom and content providers as they try to sort out how 3G technology will be introduced worldwide.

However, customers don't care about the technology. They just want to use the technology to talk with one another, get data on trades, and carry out transactions. The problem is that mobile Internet providers don't have a clue what customers really want from m-commerce and the wireless Internet. Chapters 1–6 lay out a road map for marketers on how to find out what customers want, and then how to implement the latter's choices for the mobile Internet. With hard work, lots of money, and a little bit of luck, m-commerce will be up and running in Japan in 2001, Europe in 2003, and in the US in 2005.

Real options

Here are a few investment choices.

3G cell or mobile phones, or miniature information appliances

- Pursue Nokia.
- Postpone Ericsson and Siemens.
- Terminate Motorola.

3G technology infrastructure

- Pursue Qualcomm's W-CDMA or CDMA 2000 so long as one of them merges into the universal standard, or UMTS.
- Postpone WAP unless it too merges into UMTS, or becomes one of the two dual modal links into the universal standard of UMTS.
- Terminate AT&T's TDMA and other technologies that do not have sufficient possible users to show sustainable market share in the major markets of the world.

CHAPTER #2: PROMOTION MARKETING

Pay attention to the alliance of NTT DoCoMo-AOL Japan. Marketers push DoCoMo's popular iMode wireless technology and AOL's widely used "Buddies List" throughout Japan, sometime soon into Europe, and much later into the US, China, and elsewhere in the world. Within three to five years, users will be of sufficient size to pull this partnership of connections and content through the alternative channel of distribution now known as the fixed-wireless or mobile Internet. Eventually, wireless m-commerce, perhaps through a wireless Ethernet network, will replace the current PC-based, fixed-wired Internet.

- *Key phrase.* Alliance of connections and content for cell or mobile phones, and other miniature information appliances.
- *Crucial marketing strategy.* Conquer new market space through the promotion and advertising of fixed-wireless, satellite-based, and Ethernet network-based m-commerce so that the expansion phase of the product life cycle is a fast-paced concave curve rather than a slower-paced "S" curve.
- *Recommendations.* Open up and interlink platforms, distribution, and content. Put together an entrepreneurial network that includes telecom providers, contract manufacturing, content providers, venture capitalists, order fulfillment, and sophisticated management advice. Grow by purchasing support services to capture the scale economies of the mobile Internet.

New market space through alliances

So many marketing opportunities, expectations and questions, but only a few good decisions so far. AOL's walled garden in which it branded its content (such as "You got mail," sports scores, entertainment news, stock analyses, gift buying, playing whatever, and many other items) was a window in time that other portals and telecom firm now want to open once again. Users want longer connect times to do all these things either via a DSL line hooked up to their PC, a cable modem wired into their TV, or a wireless Ethernet connection. Also customers can't wait for AOL to become a universal Internet telephone carrier and replace the current list of telecom providers. AOL, Yahoo! and other portals see themselves as the last guys standing in the fight to keep Web customers and their transaction revenues within the walled gardens of the portals, and to keep the telecom carriers from getting any or most of these mobile wireless revenues. The name of the game is burn rates, positive cash flow, sales, and earnings. AOL buys Time-Warner today, and perhaps AT&T tomorrow. Vodafone and Vivendi create the Web portal, Vizzavi, and Telefonica of Spain buys the Web portal, Lycos. Everything is up for grabs in the mobile Internet business.

M-commerce has become a movable feast. Technological change, removal of the barriers to enter the industry and reductions in the mobility barriers within the industry, shifts in customer demand, and the lack of a clear first-mover advantage among wired telecom carriers, portals, or wireless Internet firms combine to make profit a moving target. Value creation and value delivery continue to migrate from the old to the new, from the past perfect to the future perfect, from size, scale and market share to the unknown answer of a customer's basic marketing question: "What do I get?" At present, victory in the creation of new market space comes in the flexibility of the concept, the focus on revenue, and a great business design for capturing customers and putting them within the walled garden. Bigger is not always better, but big and broad connections may do the trick in the new world of the mobile Internet.

Real options

Here are some investment choices.

Fixed-wireless acquisitions and partnerships

- Pursue Vodafone's GSM acquisitions of AirTouch and Mannesmann, and NTT DoCoMo's W-CDMA alliance with the Dutch-owned telecom, KPN.
- Postpone Deutsche Telecom's GSM acquisition of VoiceStream Wireless, and postpone the GSM and CDMA alliances of Vodafone and Qualcomm respectively with local Chinese firms.
- Terminate nothing because all partnerships, alliances and equity deals are up for grabs.

Fixed-wireless Internet connections and the purchase of content

- Pursue the alliance of NTT DoCoMo-AOL Japan; and the alliances of telecom companies with hotels, airlines, stock brokers, banks, and other service providers.
- Postpone the alliance of Sprint-Yahoo!; Sprint's links with Amazon.com, Bloomberg, Fidelity, and, most recently AOL; and Yahoo!'s acquisition of the content-formatting firm Online Anywhere.

- Terminate Pacific Century Cyberworks's fruitless attempts to create content on its own.

Businesses that get a place on the wireless screen or the "home deck" and take a cut on every book, CD, or plane ticket sold via the mobile Internet

- Pursue Japanese telecoms (such as NTT) and European handset makers (such as Nokia) who have the best access to the pockets of local users.
- Postpone US telecoms, such as Sprint, Verizon, and other Baby Bells who sell both mobile phones and rate plans to users with deep pockets, but do not have the technology in place to take advantage of 3G m-commerce.
- Terminate nothing because the telecom providers, which get zero revenue for transactions and advertising on the installed-based of the fixed-wired Internet, will demand substantial revenues from the content sold over the wireless Internet.

CHAPTER #3: PRICE MARKETING

Watch marketers compete for twenty-somethings Gen-Y because this age group wants interactive sports and entertainment, on-line stock-trading, and m-banking via their mobile phones. Also study how marketers seek market share from thirty-somethings Gen-X because this age group wants on-line stock-trading. Moreover, observe how marketers postpone a hard sell on forty-somethings boomers because this age group is slower to shift from the PC-based fixed-wired Internet to the cell phone-based fixed-wireless or the mobile Internet. Finally, note how marketers terminate investments for older age groups because they have more difficulty with technological diffusion.

- *Key phrase.* Decisions about training all age groups on how to use mobile phones or miniature information appliances or both.
- *Crucial marketing strategy.* Lower the cost of handsets for teenagers through commodity pricing, and capture additional revenue from them and business executives by selling "always on" connections, customer-centered content, and microbilling plans for m-commerce.

▦ *Recommendations.* Organize viable value propositions around price transparency. Put together different offerings for voice, video or data transport; with or without information, sports or entertainment services; delivered over cable, copper, or optical landlines or using fixed-wireless or satellite technologies; or wireless Ethernet networks to residential or business customers. Grow by crossing technology, industry, and market boundaries to capture scope economies for the wireless Internet.

4 Ps marketing decisions

There have been few good marketing decisions so far because even teenagers and twenty-somethings are still learning how to navigate the wireless Web. Today's walled gardens of US telecom carriers and their content partners are similar to the homepages for Netscape and Microsoft as default settings on browsers. Users eventually found a way to pick their own start pages for the wired Internet. According to Amanda McCarthy of Forrester Research, US:

> *"... carriers won't be able to outrun content aggregators ... Users will discover how to avoid a carrier's content as new technologies like voice browsing let users navigate the mobile Internet more easily. By 2003 ... content providers will have no need to cut revenue deals with the carriers."[1]*

Both AT&T and Verizon resell airtime to the ISPs, such as GoAmerica and OmniSky, so the latter's content on Palm and Pocket PCs may become important wireless brands. The carriers get some revenue to use in their long-distance and cable businesses, and the content aggregators get the rest of the revenue to build up their brand names. In the early years, the competitive market will have too much supply chasing too little demand.

In fact, demand is unknown. Whether users will want the content offered by carriers, aggregators, and others within their walled gardens is unknown. Whether users will pay for content that looks and feels similar to content from free sources is debatable. Basically demand cannot be measured or quantified.

Hence, marketers don't know whether demand is large enough in numbers of users to be sustainable over time. Both telecom carriers and content aggregators could be moving targets ready to fold once something better comes along.

Nokia and other manufacturers of mobile phones, miniature information appliances, and handheld devices have begun to put Web links into their smart cell phones. They too are forming partnerships with content providers and, even more importantly, with on-line merchants, such as brokerages, banks, hotels, airlines, supply chains, retailers, and local transit firms.

Which group has content as its core competency? Not the wired and wireless telecom providers, such as AT&T, Verizon and Sprint. Their dumb fat pipes are no match for handheld information appliances. Not even traditional content aggregators. Their content within walled gardens is not targeted to the real needs of those who will pay for content on their handheld devices. Which group has content as its core competency? Here is the surprise. The alliances of NTT DoCoMo-AOL Japan, and of Nokia with CNN, MapQuest, and Weather.com use their content to create and deliver value on handheld phones that act as pagers. With headsets, users can bypass both telecom and content providers and buy directly from Nokia, Palm, Handspring and Sony.

Is core competency in content really that important? DoCoMo as the ISP provider in Japan blew all competition aside with packet switching and iMode phones. AOL Japan decided to join rather than fight DoCoMo. Northern Europe has no one dominant telecom or content provider; however, thanks to Sonera and Nokia, the Helsinki Virtual Village has wireless digital services covering the entire Finnish capital; in fact, SMS wireless has 95 percent market penetration in Finland. When the wireless spectrum for 3G is auctioned off in the US, perhaps as early as March 2001, AOL, Cisco, Enron and Virgin may make bids so high that the telecom providers will not be able to put up enough money and be shut out of their future.

Price is everything. The licenses may cost $100 billion. Then the winners will have to spend another $100 billion installing the 3G infrastructure. Finally, they may have to spend a third $100 billion paying for the marketing costs. These costs need to be recovered because debt must be paid down before investors look at balance sheets and decide to drive down stock prices. Hence, users will not have a free ride with content from the 3G mobile Internet of the future. If handheld manufacturers think creatively, the cell phone could become a smart card or credit card in which the wireless carrier either owns or goes into partnership with a bank to provide financial services.

Here is the face of competition in the mobile Internet industry.

- *Price marketing with substantial discounts.* All types of providers are battling to own customers, and this affects their pricing strategies. As early as 2003 in Europe and later in the US, supply will outpace demand. Customers will have to sift through content on a 30-day free trial, get airline frequent-flyer points for signing up, and then do it all again a few months or a year later for even more points. Hence, first-movers, mass affluents, and well-informed customers will ask for and get price deals, discounts, and free goods. Customers will relive their search and switch routines that they perfected in the long-distance wars. Price marketing is the name of the game in the mobile Internet.

- *Price competition without barriers.* None of these firms will just be in their traditional business anymore, and most won't be sure what businesses they are actually in. Everything is up for grabs. Success depends on how voice, data, transaction and content services are priced in competition with others doing business in the wireless or mobile Internet. The traditional entry and mobility barriers are unimportant because venture capitalists have so much cash to throw at alternative wireless solutions that no finish line exists for the mobile Internet. Price competition will make or break telecom providers and content as they build up supply, sell services, and pay down their debt.

The flood of new marketing opportunities for the mobile Internet could be the final push to merge the old and new economies into something altogether new. Hence, our emphasis in this book is on the *new* marketing concept, a *new* set of marketing strategies, and a *new* marketing organization.

- *Where do we create value?*
- *How do we deliver value?*

▓ *What do users get from mobile phones, m-commerce, and the wireless Internet?*

These questions frame our analysis of segmentation, targeting, and positioning.

Real options

Here are some good guesses about future investments.

The race for revenue from 3G-based content
▓ Pursue the most probable winners, NTT DoCoMo-AOL Japan, and Nokia.
▓ Postpone the possible winners, Enron, Virgin and other bidders for 3G licenses in the US.
▓ Terminate the least probable winners, the telecom providers, such as AT&T unless it is willing to convert TDMA to the iMode standard of W-CDMA.

The race for revenue from creative 3G partnerships
▓ Pursue Nokia as its puts the content of financial services on its wireless screen or "home deck," and goes into an alliance with Merita-Nordbanken, the merged Finnish-Swedish bank.
▓ Postpone voice-over-IP service to small business until the adoption rate grows large enough for marketers to measure demand.
▓ Terminate nothing because future marketing strategies will be designed to drive prices down and produce the switching of mobile services by customers.

The race for how customers experience products and services
Marketers now have sufficient experience with the wired Web, and they now know that the brand is the experience on the Internet. Most Web brands don't take advantage of the Internet's ability to customize browsing, and its promise of efficient and timely transactions. Will the wireless Web be any different? Only DoCoMo's iMode phone and Nokia's electronic wallets convey to users

that experience is the brand, and good experiences make the brand relevant to teenagers, business executives, and other true believers in mobile phones, m-commerce, and the wireless or mobile Internet.

CHAPTER #4: SEGMENTATION

Increase the knowledge of marketers about the possible customers for m-commerce through an analysis of market segments that cross national frontiers, For example, teenagers demand short-messaging services, mid-career business executives want voice and data communications, and some families are ready to try their hand at the purchases of goods and services via m-commerce.

- *How do customers experience mobile phones, m-commerce, and the wireless Internet?*
- *Are their intellectual, emotional, and sensory senses enriched by handheld devices, especially, by cell phones, PDAs, and wireless laptops that are Web-enabled with products and services?*
- *Can users browse through these offerings, engage in marketing-related activities, and complete transactions?*

Look at the ads for mobile phones. Although W-CDMA may be a better product than GSM in a functional sense, iMode differentiates its product by offering *manga* cartoons, Pokémon characters, and other fun things. Nokia differentiates its mobile phones by revamping the way people get and spend electronic cash through electronic wallets. AOL is rolling out new concepts by offering Internet-based phone services so that all aspects of the wireless Internet will stay within the firm's walled garden.

In all of these examples, functional features, and promotional appeals based on the value equation of price-quality-service tell only part of the story. Some non-functional, intangible attributes are the starting point for creating a value-based experience for customers. These experiences that differentiate one wireless product from another mobile product form the basis of how marketers carry out actionable segmentation.[2]

- *Key phrase.* Broad demographic data on income, age, gender, and ZIP and postal locations; more focused information on values and lifestyles; and translate them into marketing knowledge about customers.

- *Crucial marketing strategy.* Focus on actionable segmentation in which marketing knowledge about segments may be similar whether the mobile Internet products and services are sold in Japan, Europe, the US or elsewhere in the world.

- *Recommendations.* Pay attention because customers do take functional, tangible product attributes for granted. They know the features and benefits, and they understand that all providers will match prices and quality. Since these offers often do not differentiate among good products, customers have no reason to switch from one to the other, and marketers cannot capture additional revenue from their tried and true advertising campaigns. Therefore, dazzle customers with information that stimulates their interest in improved lifestyles. Give them new experiences.

Data, information and knowledge

Let's focus on one good decision about how a new wireless product is giving a better experience to one international segment, and how these national citizens of many countries are incorporating this new mobile Internet product into their global lifestyle. They asked for a brand to give them the experience, and now the experience is the brand.

Laptop computers can now be linked to the Internet via tiny PC cards that are plugged into these portable computers. They are all tied to the Ethernet wireless office networking standard (802.11b) whose co-inventor, Robert Metcalfe, framed his now famous Metcalfe's Law: "The usefulness, or utility, of a network equals the square of the number of users." This is an open standard that allows anyone to adopt it and improve on it. In fact, 802.11b is catching on so fast that it is replacing alternative wireless competitors, such as Local Area Networks (LAN's). Also the price of chip sets for 802.11b is falling so fast that the set up of a wireless Ethernet office network is now cheaper than the traditional wired Ethernet office network.[3]

Aerzone, Mobilstar and Wayport are rushing in to lock up valuable sites at university campuses, corporate office parks, hotels, restaurants, sports stadiums, Starbucks coffee shops, and airports. For example, United Airlines has entered into an alliance with Softnet Systems, a subsidiary of Aerzone, to install 802.11b in Red Carpet Club airport lounges, and at its gates and terminals. The firm's customers want mobility whether they are in Chicago, San Francisco, Hong Kong, Frankfurt or anywhere among the Star Alliance partners of United Airlines. These Premier, Premier Executive, and 1K Mileage Plus customers fly often, pay business-class air fares, and demand perks above and beyond what other air travelers get. It does not matter whether they are Americans, Hong Kong Chinese, Germans, or whoever; they all use the same wireless Ethernet network as mass affluent customers of United Airlines.

Since some of these sites will be open to travelers and non-travelers alike, Red Carpet Clubs will not only be places to wait for air flights or meet other travelers for airport meetings, but they will become a place to go to do one's own personal business without actually taking a trip. Also Starbucks may become a "high-loiter" retail shop as customers sip coffee, read their email, surf the Web, send out business proposals, and do all things they used to do in their offices or at home. Through Wayport the lobbies of hotels in Dallas-Fort Worth and Los Angeles are becoming another set of wireless meeting sites for folks who may not be staying at the hotel itself, but want to do their corporate or personal business away from their offices and homes.[4]

These actionable segments – frequent and non-flyers, coffee and non-drinkers, and hotel and non-guests – are customers for low-cost wireless Ethernet networks. Through Aerzone and Wayport companies and millions of computer customers are building their own high-speed data networks without wires, fixed-wireless, and 3G wireless systems. If the current set of actionable segments among the mass affluents from Gen-Y and Gen-X are joined by the upwardly mobile middle-class groups from the same age groups, this 802.11b wave may just swamp all other data networking standards whether they are iMode's W-CDMA, WAP, and UMTS.

In 2001, the 802.11b wireless Ethernet standard will become a common built-in feature on almost all makes of laptop computers. How DoCoMo and Nokia react to this substantial threat from IBM, IBM-clones, Apples, Sony,

Toshiba, and other manufacturers of portable computers is the crucial question for the future of the mobile Internet. It is possible that fixed-wireless and 3G have seen their better days, and those who have invested in them will not recover their costs from the auction and building the infrastructure. Or the wireless Internet will become what the wired Internet was in its early past – that is, a self-assembling world of networks with no one provider in control. If this happens, content may just be free in the mobile Internet world just like it is in the wired Internet world.

Real options

Here are some investment choices.

The quest for ownership of actionable segments of customers.

- Pursue the ability of DoCoMo and Nokia to stage experiences for 3G users, and to differentiate their products and services by dazzling their senses, touching their hearts, and stimulating their minds. These brands are giving users experiences that enhance their lifestyles. Pay attention to how Do-CoMo and Nokia deal with the emergence of the wireless Ethernet network standard and whether they will be as creative with this new technology as they were with previous wireless technologies.
- Postpone investments in their competitors unless they show they are being more creative with the introduction of 802.11b in the products and services.
- Terminate nothing because everything is up for grabs.

The quest for creative wireless Ethernet network partnerships

- Pursue both Aerzone and Wayport, and their partners from the airlines, hotels, and other businesses. In terms of United Airlines and Starbucks, the introduction of the wireless Ethernet network standard could be the most important competitive tool that pushes United ahead of American and Delta, and Starbucks ahead of Seattle's Best and other coffee chains. For those who are willing to pay for a full-fare business-class ticket and a more expensive cup of coffee, a service that enhances mobility and provides un-limited bandwidth creates and delivers value for their best customers.

▨ Postpone investments in their competitors.

▨ Terminate nothing because everything is up for grabs.

The quest for experiences as brands

▨ Pursue those wireless telecom providers, manufacturers of mobile hand-held devices, wireless Ethernet network providers, and suppliers of mobile Ethernet services to actionable segments in global markets that market a wireless experience anywhere, anytime. Their customers want "mobil-ity" everywhere. They are driven by the impulse to connect to their email, and the emotion of getting access to sufficient bandwidth for Web surfing. Therefore, successful providers and suppliers ask the following questions: What wireless products fit this consumption situation? How to design and package these products to make them appealing? How to communicate "What customers get" from these new mobile products and services.

▨ Postpone investments in those competitors that are not offering brands as wireless or mobile experiences.

▨ Terminate nothing because everything is up for grabs.

CHAPTER #5: TARGETING

Do data mining about the probable customers for m-commerce through an analysis of target groups within national markets. For example, "Supli" teen-agers in Japan are girls who drink near-water and who want *manga* cartoons on their iMode cell phones; Nokia-users in Finland, Sweden and Estonia are business executives who use their electronic wallets to pay for soda drinks and parking spots with their WAP mobile phones; and customers of Vodafone AirTouch and VoiceStream Wireless in the US are the upwardly mobile middle class who use their North American cell phone numbers to make hotel reserva-tions in 70 countries worldwide.

▨ *How do marketers gain a true insight on what customers experience from the mobile Internet?*

- *What types of experiences may marketers look for in their analysis of target groups?*
- *Can these experiences lead to decisions about brands of telecom providers, mobile phones, and Ethernet networks?*

For example, both the wireless Internet and the wireless Ethernet networks are trying to reinvent the m-commerce Internet experience. The Red Carpet Clubs create the atmosphere of a private club for Premier, Premier Executive, and 1K Mileage Plus members who think they should have a unique personal virtual mail carrier, sales person, and butler. Also they feel good because they have mastered the new wireless technology. The problem lies in carrying an Internet experience from one country to another because the willingness to show empathy with the mobile Internet differs from culture to culture. In the case of wireless technology, marketers must appeal to the users' ability to think through how they will solve their wireless problems. Both the mobile Internet and the wireless Ethernet networks offer users alternative ways of doing their business and getting the job done. Finally, users see DoCoMo, Nokia, Ethernet networks, and Red Carpet Clubs as part of their self-identity.

These experiences form the basis of how marketers carry out actionable targeting. We start with demographic data, values and lifestyle information, and translate them into knowledge of brands as personal experiences and lifestyle experiences as brands. We look for intangible attributes as the basis for creating a value equation of price-quality-service for each target group. We conclude with a list of experiences that relate the wireless Internet to the fundamental consumer question: "What do I get?"

- *Key phrase.* Mix and match knowledge about age, income, gender, ZIP code, values, lifestyles, needs, wants and desires, ethnic backgrounds, work, family life, and technological diffusion, and translate these data and information into knowledge about the experiences of target groups.
- *Crucial marketing strategy.* Focus on actionable targeting in which marketing knowledge about target groups is not the same for either the wireless Internet or the wireless Ethernet network in Japan, Europe, the US, and elsewhere in the world because their cultures differ widely.

■ *Recommendations.* Pay attention that customers want intangible product attributes. They don't know which of their experiences will relate well to the wireless Internet. Marketers must use all their promotional tools and techniques to convince customers they will enjoy their experiences with the mobile Internet. Therefore, provide customers with new kinds of experiences that can be delivered on a timely basis.

Diffusion of technology

"The Internet model exists. The wireless model does not," says Henry Nilert, the co-founder of the Finnish wireless portal, Iobox, which was recently acquired by Telefonica Moviles and Spain's Terra Networks.[5] Nevertheless, brands will be built and market share gained once brands become experiences, or experiences become brands. "The demand is there today," says Nilert.[6]

Three American content providers are trying to establish their US wireless model in Europe. First, AOL introduced its wireless portal giving its 20 million customers cell phone access to email and Web services, such as MoviePhone and MapQuest; and AOL also invested in Mviva, a wireless portal that is owned by a European mobile phones retailer, Carphone Warehouse, that will feature AOL content behind AOL's walled garden. Second, Yahoo! is providing content to European telecom providers, such as Telecom Italia Mobile and Finland's Radiolinja. Finally, Microsoft is trying to get its MSN services on the cell phone screens or the "home deck" of handheld mobile devices.

Most US content providers assume the big screen PC-based Internet world. However, most Europeans do not have PCs. Instead, they connect to the Internet through handheld wireless devices. Their cell phone screens are much smaller and confined to 2G WAP technology that is only good for short text messages. Thus there are real cultural differences in how messages and data are delivered in the US and Europe.

European telecom providers, such as British Telecom, Sonera, and Vizzavi (itself a joint venture between Vodafone and Vivendi), have set up wireless portals to provide the immediate, high-level demand among teenagers for mobile short-text message, and the anticipated demand among business executives for data services using 2G GSM. The bet is that European traffic will flow from the installed base of wired PCs to mobile handheld phones because more Europeans have cell phones than PCs, which is just the reverse of what exists in the US. Clearly, it is a mistake to import the US PC-based Internet model for use in the European wireless Internet market.

The American-owned content providers are failing to carry out actionable targeting in Europe. Even though the target groups are similar in age, income, jobs, and lifestyles – for example, teenagers or business executives – their received wisdom about what equipment to use to gain access to the wireless Internet is very different. Hence, marketers must take two different approaches, one for the US and another for Europe, in rolling out the new marketing concept, implementing two new sets of marketing strategies, and putting them altogether in two new marketing organizations.

The most successful wireless data service is NTT DoCoMo. It makes no money on advertising and transactions. Rather, over 80 percent of its revenues comes from subscription and usage fees, and 20 percent of its revenues comes from its cut of the fees charged by 10,000 content providers for the content delivered over iMode. DoCoMo does a good job offering target groups specific content to Japanese "Supli" teenage girls, unmarried young male salarymen, office ladies, married adults with one wage earner, and business executives.. DoCoMo takes the initiative in signing up content providers, guaranteeing their products and services, collecting fees for content use, and packaging them according to the values and lifestyles of each target group. This Japanese model may be the one to follow in Europe by telecom providers, American and European content providers, and mobile Internet networks.

Marketers have a big task ahead. They must decide which signals and trends to scan to define the significant technologies for tomorrow's telecom world. Some will pause and delay the introduction of new technologies. Some will decide the present is the future and stick with the familiar. Some will be reluctant to commit themselves to new technologies because demand is insufficient to make money within the first two years. These are all reasons for failure. The task for marketers is to find out which technologies provide good experiences for users, or which experiences offer a high-level of brand awareness to users.

Real options

Here are some specific investment choices.

Data, information, and knowledge about target groups

▪ Pursue teenagers as a mass-market opportunity for short messaging services, and business executives as the mass affluent market opportunity for voice and data services.

▪ Postpone those target groups that offer no positive cash flow within the first two years.

▪ Terminate no target groups because the mobile Internet is the wave of the future.

Wireless Internet services

▪ Pursue fixed-wireless, satellite wireless, and wireless Ethernet networks.

▪ Postpone none of them because demand is insufficient to determine which of these three wireless services will win out.

▪ Terminate no wireless technologies.

Wireless models

▪ Pursue DoCoMo's approach to delivering wireless content services, and determine which of its approaches will translate well in Europe and the US. Also pursue Vizzavi's approach to delivering similar wireless services in Europe.

▪ Postpone investments in US approaches to delivering wireless content services unless they are modified to match up with the real cultural differences in Europe, and watch how AOL modifies its approach in Japan and Europe because of its new DoCoMo partnership.

CHAPTER #6: POSITIONING

Position m-commerce products and services (such as, sports, entertainment, hotels, stock brokers, Internet banking, and other dot-coms) for sale to income-producing target groups. For example, watch traditional banks go into partnerships with or buy on-line stock-trading firms so that the former can learn how to create and deliver value in Internet banking; and decide whether venture capitalists should terminate investments in m-banking for better deals in interactive TV, on-line stock-trading, and sports marketing.

- *How do marketers mix and match the experiences of customers with products and services with what target groups expect from brands?*
- *What types of positioning strategies are most effective in Japan, Europe, the US, China, and elsewhere in the world?*
- *Can these marketing efforts lead to decisions about which of the following mobile Internet systems is best?*
  - *Fixed-wireless* (Qualcomm's W-CDMA, and DoCoMo-AOL Japan);
  - *Mobile Internet* (GSM-Sonera-Nokia-Virtual Helsinki together with Merita-Nordbanken-Ericsson; Vodafone and Vivendi's joint venture, Vizzavi. Many other European and American combinations);
  - *Wireless Ethernet networks* (Aerzone and United Airlines's Red Carpet Clubs, or Wayport and the better hotels).
- *Can customers get answers to the question: "What do I get?"*

W-CDMA offers the Japanese a 3G infrastructure in May 2001, 10,000 content providers, AOL's "Buddies List," and 13 million persons to talk with throughout the Japanese islands. If DoCoMo works out its deal with the Dutch firm, KPN, and finds a suitable US partner, then both Europeans and Americans may share W-CDMA technology, too. The experiences of Japanese customers is warm and fuzzy, happiness in a fast-paced world, without the need to think about technology.

GSM offers Europeans a 2G infrastructure, a few American and European content providers, and persons to talk with in 14 European countries and 70 worldwide. If GSM converts to UMTS with a 3G infrastructure, the improved WAP may be competitive with W-CDMA. The experiences of European customers is OK; however, they made it clear that they want what the Japanese customers of DoCoMo have in terms of 3G services. As a consequence, the European firms are no longer enthusiastic about the long-term prospects of GSM even as they ready themselves to face the high cost of converting to 3G.

The wireless Ethernet network is the newest technology on the market. It has all the earmarks of causing chaos in the wireless mobile Internet market. Let's call it what it is: 802.11b is a disruptive technology. Nevertheless, customers like it because it gives them mobility and bandwidth. If its demand grows and is sustainable, then the wireless Ethernet network will be a formidable challenger to both W-CDMA and GSM.

- *Key phrase.* Do a real options analysis of alternative m-commerce investments and decide which to pursue, which to postpone, and which to terminate, and translate these results into knowledge about actionable positioning.
- *Crucial marketing strategy.* Focus on actionable positioning in which all three types of mobile Internet access are tried. Then choose the wireless Ethernet network to roll out in all new interactive TV, sports marketing, online stock-trading, and Internet m-banking situations.
- *Recommendations.* Pay attention that customers want both tangible and intangible product attributes. They don't know which of their experiences will relate well to the wireless Internet, especially to the wireless Ethernet network. Marketers must use all their managerial skills of risk analysis, financial skills of investment analysis, and all their marketing skills of 4 Ps strategy analysis to convince customers they will enjoy their experiences with the mobile Ethernet network. Therefore, provide customers with new kinds of experiences that can be delivered on a timely basis and at a cost they can afford.

Rules of thumb for investments

We are almost at the end of our tour of the world's keen interest in mobile phones, m-commerce, and the wireless Internet. Technology comes and goes, and morphs into expectations about brands by customers. All this may seem confusing, and it is to some. Predictions about which technology will prevail are fraught with extreme downside risk.

My strategy is simple if classic: follow the money. There is a considerable lot of it in Japan, Europe, the US, and in China. Throughout the book we have written about the diffusion of mobile wireless technology in all three developed countries, and we know what target groups in each country expect from the wireless Internet. The industry worldwide is still up for grabs. Let's work through one more example and see where we come out in our marketing analysis of mobile phones, m-commerce, and the wireless Internet.

The Chinese mobile population has swelled in the last few years, as China called on Vodafone, Qualcomm, and others to come in and do deals with China Mobile and Unicom respectively. These two foreign-owned firms brought GSM and CDMA with them. They paid local providers to provide Chinese-language sites for stock market information from Shanghai, Hong Kong and elsewhere in the world. These foreign-owned partners have targeted China's elite. Here are the values and lifestyles of China's elite in October 1999:[7]

- The urban Chinese take in 70 percent of the wealth although they are considerably less than half of the population of mainland China.
- These city folks have stuffed their homes with appliances; their homes contain the following goods: color TV (96 percent), telephone (78 percent), pagers (64 percent).
- However, only a few own stocks (11 percent) or use the Internet (8 percent).

One year later in October 2000, here's another look at their values and lifestyles:[8]

- At home, the urban Chinese have a desktop computer (70 percent), a printer (35 percent), and a fax machine (25 percent).
- In their tote bag, they carry a mobile phone (32 percent), and a PDA (12 percent).

Between these two years, the Chinese government launched its latest ideological campaign. It said that the party now represents the interests of advanced social productive forces, in short, those who are working in high technology. Such change by redefinition means money can be made in mobile phones, m-commerce, and the wireless Internet.

Sina.com, one of the largest portal sites in greater China, has both Chinese-language and an English-language sites. Sina.com and others are thriving in China by creating new competitive market space. According to George Wang, the chief executive officer of Cinon.com, a Chinese-language financial Web site, "China is where the big money is."[9]

For example, China Mobile is adding around two million Chinese subscribers a month and it has overtaken Vodafone as the world's biggest operator. Within China 60 million people are mobile subscribers; this makes China the number two market after the US, and it could be number one any day now. Also China Netcom, a company that builds fiber optic networks, is trying to catch up to the Chinese demand for broadband Internet access. Moreover, GWcom, which is based in California but has a wireless portal in Shanghai called byair.com, provides on-line stock-trading, m-banking, trade and commerce, news and information; the firm offers stock-trading via Palm handheld devices in which users get charts, financial information, and the ability to execute buy and sell orders. And many other deals.

China is shifting to the digital lifestyle. During 2001, China will migrate to 2.5G and host about 100 million Chinese on its several wireless networks. Most of these are fixed-wireless systems that use GSM, CDMA, and locally produced wireless technology. All the urban elite will be connected to one or more wireless system, and some will soon demand a wireless Ethernet system, too. Similar to countries in the West, the younger age groups are the first to experiment with cell phones; then came the more senior government officials and business executives; now wireless phones are beginning to spread to others in China. As the costs come down, mobile phones should spread like wildfire because the Chinese do not have ample landline connections throughout the country.

Real options

Here is a rank order of wireless investments that can be made country-by-country:

■ *Japan, Europe and the US.* Make these investments first because the potential market is large and the income level of potential customers is high.

■ *China.* Add to these investments as quickly as possible. Investors that come in second or third in China tend to be also-rans in the local market.

■ *Australia.* Enhance the capability of Telstra to be successful both in Australia, and in South East Asia and in Hong Kong.

■ *Mexico, Brazil, Argentina and Chile.* Start making major investments in these crucial countries.

■ *India.* Start making limited investments in Bangalore, Mumbia (Bombay), and New Delhi.

■ *Eastern Europe and Russia.* Not yet ready for major investments.

■ *The rest of the world.* Way behind in getting ready for the mobile Internet.

Since there is so much to do and the opportunity for good results is higher in the more advanced economies, most investors and venture capitalists will not invest in the rest of the world, eastern Europe, and Russia during the next few years.

CONCLUSIONS

How to conquer the wireless world? Apply a *new* 4 Ps marketing strategy to m-commerce, especially to the existing wireless platforms of GSM, iMode and CDMA, and to those mobile Internet platforms that are coming soon with 3G technology in 2001, 2003 and 2005. Here is a checklist of things to do:

■ Put information appliances, especially wireless Ethernet networks, in the hands of m-commerce users, and upgrade these enhanced mobile phones as 2G and 2.5G systems move to 3G technology.

■ Build market share with a *new* 4 Ps marketing strategy that is transparent, and carefully adapted to the expansion phase of the product life cycle in the three developed countries, but also in China, Latin America, and India.

■ Offer customers training on crucial salient product attributes, such as location awareness, voice and data transmissions, and transaction capabilities, and implement the learning requirements of the *new* marketing concept for mobile Internet.

■ Create and deliver interactive value by mixing and matching the old and new economies, and adapting them both to the needs of m-commerce, mobile phones, and the wireless Internet.

Japan's success with m-commerce has more to do with execution than brilliant vision. The same is true for Finland and Sweden. Both NTT DoCoMo and Nokia-Sonera are using m-commerce technology to create value that is consistent with the core goals of the firms and the national aspirations of their home countries. This is how others can create and deliver value in the new wireless world unfolding before our very eyes.

HOW TO BE AN M-MARKETER

Anybody who is a good marketer also can become a good m-marketer. Here's what marketers must do to be successful m-marketers.

■ *Product marketing.* Marketers introduce miniature information appliances with unique interactive content to m-commerce customers.

■ *Promotion marketing.* Marketing managers provide customers with value-added intangible product attributes that are included as part of their smart handheld devices.

■ *Price marketing.* Marketers offer both commodity and higher value-added prices as marketing managers divide m-commerce customers into those who do virtually everything on-line and those who prefer personal services from telecom, content, and financial service providers.

■ *Segmentation.* Marketers divide like groups of people across national frontiers into those who have the income, are the correct age, live in the right neighborhoods, and belong to modernizing ethnic groups as candidates for the purchase of miniature information appliances, 3G telecom services, and interactive Internet content.

■ *Targeting.* Marketing managers assemble smaller like groups of people who are bound together by their professions, such as entertainers, or by their skills, such as athletes, and by their personal tastes, habits, and values, such as info-tech geeks.

▦ *Positioning.* Marketers match possible on-line Internet products with probable customers; the former offer the latter enhanced customer relationships to try out m-commerce and the mobile Internet.

These six fundamental marketing ideas are discussed throughout this book. It is for marketers who want to sell mobile phones, m-commerce, and the wireless Internet to a new generation of telecom customers.

Endnotes

Introduction

1 "The wireless gamble," *The Economist*, October 14, 2000, pp. 17–18.

2 Greg Lindsay, "An Answer in Search of a Question: Who wants M-Commerce?" *Fortune*, October 16, 2000, p. 399.

3 Marc Gunther, "Full Stream Ahead," *Fortune*, October 9, 2000, p. 94.

4 Richard Tomlinson, "Dialing for Dollars," *Fortune*, October 9, 2000, p. 152.

5 Some of the ideas in this section come from Andy Server, "What do these guys know about the Internet," *Fortune*, October 9, 2000, pp. 113–120.

6 Sara Webb, "Consumers Remain Wary of Online Financial Services," *Asian Wall Street Journal*, October 16, 2000, p. 4.

7 Anne Queree, "Never mind the technology, show me the value," *Financial Times*, September 20, 2000, p. XVIII.

8 *Ibid.*

9 Rod Newing, "Precision marketing vital to mobile promotions," *Financial Times*, September 20, 2000, p. XX.

10 E.S. Browning and Greg Ip, "Reality Check," *Wall Street Journal*, October 16, 2000, p. A1.

11 John Markoff, A High-Technology Festival takes a High-Anxiety Turn," *New York Times*, October 18, 2000, pp. A1, C22.

12 Tom Lester, "Value creation ratios in search of a rationale," *Financial Times*, October 13, 2000, p. 12.

PART 1: VALUE CREATION

Chapter #1: Marketing Wireless Products

1   Ian C. MacMillan and Rita Gunther McGrath, "Discover Your Products' Hidden Potential," *Harvard Business Review*, May–June 1996, pp. 58–73.

2   Stephen Baker, "Yes, It Really Is The Next Big Thing," *Business Week*, May 29, 2000, p. 164.

3   MacMillan and McGrath, "Discover New Points of Differentiation," *Harvard Business Review*, July–August 1997, pp. 133–145.

4   Fiona Harvey, "Calling the Future," *Financial Times Understanding WAP*, Summer 2000, pp. 24–25.

5   David Wessel, "Gadget Envy," *Wall Street Journal*, August 3, 2000, p. B1.

6   "Wireless in Cyberspace," *Business Week*, May 29, 2000, p. 144.

7   David Kenny and John F. Marshall, "Contextual Marketing: The Real Business of the Internet," *Harvard Business Review*, November–December 2000, p. 124.

8   "High-Tech Equipment Makers Confront Bad-Debt Risk Due to Loans to Customers," *Wall Street Journal*, November 24, 2000, p. B1.

9   Caroline Daniel, "Warning signals for Europe's mobile makers," *Financial Times*, August 10, 2000, p. 11.

10   John Forsyth et al., "A segmentation you can act on," *McKinsey Quarterly*, 3 (1999), pp. 7–15.

11   Andrea Petersen, "A Nascent Industry in the US Looks to Blossom," *Wall Street Journal*, August 18, 2000, p. B1.

12   Norm Alster, "Cell Phones: We Need More Testing," *Business Week*, August 14, 2000, p. 39.

13   Saikat Chaudhuri and Behnam Tabrizi, "Capturing the Real Value in High-Tech Acquisitions," *Harvard Business Review*, September–October 1999, pp. 123–130.

14   Patrick Harverson, "A key player in sports team," *Financial Times Survey: Information Technology*, August 2, 2000, p. I.

Chapter #2: Promoting New Market Space

1   "Good-Bye to Pumped-Up Profits?" *Business Week*, November 20, 2000, p. 92.

2   The ad appeared in many papers including *New York Times*, August 11, 2000, p. A9.

3   "Deutsche Telekom's Wireless Wager," *Business Week*, August 7, 2000, pp. 30–32.

4   William Boston, "Speed Dial: Siemens Grabs Cell Market," *Wall Street Journal*, June 23, 2000, p. A16.

5   Jeffrey F. Rayport and John J. Sviokla, "Managing in the Marketspace," *Harvard Business Review*, November–December 1994, pp. 141–150.

6   Kevin Lane Keffer, "The Brand Report Card," *Harvard Business Review*, January–February 2000, pp. 147–157. Indrajit Sinha, "Cost Transparency: The Net's Real Threat to Prices and Brands," *Harvard Business Review*, March–April 2000, pp. 43–50. Peter Sealey, "How E-Commerce Will Trump Brand Management," *Harvard Business Review*, July–August 1999, pp. 4–7.

7   This section is a summary of a research paper prepared by Georgi Zhikharev on the application of real options to marketing iMode phones. Zhikharev is an International Marketing and Finance MBA student at DePaul University in Chicago.

8   R. Clark, "The NTT DoCoMo Success Story," *America's Network*, 104:4, March 1, 2000, pp. 46–50.

Chapter #3: Pricing M-Commerce Services

1   Paul Krugman, "To Boldly Go," *New York Times*, November 6, 2000, p. A 23.

2   Laura M. Holson, "Econpanies and Sprint Plan Venture, *New York Times*, August 28, 2000, p. C8.

3   The phrase is taken from Michael Lewis, *The New New Thing*, New York: W.W. Norton & Co., 1999.

4   Ralf Leszinski and Michael V. Marin, "Setting Value, Not Price," *McKinsey Quarterly*, Number 1 (1997), pp. 99–100.

5   *Ibid.*, p. 100.

6   Nicole Harris and Nikhil Deogun, "VoiceStream Wireless Agrees to Purchase Powertel for $5.9 Billion in Stock, *Wall Street Journal*, August 28, 2000, p. A3.

7   Leszinski and Marin, p. 106.

8   William Gurley, "Making Sense of the Wireless Web," *Fortune*, September 4, 2000, p. 378.

9   "Fool on the Hill: How to Value Telecom Carriers," <http://dailynews.yahoo.com/h/mf/20...w_to_value_telecom carriers_1.html>, August 25, 2000, (Accessed August 26, 2000). "Convergence Emergence, Part 2: The 'Sunk Assets'," <http://www.fool.com/news/foth/2000/foth000808.htm>, August 8, 2000, (Accessed August 26, 2000).

10 Rebecca Smith and Aaron Lucchetti, "Sink or Swim: Rebecca Mark's Exit Leaves Enron's Azurix Treading Deep Water," *Wall Street Journal*, August 28, 2000, pp. A1, A10.

11 Mark Landler, "Wheeler-Dealer, Tycoon, Trader; Hutchison Whampoa Earns Billions and Can Even Say No," *New York Times*, August 25, 2000, p. C1.

12 Smith and Lucchetti, pp. A1, A10.

13 Landler, p. C2.

14 *Ibid*.

15 Gren Manuel and Anette Jonsson, "Hong Kong Firm Decides That Money *Is* An Object," *Wall Street Journal*, August 21, 2000, p. 13.

16 William Boston, "Europe's Wireless Auctions Wind Down. Now What?" *Wall Street Journal*, August 23, 2000, p. A17.

17 Leszinski and Marin, pp. 99–115.

18 TV and print advertisements were created by Wieden & Kennedy of Portland, Oregon for Robertson Stephens. Noreen O'Leary, "Banking on a better view from on high," *Financial Times*, August 20, 2000, p. XXIV.

19 John Willman, "Branch equity," *Financial Times*, July 7, 2000, p. 10.

20 *Ibid*.

21 *Ibid*.

22 Heather Timmons, "Online Banks Can't Go It Alone," *Business Week*, July 31, 2000, pp. 86–87.

23   *Ibid.*

24   Mark Vernon, "Control of costs is crucial," *Financial Times*, July 19, 2000, p. VII.

25   Geoffrey Narin, "Web-based call centres: Banks show renewed interest," *Financial Times*, July 5, 2000, p. IX.

26   Philip B. Evans and Thomas S. Wurster, "Strategy and the New Economics of Information," *Harvard Business Review*, September–October 1997, pp. 72–82.

PART II: VALUE DELIVERY

Chapter #4: Segmenting International Markets

1   Carolyn Whelan, "The Long and Wireless Road: One Farsighted Navigator Weighs In," *Fortune*, November 27, 2000, p. 286. "Asia's Future," *Business Week*, November 27, 2000, pp. 132–144.

2   Data are from a report by Renaissance Strategy Worldwide. It is cited by Michael Santoli, "Broadband's Mantra," *Barron's*, September 11, 2000, p. 17.

3   Andrew Fisher, "Consumer enthusiasm promises lucrative future," *Financial Times*, September 6, 2000, p. V.

4   *Ibid.*

5   *Ibid.*

6   *Ibid.*

7   *Ibid.*

8   Scheherazade Daneshku, "Check in, plug in, log on,' *Financial Times*, September 8, 2000, p. I.

9   *Ibid.*

10   John Markoff, "Silicon Valley's Primal Spirit Lives On, in a Part of Beijing," *New York Times*, August 4, 2000, p. A4.

11   "Wired China: The flies swarm in," *The Economist*, July 22, 2000, pp. 24–28.

12   See <www.willshop.com>.

13   Irene M. Kunii, "Tokyo's Valley of the Netrepreneurs," *Business Week*, September 6, 1999, pp. 92.

14 Alexandra Harney, "Thirst for soft drink with a bit of fizz," *Financial Times*, July 23, 1999, p. 16.

15 John Burton, "Share dealing gallops ahead in South Korea, *Financial Times*, September 6, 2000, p. VIII.

16 "Korea's Digital Quest," *Business Week*, September 25, 2000, p. 68.

17 Sheila McNulty, "Equipping a nation for the new economy," *Financial Times*, September 15, 2000, p. 12.

18 Virginia Marsh, "Telstra attacks costs to regain fighting weight," *Financial Times*, September 21, 2000, p. 22.

19 Tony Horwitz, "In Sydney, the Games Are Hot," *Wall Street Journal*, September 19, 2000, p. A6.

Chapter #5: Targeting National Markets

1 "A Survey of E-Management," *The Economist*, November 11, 2000, pp. 5–40.

2 "The Lex Column: Click, clunk," *Financial Times*, September 27, 2000, p. 18.

3 Katherine Campbell, "Fledglings learn not to follow the flock blindly," *Financial Times*, September 13, 2000, p. V.

4 Cait Murphy, "The Next French Revolution," *Fortune*, June 12, 2000, p. 158.

5 James Mackintosh, "Portals open new paths to profits, "*Financial Times*, May 26, 2000, p. VIII.

6 David Rosenberg, "Education Battlefield," *Red Herring*, September 2000, p. 281.

7 Tom Stein, "Group Therapy," *Red Herring*, September 2000, p. 254.

8 Sharon Cleary, "Speak and You Shall Receive," *Wall Street Journal*, September 18, 2000, p. R25.

9 Sadanand Dhume, "Wired Warriors," *Far Eastern Economic Review*, October 5, 2000, p. 35.

Chapter #6: Positioning Local Goods and Services

1 "A survey of e-management," *The Economist*, November 11, 2000, p. 36.

2   "PCCW Devalued," *The Economist*, October 7, 2000, p. 81.

3   Anthony Perkins, "Coming Soon: Interactive TV," *Asian Wall Street Journal*, October 3, 2000, p. 8.

4   *Ibid.*

5   Richard Covington, "Two-Way TV, a European Hit, Has Misses Too," *International Herald Tribune*, September 25, 2000, p. 11.

6   Christopher Parkes, "Satellite TV refinds its roots," *Financial Times*, October 7–8, 2000, p. 9.

7   Clara Li, "IPO boosts Web banking," *South China Morning Post*, October 1, 2000, p. 3.

8   Louise Lee, "Speaking the Customer's Language-Literally," *Business Week*, September 25, 2000, p. 178.

9   Alexandra Harney, "Controversy amid online optimism," *Financial Times*, September 6, 2000, p. VIII.

10 *Ibid.*

11 Tony Barber, "Direct broker plans expansion abroad," *Financial Times*, October 25, 1999, p. IX.

12 Louis Beckerling, "HSBC joins world online-service elite," *South China Morning Post*, October 11, 2000, p. B3.

13 John Willman, "Private banks take everyone into account," *Financial Times*, October 10, 2000, p. 19.

Conclusions

1   Brad Stone, "A War of Inches," *The Industry Standard*, November 2000, p. 78.

2   Bernd Schmitt, "Marketers seeking sense in sensibility," in "Mastering Management," *Financial Times*, October 23, 2000, pp. 12–13. B.H. Schmitt, *Experiential Marketing*, New York: Free Press, 1999.

3   John Markoff, "New Economy," *The New York Times*, October 30, 2000, p. C5.

4   Tim Jackson, "Networking in the fast Lane," *Financial Times*, September 26, 2000, p. 13.

5   Amy Cortese, "Up Against the Wall," *The Industry Standard*, November 2000, p. 117.

6   *Ibid.*, p. 116.

7   Brian Palmer, "What the Chinese Want," *Fortune*, October 11, 1999, pp. 229–234.

8   "The Gadget Count is Rising," *Far Eastern Economic Review*, October 5, 2000, p. 68.

9   Connie Ling, "Sizing Australia's Chinese Net Worth, *Asian Wall Street Journal*, October 16, 2000, p. 13.

Index